A M E R I C A N
ROUGHSHOOTING

EDWARD K. ROGGENKAMP, III

HOWELL
BOOK
HOUSE

This English print by P. Reinagle, engraved by I. Scott was published in London by Richard Bentley in 1846. It depicts the origins of roughshooting with the dogs flushing birds before the guns.

Howell Book House
MACMILLAN
A Simon & Schuster/Macmillan Company
1633 Broadway
New York, NY 10019

MACMILLAN is a registered trademark of Macmillan, Inc.

Roggenkamp, Edward K.
   American roughshooting: the practice and pleasures of sport hunting/Ed Roggenkamp.
       p.   cm.
   Includes bibliographical references.
   ISBN 0-87605-427-0
   1. Upland game bird shooting—United States.   2. Bird dogs.
I. Title.
SK323.R64   1996
799.2'42'0973—dc20   95–34344
                                        CIP

Manufactured in the United States of America

10 9 8 7 6 5 4 3 2 1

To my family—Rheva, Kara and Ed. Their strength, independence and personal achievements have allowed me to pursue my interests, hobbies and a demanding business career.

SPECIAL THANKS

To my wife, Rheva, for her valuable assistance in the completion of this book. Without her many hours of editing, proofing and advice, it would have never come to fruition.

To Linda Lederle, for her conscientious typing and word processing. Her skills, patience and pleasant nature put the manuscript into form.

To Ann and Jerry Keiser, for transcribing the tapes of the interviews.

And, to Steve Ellis for completing the illustrations.

CONTENTS

HONEST, RELIABLE, PRACTICAL ADVICE FROM THE EXPERTS

Unfortunately, some of the most knowledgeable people with great expertise about the sport of roughshooting are also the most unlikely to ever take the time to write it down on paper. That formality is not their style. As I set out to compile this book, one of my objectives was to gather the practical thoughts and opinions of such experts and share them with you, the reader. I only wish it were possible for you to have tagged along for the interviews. It was great fun and very enlightening. I've known each of these characters for years, and in every case, I've grown to respect their knowledge and talents in their chosen fields.

Over the years I've been given some amusing and unrealistic advice about guns, dogs and hunting. I remember a snooty sales clerk in the shop of one of London's "best" gunmakers. He advised me that no used gun costing less than $5,000 was safe to fire. If he was right, about ten million Americans are in grave danger.

Another time, I watched as a well-heeled, well-read chap and his wife showed up at the skeet range of a prestigious shooting club with a matched pair of beautiful 28-gauge over-unders they had ordered from a highly respected Italian gunmaker. The people were beautiful; their clothes were beautiful; the guns were beautiful; the club was beautiful and the day was beautiful. On the skeet range one shot five out of twenty-five and the other shot three of twenty-five. What they needed was some practical advice about how to get started in shooting sports.

In the area of dog training, I have gone to people who train dogs for roughshooting. I did not go to any big-name pointer or retriever field trial trainer for advice. What they do is great sport, fun and exciting, but it has very little relevance to everyday roughshooting. If you were buying a horse for a family member to ride and enjoy, would you go to Wayne Lukas or Ron McAnally, even though they train some of the finest, fastest thoroughbred racehorses in America? I doubt it.

I believe the advice these experts have given is of value to the roughshooter.

Ed Roggenkamp—in his element.

FRIENDS AND MENTORS

Many of the ideas and opinions in this book are not mine alone; they were distilled after days of watching the success of my hunting partners and many hours of conversation sharing ideas with these same friends. To all my hunting cronies—thanks for the memories:

Leon Vaughn—A gentleman and consummate Iowa pheasant hunter with fifty years experience. *Frank Sylvester*—One of the world's best grouse and woodcock hunters. *Dominick Santerelli*—Fine company and an excellent and safe grouse hunter. *George Wilson*—My dog training and hunting comrade; the kind of easygoing man you can spend days with. *Chad Betts*—Really knows his stuff; a fine hunter and great dog trainer. *Erik Warren*—A good shot who truly knows and understands shotgunning. *Peter Casella*—A hard hunter and a good friend. *Bob Michel*—Was always ready to try the next covert; rest in peace. *Keith Anger*—A believer in magnum shells and five-shot magazines. *Bill Welk*—Loves the joy of the hunt—good friends, good food, good places. *Wil Avril*—Steady, safe and reliable; a thinking man. *Jerry Babin*—Knows the Canadian bush like the back of his hand, and a laugh a minute. *Ham Schirmer*—A dedicated traditionalist and a talented hunter. *Tony Hopp*—Another busy executive who finally figured out how to match his lifestyle with a good dog. *Bob Burger*—Always added a level of class to the sport; owned the best camp in the North Woods. *Roy Hopkins*—One hell of a fine shot; knows over-unders. *Bill Kennedy*—A good gun dealer who helped me in my gun searches. *John Dallas*—Shoots a howitzer, and very well; a magnum loader. *Derek Sylvester*—Takes after his father; a dedicated hunter, mile after mile. *Tom Meyer*—A Minnesota hunter with good taste in side-by-side guns. *Fred Gray*—Always ready to walk another mile. *John Blanock*—Colonel John, a dog training comrade and a fine gentleman.

THE EXPERTS, MY COLLABORATORS

To you I extend my special thanks for your time, your candor, your thoughtfulness and your willingness to share your experience: Dean Brunn, Jerry Cacchio, Herschel Chadick, Mark Crudgington, Dan Dessecker, Keith Erlandson, Alan Gwynne, Harry Henriques, Dale Jarvis, David Jones, Pat Lieske, Charlie Mann, Dr. Denny Scherer, Lee Seinkowski, Roger Wells and Nidal Zaher.

PART I
BIRDS

CHAPTER 1
AMERICAN ROUGHSHOOTING

American roughshooting, in its truest sense, is a Yankee version of the old English walk in the rough, shooting whatever game—feather, fur or water-fowl—that jumped out from the path of the hunter and his dog. So although Americans did not invent roughshooting, we have practiced it so long and so enthusiastically, in our own personalized way, that it now has deep American roots. In fact, almost all American upland bird hunting could be considered roughshooting by my definition, since very little driven shooting is available in the United States. With the introduction of different birds such as the ring-neck pheasant and the chukar partridge, different dogs such as the Vizsla and the upland Labrador Retriever, and new styles of guns, American roughshooting is sure to continue to change.

There are still many places in the United States where a hunter could go out for a mixed bag, but for more practical reasons, most American roughshooters limit their bag on any day to only one or two species. I recall days in Iowa when we shot pheasant, quail and mallards, or in Minnesota when we shot grouse, woodcock, snipe and teal. But steel shot is now required by law for waterfowling, and many of us forego shooting steel in our older double-barreled game guns. That effectively eliminates waterfowl from the roughshoot bag, and as for fur, it just doesn't appeal to most bird hunters; few hunters care to work their best dogs on a mixed bag of fur and feathers.

The vocabulary used in this book may require some definition. It seems strange that millions of us roughshoot every year, but if you go to a well-stocked library and scour every dictionary, you will be hard-pressed to find the terms of our sport defined. You can find *roughrider* and *roughshod* but not *roughshooting*. Nor is upland game defined anywhere. Consequently, I have developed my own definitions, and I hope you will find them helpful.

Roughshooting—My simple, one-sentence definition of roughshooting is: *Upland bird hunting on foot in rough cover.*

Although this definition is simple, direct and to the point, some would consider it too narrow, so it could be expanded a bit to add clarity.

American Roughshooting—The sport of hunting ground-dwelling, wild-propagated, upland game birds using the practice of walking in and through native habitat—preferably using dogs to find and flush the birds, which are then killed in flight, using a shotgun, then retrieved.

Either way it is easily understood.

There is a definition of *upland* in my *Webster's New Twentieth Century Dictionary, Unabridged*:

Upland—1. Up' land, n. high land; ground elevated above the lowlands, as of a region or country 2. Up'land, of or pertaining to upland, growing on upland.

So I take it that *upland game birds* defines game birds most commonly found on dry ground. That excludes ducks, geese and rails, and although woodcock need moist ground to survive, they seldom are found in swamps. Woodcock are considered an upland bird.

This book focuses on the four most widely distributed upland game birds—ring-neck pheasants, ruffed grouse, woodcock or bob white quail—that American roughshooters spend the majority of their time, energy and dollars hunting. But America's woods and fields host many other great game birds, each with a restricted range. Those hunters fortunate enough to tackle the less common birds in their native habitat will have a great time adapting their techniques and skills to successfully hunt those species.

Most hunters, due to time and logistical constraints, limit the scope of their roughshooting to one or two species, and their focus helps them develop proficiency. Given the opportunity, most good, adaptable hunters could quickly broaden their talents to become proficient on other species. The basic skills are the same. Unfortunately, for most of us, there is never enough time to hunt all the coverts we want to hunt, test our skills on all the different game bird species that interest us or cross every mountain ridge on a bracing, autumn morning.

WHY IS ROUGHSHOOTING SO SPECIAL?

I grew up roughshooting. Since we didn't own a bird dog, our hunting was a long hike in the woods or fields, shooting whatever our feet flushed, fur or feather. It was great fun and I spent many happy days doing it.

Somewhere in my twenties, I lost interest or got involved in other more voguish sports like golf and tennis, and they were fun for a while. But in my thirties, I rediscovered bird hunting in all its many forms, and I embraced it with a zeal that surprised me. I had always been one to flit from one hobby or interest to another, but when I got back into shooting, I stayed with it. I swallowed the hook as completely as anyone could. I tried every kind of bird shooting—sitting in blinds, sneak boats, quail safaris, pass shooting—but my real love was hard-going hunting with a bold and hard-driving dog, the kind of hunting that makes me sweat. That is the real roughshooting. That is my nature: active, pushy, involved. I'm a doer, not a watcher and I'd rather shoot pinball than watch the Superbowl.

Many times I lie in bed after a hard day afield and ask myself why I've enjoyed the hunt so much. The answer is always difficult to grasp because I like it all. I love to watch the dogs work. I enjoy being outside in the weather. These are moments of great excitement, interspersed with traveling miles of countryside. The exercise makes me feel terrific, and the dull ache from a day's hunt provides a relief from too many days in the office.

Intense personal involvement is the essence of roughshooting. Here Ham Schirmer walks in behind his English Setter "Davis" to flush either a grouse or a woodcock.

Roughshooting is simply special, and for those of us who have caught the fever, it is a daily thought twelve months of the year, not just for two or three days during bird hunting season. Many years ago, the late Dr. Harry B. Bigelow, a noted marine biologist and consummate grouse hunter, uttered a notable statement: "About the time a man learns to hunt grouse, he dies!" Accomplished roughshooters develop and apply a complex set of skills: reading the cover, formulating a strategy, controlling a high-powered dog, orienteering and quick shooting, all performed during a period of strenuous physical activity, sometimes in very adverse weather conditions. This sport is not for the armchair cowboy, which is why accomplished roughshooters account for only 2 or 3 percent of all the hunters who purchase a small game hunting license in any given year.

My skills and knowledge were developed under the quiet tutelage and mentoring of some very accomplished roughshooters, men who approached the sport with a passion and were willing to share their knowledge and their coverts with me. Any of them could have written this book, but they were too busy living every day.

As one becomes a serious and accomplished roughshooter, *three major decisions* are made, consciously or unconsciously. Where to hunt and which bird to concentrate on? Which style dog to own? And what type gun to shoot? Every hunter makes those decisions. This book may help you evaluate those decisions more directly.

You certainly won't agree with everything I write. Sometimes your opinions and mine will be very different. This book also includes the opinions of some very knowledgeable collaborators: dog trainers, hunting guides and gunsmiths who can be called "experts." I think you will find their opinions enlightening and thought provoking.

THE FUTURE OF ROUGHSHOOTING

Autumn days cause a yearning for the hunting fields in the heart of every dedicated outdoorsman, a calling akin to the urges that drive geese south in the fall. This tradition, a rite of the season, a ritual that bird-shooting sportsmen have sometimes carried to the level of an art, is marked by fine dogs, high quality guns, elaborate social settings, deep friendships and a rigorous adherence to a code of ethics.

Our sport is taxing and time consuming, but it can be properly enjoyed by any physically fit person willing to learn the necessary skills. Unlike English or European roughshooting, American roughshooting has never been reserved only for the elite.

As with virtually every aspect of American life, roughshooting today is more of a do-it-yourself sport. The days of armies of dog handlers, cooks and guides are long gone. That has been replaced by a whole generation of physically active sportsmen who not only hunt in the fall but ski, mountain hike, white-water raft, sail, fly-fish and jog. These are people who search out life rather than waiting for it to pay a visit.

Roughshooting is also a high-profile blood sport using firearms, and therein lies the portent of restrictive legislation. I see three threats looming on the horizon. The first is antigun legislation, prompted by a wave of wanton killing in our streets. Unfortunately, many well-meaning citizens associate the treasured old side-by-sides in my locker with street violence. To them a gun is a gun. Antigun laws will pass and the honest hunters need to separate themselves from the AK47 and Uzi crowd. The second threat is the animal rights groups that are simply against any form of blood sports. Our best counter to that argument is a strict adherence to a high code of

ethics. The third threat is the wave of slobs in the field that hunt without permission, break fences, trample crops, litter the landscape and violate the game laws. We are guilty by association. That type of hunter gives us all a bad name and they are driving many farmers into a "pay-to-hunt" mentality.

Maintaining large amounts of proper habitat is the key to the future of roughshooting in America, and every hunter has an obligation to support the environment that supports wildlife.

What separates the roughshooter from the meat hunter is an appreciation for the best traditions of the sport, a zeal to develop a high level of skills, and willingness to support

what is best for our environment. The future of the sport is in the hands of the roughshooters. Traditional roughshooters vote, pay taxes, obey laws, support wildlife conservation and environmental causes, and conduct themselves responsibly. This core of ethical sportsmen must chart the path and set the standards for the sport.

HOW THIS BOOK IS ORGANIZED

This book is laid out in a collective style, like patching together a series of five booklets (or sections), all bound together by a common theme. The first section discusses the four great game birds of America and how to

pursue them successfully. Section two covers the wide and wonderful varieties of gun dogs available today. It goes on to discuss matching your style with the dog's style, the dog skills needed to succeed and maintenance and training needs of a fine dog. Section three covers the tools of the sport—game guns in many shapes, sizes and grades. It focuses on selecting a gun to fit your shooting style and

Trucks, fancy and stylish, are today's roughshooters' preferred mode of travel.

how to hone the skills to shoot better in the field. Section four is about the finer things in life—good friends, good food, good drink, good times and how to easily enjoy them regardless of how remote the spot. Section five is a random group of thoughts, ideas and suggestions on the style and ethics one brings to American roughshooting and maybe life in general.

Three of the four sections of this book relate to birds, dogs and guns. Which bird you choose to hunt affects your choice of a dog and a gun. If you are a dedicated quail hunter and will generally hunt in the South, the type of dog and gun you choose will be considerably different than an Iowa pheasant fan. If you follow the seasons to hunt pheasant on the prairies, grouse in Minnesota, woodcock in Maine and quail in Alabama—all with one dog and one gun—you will need to make some compromises, for all the choices are intertwined. The selection and training of a multitalented gun dog is complex, and most of us have more than one gun, whether we need it or not. That may hurt our shooting more than it helps.

Miscellaneous Subjects

In many places this book is a collection of random experiences, observations and opinions. Sometimes it was difficult to find the proper placement within the context of the book, or perhaps the discussion applies to more than one category. In those cases I have tried to place the subject in the most relevant area. For example, the subject of Conservation Reserve Program (CRP) property is in the pheasant section, since CRP has more impact on pheasants than on quail.

Two-trigger guns are discussed in the side-by-side section, since that is where two triggers are most often found. Backing another dog's points is discussed in the pointer and setter section, since these dogs are most generally expected to back solidly.

The dog's—ah yes, the wonderful, exciting, stylish dogs that make roughshooting so interesting. Shown here a German Wirehaired Pointer, "Levi," (left) and an English Pointer, "Blackie," (right).

Much of this book reflects ideas that I gathered from my hunting partners—at least those subjects we batted back and forth during the long drives to the shooting places or over dinner after a long day of hunting. In many cases these ideas are other people's knowledge, experience or beliefs that I have lived with so long and embraced so fully that I now sometimes believe they were my ideas originally. I hope my friends will forgive me if I've appropriated their thoughts.

Throughout most of this book I use the masculine pronoun *he*: *he* the hunter, *he* the dog. There is no particular reason for this. In my experience most roughshooters are men, although I know of some very proficient women hunters. Although my dog references generally use the masculine pronoun *he,* in practice about 90 percent of my hunting dogs have been female.

I always refer to the vehicle as a *truck.* Today the vast majority of hunters drive a truck of some type, be it a four-wheel-drive sport utility truck, a minivan, a suburban or a pickup truck with a dog box or a bed cap. Cars and station wagons are extremely rare in the hunting world today.

C H A P T E R 2
PHEASANTS IN AMERICA

The majestic ring-necked pheasant, a bird of uncommon cunning and grace, first came to our shores from its native China in 1881. It flourished first in the Willamette Valley of Oregon, but soon spread its range across the United States through propagation and transplant. During its prolific periods, the pheasant grew in wildly abundant numbers in states as far removed as California, Washington, Nebraska, Iowa, Michigan, New York and Maine. But its stronghold was always the fertile farmlands of the northern grain belt, from the Dakotas through Pennsylvania. No one really knows for sure why the huge pheasant populations of the 1950s and 1960s suddenly fell during the 1970s and 1980s. Experts cite many possible causes including: the end of the soil bank program; the change in farm practices that left little undercover for nesting; and pesticides, disease, viruses or genetic deficiencies. Today the wild ring-necked pheasant populations in many former strongholds like Ohio, New York and Pennsylvania are sparse, and the decline has appeared to be long term and irreversible in these areas. However, a significant development occurred in the early 1990s when the Sichuan strains of ring-necked pheasants were introduced in Michigan. This introduction, which seems initially to be successful, is expected to instill renewed vigor, wariness, nesting practices that enhance survivability and more realistic habitat needs. The Szechuan, which readily mates with native ringnecks, may be the key to renewed pheasant populations in the northeastern section of the United States from Michigan to Maine.

Fortunately, there are still pockets of strong ring-necked populations in the plains states of Iowa, Nebraska, Kansas and the Dakotas that continue to reproduce vigorously. Throughout the great plains, many states are currently in a strong upswing period of bird populations, approaching or even exceeding the record years of the 1950s and 1960s. Most knowledgeable wildlife experts credit the Conservation Reserve Program (CRP) for all of the growth in bird numbers.

This is all great news for today's very mobile hunter, who has both the time and the resources to travel to the areas that produce birds. However, the current wave of prosperous hunters, able to roam the nation in search of great hunting opportunities, is taxing and testing the time-honored traditions of free pheasant hunting on private land. Many states and many farmers have come to view "out-of-state" hunters as a revenue source, and this raises grave concerns that wild birds will turn into a cash crop for landowners, as they are in England and Continental Europe, where only the rich can afford to hunt on privately controlled land. I've lived and hunted in pheasant country most of my adult life and spent many wonderful days afield. I also developed some of my best personal friends, both hunters and farmers, during pheasant hunting trips through the American heartland. I'd hate to see that American legacy wiped out by "cash only" shooting.

MATCHING WITS WITH A PHEASANT

No two days of pheasant hunting are ever the same, for every day the birds move around their locale and constantly shift habits and habitat to avoid the hunter. Over the years I have come to respect the ringneck as the most intelligent of the big four game birds and the one that, through its cunning and shrewdness, is most able to elude my efforts.

On opening day, the young birds may not understand the realities of their world, but they either wise up quickly or perish. By midseason only the wise or the very lucky birds have survived. Therefore, successful hunting for pheasants requires a careful study of the situation and the development of geographic tactics. A well-developed plan for attacking a piece of cover can raise your chances of success by 25 to 50 percent. My experience tells me that if we were able to track all the birds that sneak out the escape routes, or run far and fast always staying beyond gun range, we would account for at least 50 percent of the birds. Careful planning and pincher tactics are what you need to successfully hunt these wily pheasants.

I have never been a deer hunter, but I once read a report of an experiment where two very experienced deer hunters (with radio tracers) entered an eighty-acre enclosure that contained two wise old bucks also wearing radio transmitters. As the observers tracked both the deer and the hunters, they learned that both moved in convoluted paths within these eighty acres of prime habitat, constantly playing hide-and-seek. At times the deer and the hunters were in extremely close proximity, but the hunters never saw a deer the entire day. In many ways that experiment replicates pheasant hunting without either a geographic strategy or a good dog.

Before hunting a piece of property it is prudent to map out a plan, where three rules generally apply:

1. Try to work into the wind. The dog's nose works best into the wind and it will usually find and trail birds better going into the wind. An into-the-wind direction also muffles the noise you make, allowing you to get closer to the birds. Any loud, unnatural noise will spook birds, so work quietly into the wind as you approach.

2. Sweep the cover clean as you go, working out all of the cover much as you would sweep dirt ahead of you on a sidewalk. Try to keep birds from running around you. Visualize herding the unseen birds as you go.

3. Walk out all the little escape routes—especially if your dog shows any birdiness as you start into the little fingers of cover.

Over the years I've probably shot as many birds from the tiny fingers of cover as from the big main bodies of the sloughs. In most cases these were birds that my dog and I had pushed into a flight-to-escape situation. I especially remember a day in western Iowa when my dog and I found our three-rooster limit, but each was at the far end of a long and winding finger of cover. The dog pushed each bird until the cover petered out and the bird had to fly in order to escape. The shots were long but the strong loads of number fives were up to the task. You must be prepared to do some serious walking in this process. You'll be squeezing out miles of cover, including some long walks across bare ground to gain position. You need a dog that will adapt its methods to match various types and

Country roads, many a mixture of gravel and mud, lead to the best pheasant covers in the midwest.

Wil Avril's grin tells the story.

sizes of cover at your direction, sometimes running wide and fast to sweep large expanses, and other times staying close and working slowly in order to push out a small finger of cover. An adaptable dog is a great asset in pheasant country.

Mature and experienced pheasants are very wary and most will run ahead of the noise of the hunter and the dog. I always try to visualize my efforts as herding the birds, pushing them into a situation where they must fly in order to flee. Of course, not all of the birds can stand the suspense and some will panic and fly long before you reach the end of a piece of cover. Others will try to hunker down in the cover and a few will hold extremely tight until you pass. This is where a reliable dog with a good nose will root out the birds and produce many of your most memorable shots.

PHEASANT WEATHER

Perfect weather for pheasant hunting dawns crisp and clear with a morning dusting of ice diamonds that shimmer on the grass, then slowly melt, as the sun warms the morning to perfection. Then add a gentle five mile-per-hour breeze and enough moisture in the air to enhance scenting. Under these circumstances, good dogs exhibit a brilliant use of their olfactory talents and great stamina. Unfortunately, days of perfect weather may not always happen for you, especially if you have squeezed your long-planned hunting trip into a busy work calendar. Perfect days are fairly common on the rolling prairie—they just seldom seem to happen when I'm on hand to enjoy them. But I come to hunt and hunt I do, regardless of weather conditions.

My trips to the midwest have run the gamut from hot, dry, eighty-degree scorchers that burned out the dogs in only a few hours to brutally cold, windy, snow-swept days that chilled us to the bone. One year we hunted Iowa in several inches of snow and thirty mile-per-hour winds. A trip to Wal-Mart for insulated sweatshirts and gloves saved the trip. The weather also determines when the farmers can harvest the crops. If the corn is still standing due to late rains, the birds will be hiding and feeding in the standing corn. They cannot be easily hunted under those circumstances in the corn, especially with dogs.

THE BEST PHEASANT COVER IS INVISIBLE

My favorite and most productive cover is often invisible. Invisible, that is, from the road or the highway. It is not the big rolling areas of CRP ground, although that is a major source of pheasant production. My favorite spots— the places that fill my mind with beautiful memories of sunlit days, competent dogs finding birds, long crossing shots that scored and long difficult retrieves completed—are almost all little fingers of invisible cover.

The places where birds can be found have changed over time as farming practices have significantly altered the birds' habitat. At one time, some of the best pheasant cover in America existed on the large tracts of almost dead level ground in north central Illinois, northern Iowa, eastern Nebraska and southern Minnesota. That "table top" flat terrain also accommodated some of the finest farmland in America. It was, in fact, so productive that many farmers switched to 100 percent grain production. They sold off their livestock, removed all the fences and cleared all the ditches so they could plow from horizon to horizon. Unfortunately, this practice also reduced pheasant habitat, almost all of those weedy, brushy, trashy ditches and fence rows where pheasants could hide and raise their broods. Then, in the 1970s, the farmers took to fall plowing to have the ground basically ready to quickly plant crops in the spring. If the ground is turned in the fall, spring planting requires only a couple of quick passes with disc, harrow and planter. With more efficient farming practices came the use of herbicides so strong and error free as to make a corn crop weedless. Soon there is absolutely no place for a pheasant to hide, survive predation or raise a brood. By the early 1980s, pheasant hunting in northern Iowa had seriously declined to the point of not being worth the sportsman's effort.

The pheasant habitat gradually shifted to the rough edges of the great plains, the rolling prairies where deep weed-entangled waterways provided year-round sanctuary to an ever-increasing population of pheasants. These are *the* spots, small hidden patches of cover, many so small as to be invisible from the road. These are the hidden oases of cover that support a surprising number of pheasants. But these spots are not for the lazy nor the timid. These spots exact a toll of sweat and miles of walking. Getting to them involves climbing and hiking, crossing fences, jumping streams and pushing through waist-high tangles of brush, briars and prairie grass. Most importantly, it involves knocking on doors and asking permission to hunt.

Last fall in one of my favorite parts of the Midwest—in a county I had hunted dozens of times before—an old friend invited me to hunt in one of his favorite spots. Even though I had often driven down this highway, I would have never expected the wonderland of ditches and cover that bisected this two hundred-acre field. From the road it looked like a clear, flat corn stubble field corner to corner. But my impressions were dead wrong. Subtly camouflaged by the rolling hills was a treasure trove of hiding places. On that morning, while my young dog found and flushed four roosters, she also found and worked 15 or 20 hens. It was a great learning experience for her and a thrill for me. I love to watch the strong and bold flush of a startled hen.

Working these dense patches of cover again challenges your tactics and dog control. A dog running wildly, out of control and hunting on its own with little or no regard for you or your tactics is the wily rooster's best friend. That dog gives your quarry ample warning of your approach and results in a spectacular wild flush, a hundred yards or more from your gun. The invisible covers of the American pheasant range are the tactical hunter's dream.

NOT ALL PHEASANT SHOTS ARE EQUAL

How pheasants are found and flushed and the position of the gunners significantly affect the amount of shot required to down a bird. The flight path of the bird and the angle of the shot make a tremendous difference in the force needed to drop it. In England, birds are often shot by stationary gunners, as the birds are driven (fly) toward and over the gunning stations (called butts). Since the birds are flying toward the guns, the shot charge is concentrated on vital areas—the head, neck and chest. At this angle a small amount of shot can have tremendous impact on the bird, even from great distances.

Conversely, when we roughshoot pheasants in America, we generally flush the birds at a significant distance from us and they fly directly away. When the birds are flying away, the shot is striking a less vital part of the bird and must penetrate through heavy rear plumage

I snagged this photo off the wall of Lee Seinkowski's office. The German Shorthaired Pointer helped put together a very successful season. "Yukon" is owned by Fred Tilsner of Kenosha, Wisconsin, and trained by Lee Seinkowski.

to reach vitals. Generally speaking, the wilder the bird, the
farther ahead of the guns it
will flush, so the shots are
longer. Rugged old roosters,
two or three years old, have
heavy muscling, dense feathers
and stronger escape instincts
than yearlings or released
birds. Seldom will one or two pellets do the job at this range and angle.
Hence, American roughshooters tend to use stronger loads with more shot
and larger shot sizes than their English counterparts.

People hunting over any breed of flushing dog tend to use a bit more
gun than those shooting over any of the Pointers or setters, for obvious reasons. Birds flushed by flushing dogs are a bit farther from the gun. Over
flushing dogs an extra measure of shot from a larger gauge gun is helpful.
This is even more true with spaniels than with retriever breeds. In my experience the spaniels will consistently quest farther from the gunner than a
retriever, thus making the shots longer and more challenging. When using
a spaniel, the tiny gauge guns often do not pack the firepower to get the
job done consistently.

PHEASANT HUNTING STRATEGIES, TACTICS AND TIPS

To hunt the wild rooster successfully you need a basic understanding of the
birds' behavior, which varies as they become older and warier. On any particular day weather can also significantly alter the bird's actions. There is little doubt that the easiest and most predictable hunting occurs on opening
day when the young naive birds sit tight. But the challenge gets progres-
sively more difficult as the season wears on and weather conditions worsen.
A new crop of naive young roosters may be ignorant of the ways of the
approaching hunter, but after being dusted with lead a few times, the survivors grow leery and begin to run away from the approach of any man,
regardless of why he has come to the bird field.

During the early season before the crops are completely harvested, the
birds will spend most of the daylight hours in the fields of standing corn or
milo. Here they feel safe with a full supply of food and shelter. Pheasants
learn to elude their natural predators by running away through the tall
crops and the noise of the corn leaves alerts the birds to your approach.
Many farmers, fearing crop damage, will *not* allow hunters to enter their
standing corn or milo. But when permission is granted, a push through
standing corn in a traditional pheasant drive is a productive method of

hunting. The use of dogs when pushing through standing crops rarely works unless the dogs are extremely close working and obedient. You can easily lose a dog in a large field of corn and a wild running dog will follow moving birds until they are far out of shooting range. Once your dog is out of control, it can become disoriented by the noise of the wind in the corn, and many dogs are lost for hours in these circumstances.

As the corn or milo fields are harvested, some birds will continue to spend days in the remaining standing crops, but many will disperse into the surrounding bits of weedy cover, fence rows, CRP fields and drainage sloughs. Note: Milo is a grain crop that is grown in more arid regions of the great plains, and pheasants will eat milo as aggressively as corn. At this point the birds feed mostly on grain dropped in the fields during the harvesting process. Although it is obvious that the pheasants spend a considerable amount of time feeding in the harvested fields, few hunters concentrate their efforts in the corn or milo stubble. Milo or corn stubble, especially if trashy and filled with pockets of weeds, can on occasion hold a bird or two, but clean stubble without trash is less productive and usually involves miles and miles of walking with little to show for it. As the season progresses and the birds become increasingly wary, they seem to feed as close to the security of cover as possible, ducking back into the thick weedy growth from the crop fields as soon as any sign of danger approaches. On the days when scenting conditions are perfect, a spaniel or a retriever can trail foot scent as if following a railroad track. You can walk into a cornfield and literally watch the dog follow individual bird tracks from the corn back into the cover.

A dog with a good nose for track-ing will provide solid indicators when it is tracking a bird, often finding, losing, and then refinding the scent trail in an on again, off again frenzy. I've sometimes fol-lowed a dog as it methodically trailed a bird for a quarter mile. Eventually, the bird will stop mov-ing and flush, hopefully within gun range.

The line of hunters works through the field.

TACTICS

You must use tactics to plot how to divide and conquer a piece of cover to block the ground escape routes and force the birds into flight.

From a wildlife standpoint, CRP is to the 1980s and 1990s what the "Soil Bank" was to the 1950s. Since the advent of CRP, pheasant populations have exploded and today are at levels not experienced in forty years. CRP ground offers a special challenge for the hunter. Although CRP property has been a boon to pheasant populations, it has introduced a whole new dimension to hunting, as the giant fields offer so many escape routes and ways for the birds to run around the hunter to avoid being flushed. CRP vegetation is often very dense, and in hot weather it will wear down a dog in short order. Putting pressure on birds in a fifty-acre field also isn't easy. A well-controlled dog that will follow a track and stay within gun range is invaluable. The ideal dog runs big enough to cover the ground, while still being easily controlled to stay in range.

Such a dog can be of either a pointing breed or a flushing breed so long as it meets these criteria. Recently I hunted through a fifty-acre field in Iowa with three friends (four hunters) and two dogs. The dogs were a medium-ranging Brittany and a horizon-running English Setter. We shot five roosters in the field; two in close proximity to the Brittany as she carefully worked the trail of moving birds, and three that we walked up. The big running setter, a dog with a terrific proven nose, never indicated a bird, never pointed and never bumped a bird even though he covered three times as much ground as the Brittany. The dog was apparently running over the trails and never encountered a nesting bird.

I hunted pheasants in a huge Kansas CRP tract recently over Quinn Smith's beautifully trained eight-year-old English Setter, Lady. She found several birds almost at my feet while a partner's big-running dog on the other side of the field popped out a dozen birds at the far fence several hundred yards away from the gunner. CRP has been a boon to the guy with a controllable dog and a disaster for the guy with the out-of-control horizon runner.

Another tactic is the pheasant drive. If you get a chance to join a traditional Dakota pheasant drive, don't miss the experience. A unique way to corral a wily rooster and force him to fly before guns, the big Dakota pheasant drive parallels the driven shoots of England in some way. However, here the beaters carry guns and shoot. Usually, ten, fifteen or even twenty hunters line up twenty yards apart. They march from road to road through fields, brush, scrub trees and corn stubble, herding and driving the birds in front of their noise. It sounds dangerous, and it can be, so you hope for a master hunter with the backbone and confidence to give the group a stern lecture on gun safety before you start. You need blockers, hunters who stand at the end of the fields to shut off the escape paths for the fast-running birds. Blocking is the job for an older hunter or a guy with a bit of a health problem—a bum knee, bad back or sprained ankle. Safety here is also of the utmost importance as two groups of hunters converge. Only shots high into the air are appropriate at the ends of the fields. When approaching the blockers, shooting a low-flying rooster is strictly forbidden, just as it is in England.

I participated in a South Dakota pheasant drive at Bill Welk's Ranch. Bill Welk always gave the group a stern safety lecture before the start of the drive. He also included some retrieving advice. There were very few dogs on the line and he urged every hunter to "run directly to the spot" of the fall of any rooster. In his words, "They'll fall like a stone . . . but in twenty seconds they'll jump up and run away." Was he right! The shooters were accurate marksmen and the loads they were firing were stiff magnum shells, but at the Dakota distances a high percentage of those tough and wiry birds survived the shot to run away. On that day at least 20 percent of the downed birds were not found by the shooters. I was very surprised by the percentage of lost birds—much higher than I experience hunting over dogs.

Dogs are strictly optional in a pheasant drive, but only well-mannered dogs that work very close are of any value. A wide-ranging dog would be a detriment if it just ran ahead and flushed out the game before the line of hunters pushed through the field.

It is obvious to me that no one dog is ideal for every pheasant hunting situation, although some are more adaptable than others. A medium-ranged dog is of value in CRP covers, while a close-working dog will stay in gun range when you work fence rows and small fingers of cover. Owning two dogs of very different styles can be of great value and there is no substitute for a good retriever to find downed birds.

TIPS

I live in Michigan, where deer hunting season is a big deal. On the fifteenth of November, seven hundred thousand orange-clad hunters enter the woods ready for a big event. By law, the bird season closes for two weeks, but an army of orange-clad guys with rifles is enough reason for me to stay home and rest, especially after two months of hunting grouse, woodcock and pheasants. Here in Michigan they report the success of the first few days of the deer season on TV and radio—just like the sports scores. One morning on the way to work I tuned in to the local fifty thousand-watt station in time to hear the state's most renowned outdoor sports commentator explain that high winds in excess of thirty miles per hour had materially altered the hunting during the first few days of the season. His explanation seemed quite plausible. In his view deer rely mostly on their sense of smell and hearing to warn them of coming danger. In high, gusty wind neither sense works very well so the deer become very *"skittish."*

On the day I heard this report, I was just back to work after hunting trips to Iowa, South Dakota and Kansas, and each trip had included one day with heavy winds, sometimes gusting to forty miles per hour. The same rule must hold true for pheasants, because they were *"skittish"* as hell, often flushing several hundred yards ahead of the dogs. The high winds seem to arouse the birds almost to a state of panic. Couple that with the fact that the dogs can't find much when the wind is whipping the scent away and these days of high wind are seldom very productive.

Working into the wind greatly reduces the noise you generate and the less human voice commands to the dog, the better. The human voice seems to spook the birds more than a whistle. I think the birds' warning mechanisms are less acute on windy days and they overcompensate with extreme wariness. On a very windy day in Iowa we watched birds fly out of a huge CRP field a half-mile ahead of us as the wind carried our sound to the very spooky birds. Finding the most sheltered covers, away from the wind and then hunting into the wind is about the only tactic to use on these high-wind days.

Weather is always a factor and on especially cold, snowy or rainy days, the birds are usually in the deepest cover, hunkered down to avoid the weather. If you can find these sheltered spots, you'll have great hunting. Although the weather is miserable for the hunter, the birds tend to hold tighter. After a wet period of rain or mist, the birds are often in sunny places, warming up and drying off; south slopes are a favorite. On hot days the birds tend to stay in open areas where the air is light and the cool breezes flow.

You don't often see a flock of rooster pheasants. When you do, note it well and commit the event to memory. What I'm referring to is a group of roosters bunched up together and moving together to elude you and your dog. On almost every occasion when I have encountered such a flock, the cover was so dense as to virtually guarantee the birds' sanctuary. The birds certainly did not expect an aggressive spaniel to come thrashing in their midst.

We once surprised a rooster flock in waist-high frozen cattails, a patch more than three acres in size. On close inspection of the cattail stubble, we could see the ground was criss-crossed by dozens of small trails and paths, giving the birds untold escape routes. As I thrashed through the middle of the patch, my spaniel flushed roosters out of their shelter right and left— some behind me, some in front—about a dozen birds in all. On another occasion, we launched into a very dense strip of reedy grass covering the bottom of a deep swale. This strip was no more than forty yards wide and two hundred yards long, but the grass stalks were so stiff and so interwoven that they were almost impenetrable. However, my determined Springer thrust her way through it until she found the birds.

Another time, the roosters hid in year-old, unharvested sorghum cane. Inch-thick sorghum stalks had fallen, randomly weaving a mesh of inter-twined vegetation and the unthrashed sorghum heads had dribbled grain into the cozy mass of tunnels.

In all three cases, I just happened onto a sanctuary selected by the birds for its natural concealment and its ability to give ample warning (crackling, crashing, popping) when any danger approached. In each case only aggressive hunting by my Springers forced the birds to flight. The dog would crash into the mass of cover and spring into a frenzy of action. Most Springers give ample warning via body action when they hit scent. But in these cases (several different dogs were involved in different places and years) they reached a level of animation I had not seen before or since. In some cases the dog made so much noise crashing around that it didn't hear the bird's wings, and only the *bang* of my 12 bore told the dog that a bird had flown. I can only suppose that the level of scent enveloping the ground level of this bird haven must have put forth an aroma of pheasants so strong as to match the pungent atmosphere of my favorite restaurant in Little Italy!

On one such occasion, working a very young and inexperienced dog, I watched him go berserk on scent, but when the bird flushed twenty feet from me, I missed the rooster with *both* barrels. The young (unsteady) pup just wouldn't respond to my calls and kept hunting. Naturally, I thought he was confused by the scent of the first bird—until the second bird flushed, before my empty gun—followed only a few seconds later by a third rooster. I had an empty game bag but both the dog and I had learned a valuable lesson. He learned to stay with fresh scent even if a bird has flown, and I learned to trust that dog and reload fast.

Cover like this will also make you believe in teaching a dog to take hand signals and "hunt dead." Often your shot is the dog's first and only knowl-edge that the bird has flown and fallen. She must then rely on you for direction to the fall. I recall one bird that flew out of a deep swale and I hit it with the second barrel of my old Parker 12 gauge. It dropped just over the edge of a ridge. The fall was totally blind to the dog so I ended up yelling and gesturing and finally walking the dog to within twenty yards or so of where I thought the bird had fallen. When she finally reached the area of the fall, she showed some interest but began to cast around as if puzzled. It had now been five minutes or so since the bird had fallen. My instincts told me to *just shut up* and let her work it out. She hunted and hunted, then suddenly she was eighty or ninety yards away, nose to the ground and gaining speed with every stride. Within seconds she was two

The range of the ring-necked pheasant in North America.

hundred yards away running down a very alive rooster in an all-out foot race through a stubble field.

There are several lessons here. One, finding the birds grouped up is mainly a matter of luck. Usually they are spread out foraging or they scatter far ahead of your noisy approach.

Two, *always* reload fast and be ready for another flush.

Three, trust your dog! Let it work.

Four, teach your dog to work with you on blind or directed retrieves—completing a long, difficult retrieve is truly a thing of beauty.

Five, work the tough stuff—that is real bird cover.

CHAPTER 3
HUNTING THE NORTH WOODS
FOR RUFFED GROUSE

For all practical purposes grouse and woodcock hunting covers are one and the same. Although the age of the cover that pleases each bird may vary slightly, such differences are subtle and usually only distinguishable to the most experienced hunters. As for technique, most dedicated hunters have just accepted the fact that the best way to find either bird is to walk the ground, mile after mile.

I'm a woods hunter, as are most of the men with whom I've hunted. Other people see the grouse as a bird of abandoned homesteads. Franklin Burroughs, in his book of essays *Billy Watson's Croker Sack*, puts it this way:

> . . . their [grouse's] fondness for apples explains why they haunt the old home sites, farms sunk back into the forest, and the stone fences that once marked the borders of the fields. Further north, they are a true forest bird, but here they have become a bird of abandoned history. . . .

I've often read about the ruffed grouse's affection for abandoned farms and especially old orchards, but I think those writings hark back to the 1950s and 1960s when numerous farms across the grouse range were being allowed to return to nature. Today those thickets are composed of medium-sized timber and most of the orchard trees have died of old age. I now find grouse mainly in the new-growth areas and most often grouse and woodcock are interspersed. In an hour's hunt you may find two grouse and three woodcock all mixed along your path. Both prefer the subtle shadings of the cover you traverse. You may flush a grouse or two as you walk the young alders before you stumble onto a definite woodcock haven where the ground is dotted with "splash," a sure sign that a significant woodcock flight has touched down on this site.

THE THREE PHASES OF THE GROUSE SEASON

Grouse season includes three distinct and very different hunting phases. The first comes early, from opening day until the leaves fall—the heavy foliage season. Next comes the traditional period, when the leaves are down and the ground is bare. The final phase comes with winter, when the trees are naked and the ground is blanketed in snow.

The grouse hunting so lovingly chronicled in literature occurs in the middle period, which usually starts between October first and tenth in the north woods. A sudden transformation takes the woods from full autumn resplendence to the nakedness of winter. A woods with diverse flora can lengthen the seasonal striptease as each species sheds its coat on a different schedule, but usually the majority of the foliage drops during one or two days of a cold hard rain and strong swirling winds. It is not unusual to be poke shooting on Wednesday, firing off shell after shell at birds only half seen through a canopy of golden foliage, but by Thursday afternoon to have bird flushes fully visible through naked limbs stripped of their leaves by a night of wind and rain.

Old orchards, stone fences and abandoned farms are a part of the legend of the ruffed grouse. Combine a fine, close-working English Setter, a fine double gun and a crisp fall day, and the storybook setting is complete.

I wish I could always plan hunting trips to match the glorious middle phase of the season that I most enjoy. However, the timing of the falling leaves is controlled by a higher authority, while my timing is controlled by a busy business calendar. Some years, in the far north, my favorite phase (no leaves, no snow) is short and only a few weeks may separate bare branches from the year's first deep snow. I remember one season in the early 1990s in northern Minnesota when the branches were plucked clean by an October tenth storm and a twenty-inch snow fell a week before Halloween.

Many impatient hunters tackle the woods in full autumn foliage. Grouse and woodcock season traditionally start in mid-September in the northern tier states of Minnesota, Wisconsin, Michigan, New York, Vermont, New Hampshire, Maine and the eastern provinces of Canada. Even though I know better, after a year of anticipation, I'm always eager to race off in search of the birds even if the season is prefrost and the woods are in full foliage. Regardless of the consequences, on September fifteenth my truck heads north. Although a few native woodcock may fall to my gun, the grouse are just thundering ghosts in the trees that race my heart and make promises in my mind for the weeks to come. What I usually get is exercise, sunburn and mosquito bites. I've never been quite sure why the season opens so early except to assuage our anxious interests.

Late in the season there are many spots in the United States and Canada where the deep snowpack and the grouse season overlap and grouse shooting on snowshoes or (I suppose) cross-country skis is available. I've known several hunters who tackled grouse via snowshoe trekking, but I've never known anyone with the dexterity and balance to ski and wing shoot at the same time. Of course this is dogless hunting, for dogs cannot negotiate the deep snow for more than a few minutes.

There are times when you will be forced to hunt grouse when the ground is covered by an inch or two of powdery fluff from a sudden overnight snow squall, which is quite common in the north woods. Challenging and physically taxing, snow never seems to affect the dog's nose the same way twice. Sometimes the scent seems to lay upon the white bed of snow like a down comforter holding the essence of game close to the ground for the dog to boldly find. At other times snow seems to deaden the dog's nose or disperse the scent in a way that converts the dog into a woods thrasher that merely frightens the birds into flight.

In northern Minnesota we once hunted with dogs through two inches of wet snow and found grouse throughout the morning on the heavy edges by the pine thickets. We assumed that the woodcock had all flown out on the winds of the approaching storm, but by late afternoon the snow had melted off in spots and we were into fairly heavy woodcock shooting. I still wonder where the woodcock found shelter during that morning to avoid the snow. We sure hadn't flushed any.

Each of the three phases of grouse hunting has its own unique character and charm, but must be approached with tailored strategies, adjusted techniques and realistic expectations.

GROUSE CYCLES

In the northern areas of their range, the fortunes of the ruffed grouse rise and fall dramatically on a ten-year cycle. This is not a moderate swing of a few percentage points but an explosive population increase during peak cycles and a deadly fall during the lows of the cycle. Drops of 90 percent from peak populations are not unheard of, as these cycles undulate across the northern grouse range in coordinated waves. For years no one knew for sure why these cycles occurred, but many theories were advanced, including changes in food supply, disease, genetic weakness and predator cycles. The Ruffed Grouse Society has studied the bird for many years and devoted millions of donated dollars to developing ideal grouse habitat, but still the cycle continues. Obviously the cycle involves more than habitat consequences. The late Gordon Gullion, a director of the Ruffed Grouse Society (RGS), was America's most esteemed ruffed grouse biologist and researcher. He studied and documented more about the ruffed grouse than anyone else had. While he never completely unraveled the mystery of the cycle, he added a great deal to the knowledge of this phenomenon. Since Gordon's death, U.S. biologists, including Dan Dessecker, a young RGS researcher living in Rice Lake, Wisconsin, have continued Gordon's research.

Dan has been filling me in on the latest theories on ruffed grouse cycles. Based on current research, it appears that two factors account for the cycle. First, raptor populations significantly increase; so significantly, in fact, that a snowshoe hare cycle has developed that closely matches the grouse cycle. Dan explained it this way:

> As the raptor population builds, first it decimates the snowshoes, then the raptors move south and feed on the ruffed grouse. Finally, due to lack of food, the raptors die off or move their range again. Coincidentally, a second and perhaps more critical factor comes into play in the grouse cycle. That is a cyclical change in the nutritional value of aspen buds, the key food source for wintering grouse in the northern areas. Why the nutritional value of aspen buds falls is anyone's guess, but the combination of the up cycle of predators with the down cycle of the aspen buds' nutritional value seems to spell disaster for the ruffed grouse populations. At least that is the best current thinking.

Just how wide are the swings in the cycle? Dan cited one study from Manitoba that documented an area where the count started at a hundred drumming males at peak cycle and fell to only one drumming male at the bottom of the cycle. On average, a drop of 50 to 90 percent can be expected every ten years.

So I asked Dan, "Then what's the point of all the Ruffed Grouse Society projects if the cycle rather than habitat controls the population?" Dan explained, "If an RGS project improves an area so that at peak cycle, its grouse population is three hundred rather than a hundred birds; at the bottom of the cycle its capacity should be increased from, say, thirty birds to ninety birds! A *significant* improvement."

"So grouse have cycles just like quail have cycles?" I asked. "No," Dan explained. "Grouse have a true ten-year cycle. They are cyclical, while the population of quail (and other game birds) fluctuates mainly based on weather conditions like winter freezes or hot, dry summers that spoil the nesting season. That is a *periodic fluctuation* due to weather that has no predictable cycle." It is a point to remember: *grouse population fluctuations are cyclical,* while all other game bird populations have *periodic* and unpredictable changes.

The best covers are far from the main roads, off the beaten path, and can usually only be reached in a four-wheel-drive truck.

THE GROUSE TREES

Grouse as a species like hard growth. Not tall woods, not mature timber, but young, woody growth areas with open ground underneath. They prosper in the places that will be the forests of the future but for now are just tangles of saplings. Three trees are most commonly the home to grouse and by and large, the birds are found in either *quaking aspen, tag alders* or *hawthorn.* That's not to say that one won't occasionally be found in dogwood thickets or tall maple clusters, but the hunter who is able to drive down a winding dirt two-track and recognize these three most likely covers from afar has developed a valuable hunting skill.

Quaking aspen have beautiful straight trunks with shining silver-gray bark and golden fall leaves. Aspen, nicknamed popple, tends to grow in clusters with very high density stands of many thousand stems per acre. For some reason, when the trees reach a certain height they suddenly begin to attract grouse. A stand that held no birds one year will suddenly grow into attractive habitat the following year, while a reliable cover that held birds two years ago may grow beyond holding birds in just a short period of time. Such a subtle change is hard to see, and some of my favorite spots seem to grow out of favor every year. Quaking aspens are the beautiful shimmering mountain trees depicted so often in the black and white photographs of Ansel Adams.

The second major grouse habitat tree is the *tag alder,* nicknamed the black birch in the northeast. Tag alders are everything the aspens are not. They are dark, gnarled, crooked, tangled and brittle. While aspen grow tall and straight, tag alders are stunted and tangled into thickets, an octopus of entwining trunks. Tag alders often hold grouse but even more frequently shelter woodcock. When you walk into the tags and see a clear floor covered with white polka dots the size of quarters (called woodcock *splash*) get ready, for fast and wild woodcock shooting is usually at hand. Although grouse woods can be overhunted, the migratory nature of the woodcock keeps it passing through. A property that is barren today may be teeming with birds tomorrow, or vice versa.

This cover offers great and easy walking, but such open areas seldom hold birds.

The third major grouse tree is the *hawthorn*, a beautiful tree to look at, but a treacherous tree to hunt through. What attracts grouse to the hawthorn is both its protective overhead cover and the red, cherry-sized fruits that seem to come in waves. One year the hawthorn will produce a bounty of fruit; the next year, almost none. By the time grouse season rolls around, the tangled hawthorn crowns are steel gray in color and menacing to the hunter. The long spines (thorns!) of hawthorn are frankly dangerous to both dogs and hunters, and probably inflict more minor injuries than any spine in the woods. Major injuries are possible, for the one and one-half-inch spikes can inflict serious damage to an eye left unprotected. Dogs routinely catch a spine in the paw that must be pulled out immediately to avoid infection.

A fourth tree species, the *hazelnut*, attracts significant numbers of grouse as well, but the tree's range is limited mainly to the Great Lakes states. "Hazel," as it is known, often grows low, almost like a bush and a mix of aspen, and it seems to be almost irresistible during up cycles of the bird.

Each species of grouse tree grows in its own unique setting. Quaking aspen tend to grow in islands or patches in the midst of other kinds of cover. Tag alders grow in huge blocks of swampy, damp ground and hunting through this often takes effort. Hawthorns seem to grow on slopes as if in orchards planted by nature. There are dozens of hawthorn varieties and because their fruit is often bountiful, hawthorn trees rarely stand alone. They seed themselves and are usually found in clusters, generating and regenerating.

The best hunters take the time to observe and study the cover and trees to learn the types of habitat that hold birds and to understand how this affects the hunting year in and year out. One of the best things about grouse and woodcock fever is the availability of hunting covers. Millions of acres of state, federal and timber company land are open to the hunter, but these lands are isolated and generally in the far northern reaches of the United States. In Canada the government property is known as crown land and millions of acres are available.

COVERTS VS. BUSH HUNTING

Grouse hunting in favorite coverts differs markedly from bush hunting. Favorite coverts resemble a friendly restaurant in a far off city or a cozy hotel that you have visited many times, while bush hunting (as in *bush* plane or Canadian *bush*) is wild and foreign in an unknown place of vast proportions. Coverts are personal, but the *bush* is anonymous.

One Sunday morning I met my old friend and hunting partner R. Hamilton (Ham) Shirmer at his comfortable lake cottage in northern Michigan for a quick morning hunt. We had hunted together before but never out of his lake place. Little did I know that Ham was about to take me along to his four or five favorite personal coverts, perhaps one of the most unselfish acts of sharing that a roughshooter can muster. He was relying on the unspoken agreement between roughshooters that you will never return to another man's coverts without permission or an invitation.

Between 9 A.M. and 1 P.M. we hunted through each of the little spots, driving five to ten miles in between. The hunting was successful and a great pleasure because of the quality of the day, not because of the size of the bag. We shot some birds and Ham's English Setter made some great points, but mostly it was just a sun-dappled day that epitomizes the pleasure of grouse hunting.

On this day Ham was working the kinks out of yet another new gun and a new dog and having fair success with both. Ham believes in going first cabin. Davis, a big black and white yearling setter of impeccable breeding and the gun, a new Parker reproduction, were both up to standard. Davis was a bit wild and rank more from exuberance than obstinacy and his unbridled enthusiasm added an air of lightheartedness to the day. The pup was just plain fun to watch. At one place at the edge of an alder thicket by a patch of cattails, the youngster skidded into a high-tailed point as classic as a statue. If this was a portent of the dog's talent, Ham was in for a long career of fun with this dog. The grouse flushed out on Ham's side and flew left over the wet ground, barely clearing the tops of the cattails, then continued its path into the alders beyond the little swamp. The Parker sounded as the bird disappeared into the alders. It was one of those "now you see it, now you don't" situations, but even through the dense and alternating foliage, the trajectory of the bird was traceable. As is often the case with veteran grouse hunters, instinctively Ham calculated the bird's path and squeezed off a shot. The grouse disappeared from view. We found it downed at the base of a large spruce tree.

Ham's confident shooting through the trees reminds me of a story told by Ira Ayres, a hunting friend from New Jersey. In his youth Ira was being instructed how to hunt grouse by an uncle. After Ira had passed up several grouse shots obscured by the trees, his uncle said, "Ira, are you short on shells? Or can't you afford shells? If you're going to wait for a clear shot, you might as well stay home. Boy, when that bird flushes, point that gun and pull the trigger!" Similarly, Ham, who has hunted grouse for many years, sure didn't let a few trees slow down his shooting. Later in the morning we hunted a sandy hillside that had been clear-cut five or six years earlier and was now covered in new and densely growing aspen scarcely taller than our heads. The leaves still clung to the branches so the visibility was twenty feet at most. It was one of those shoot-fast-and-hope situations as the birds (mostly woodcock) flushed low, skimmed the tops of the saplings and dropped back into the foliage.

Bush hunting is totally different from covert hunting. Bush hunting is launching off into miles and miles of unknown territory in hopes of finding the treasure. I've bush hunted in many states and Canada with some great success and some long, weary, fruitless days. If you decide to tackle the bush, be sure you have a good compass and a modicum of orienteering skills. The overconfident hunter who disdains the need for a little caution should have a little discussion with a fellow who has slept the night lost in the bush! Having a keen feel for your way back to the truck allows you to follow the cover and the birds wherever they lead you. Once in northern Minnesota, my roughshooting partners Pete Casella, Tom Meyers and I parked the truck just off a heavily traveled north-south highway and headed in deep for an all-morning bush hunt. We went in east, so as long as we came out west we would hit the highway, and follow it back to the truck.

Fortunately the whining of cars on the road in the distance gave us a constant sense of direction, because about thirty minutes into the bush we got into the birds in volume and decided to do *follow the flush* hunting. We followed the flush of every bird until we either flushed it again or completely lost its trail. That took us into swamps and across streams and round and round in meandering rambles. Tom was shooting a little English 12 gauge that shoots the rare little two-inch shells and as I recall we saw so many birds, he ran out of shells that day, too. During the three hours or so we rambled in the ever deeper bush, none of us even glanced at a compass, remembering our phrase from the morning "go in east, get out west," a sure direction back to the truck. Each of us carried a compass and the faint whine of the trucks on the distant tarmac gave us all the assurance we needed to wander around at will in the bush, knowing the way home would be west.

GROUSE POINTS

Years ago in upstate New York, I was driving down a gravel road with my friend Frank Sylvester when he spied a likely looking grouse haven up on a ridge about a half mile behind a farmer's barn. Frank has a way about him that is most reassuring to people, even strangers. After Frank spent a few minutes with the farmer, I heard the dairyman say in his clipped upstate voice, "Sure, you can hunt partridge," and then added a few directions as to how to best reach the woods while avoiding the cows and the buildings. Sometimes I've even seen Frank charm directions to "my brother's place" or "old Ted Smith's forty acres" from a complete stranger. If you are going to hunt in America, you must soon learn how to ask permission to do so.

On this autumn day the first dog out of the truck was a chubby old veteran English Setter named Molly who wasn't very stylish but could sure find birds. We weren't a hundred yards into this hunt when she locked up on point. By the time we got in position the bird flushed wild several yards in front of Molly. We were in for a day of moving, spooky birds. It would have been easy to blame the dog for false pointing, but each point led to another and another—sometimes six or eight points—before a very erratic flush some distance in front of the dog. Despite wild flushes, we actually had quite a successful day. We assumed the scenting (as best a human can assess scenting) was giving the dog a face full of body scent; but as we moved in to flush the bird, the bird moved away and the scent dissipated. Then the dog would move up until it encountered heavy scent again and would point again!

Usually our best shots came when the bird was pinched between the dog and a barrier like a creek or a road clearing it didn't want to cross. When cornered, the birds held well for points and the shooting was excellent. Molly could find birds but she wasn't much for tracking a bird. She never dropped her head to trail a bird but simply geared down a notch or two and carefully worked forward until she found body scent again. Frank, ever the consummate hunter, knew how to calmly work her to match the day's conditions, in order to get birds into the air. These were Frank's methodical, consistent grouse dogs, not his fired up field trial dogs that might have lessened their staunchness in such a situation.

Although my observation is sure to raise the ire of pointing dog purists, I have never seen grouse hold all that well for pointing dogs. Usually the bird flushes after a series of points often including some soft points, flash points, creeping points or tracking points. Today's ruffed grouse is a wily critter too smart to stay anchored in one spot with a dog's nose a few feet away. Although the cover and the terrain is totally different, the actions of a walking grouse are often very similar to a skulking rooster pheasant playing hide-and-seek games.

No two days of grouse hunting are ever quite the same. Just when I think that I have found the magic code that will yield the birds' location with unvarying regularity, a day of exceptions emerges to throw my postulations out the proverbial window.

Personally, I categorize *prime* grouse habitat as older saplings and mixed hard growth with mod-erately clear undercover that will allow the bird's freedom of move-

A dog that retrieves well is a great asset in the grouse woods.

ment while still providing hiding spots and ample food. Imagine my surprise on a hunting trip in New York when I followed a big setter on point, off point, tail up, tail down, creep, point, creep—on a path that lead for a hundred yards in the woods and then another fifty yards into an abandoned pasture where the weeds were more than knee high. I honestly thought we were following a rabbit and I was just about ready to say to hell with this nonsense, when the grouse chose to thunder up for a shot as open as a pheasant in a parking lot. I was so surprised that I missed it with both barrels.

I was similarly surprised on another hunt in southern Indiana. There aren't many grouse in southern Indiana, but enough to give it a try as a change of pace between quail hunts. I was hunting with my brother Kelly down in the red clay hills. We were walking an old farm road between a tall, clean stand of hardwoods, mostly oak and maple, and an abandoned pasture of brushy cedars and briars. It had been a long, wet, cold unproductive day as we trudged through the mud from one likely grouse spot to another. Kelly observed that he had had about all the fun he could stand for one day. We had unloaded our guns and we were just walking and talking, not hunting. This was *not* grouse cover. Suddenly the dog got *birdie* near a grove of cedars thirty or forty yards into the center of the open field. Grudgingly, we reloaded, expecting quail or maybe a rabbit. To my surprise, out exploded a big gray grouse, which proceeded to fly a near perfect circle around the dog, the cedar trees and me. I emptied both barrels as I nearly screwed myself into the ground but the bird rocketed away into the tall, mature woods. Obviously, you can never be certain where a grouse will park itself.

I've come to believe that no absolutely perfect grouse cover exists—just some likely spots that portent grudgingly higher percentages of birds than others.

Dan Dessecker, a biologist for the Ruffed Grouse Society and a team hunter at the National Grouse Hunt, examines a ruffed grouse. During the hunt every bird is weighed, sexed, examined for health and carefully charted. These data, when compared from year to year, are very helpful in tracking the complex cycle of the American ruffed grouse.

GROUSE HUNTING STRATEGIES, TACTICS AND TIPS

Of the four game birds featured in this book, grouse are the second most likely to require a tactical approach that corners the birds into a situation where they must fly to flee. Most veteran grouse hunters agree that today's ruffed grouse is more likely to attempt an escape on the ground than the grouse of thirty years ago. When hunting with partners a dual approach using each other as herders can minimize side escapes. Working tactically and noting how each bird behaves can help you design a daily strategy. However, if you are bush hunting, you will find the barriers randomly and it is there that the birds are most likely to flush.

The covers that hold grouse vary from year to year, week to week and even day to day. Knowing (or properly guessing) which covers are holding birds today (based on wind, temperature, rain, etc.) is the key to continued success. Some grouse hunters aggressively follow every flushed bird for a second chance while others show open disdain for such practices. My own experience is that following the flight path will yield a second flush in about 50 percent of the cases, giving you much better odds than a random walk in the woods. However, the decision to follow a bird and attempt a second flush or ignore the flight and continue on the planned route of your hunt is always a difficult one.

Other strategies vary from the *patch-style* hunter who hits many small sections, rarely spending more than an hour in any one spot unless he is into

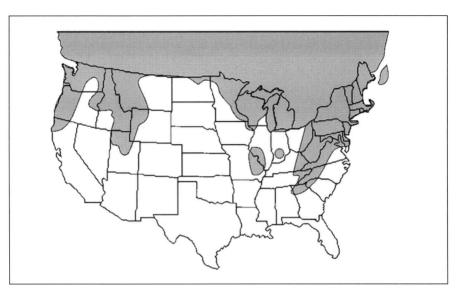

The range of the ruffed grouse.

birds, to the *hiker-style* hunter who sets off on a long-range trek of several miles, hitting widely varying types of cover along the way and arriving back at the vehicle hours later. Other hunters mix their styles based on the covers available and the types of dogs in the truck; tackling large tracts with fresh young dogs and limited patches with a slower old veteran dog.

Some hunters only walk abandoned logging roads, letting the dogs scour the heavy stuff. Trail hunting (walking the existing logging or two track trails) minimizes the amount of brush busting necessary. This tactic is most effective when you have a dog that gets in and really works out all the parts of the heavy cover along the trail's edges. However, it is my experience that the birds just move away from the edges when they hear you approach and you walk past them. Regardless of where you hunt grouse, understanding the birds *current* habits and hunting appropriately for *today* will yield the best chance of success.

CHAPTER 4
AMERICAN WOODCOCK

The woodcock is a migratory bird that spends its spring, summer and fall in the northeastern United States and eastern Canada and its winters in the deep south. The bird travels its flyway instinctively, but stops frequently along the way. It does not linger for long, just passes through. I've never lived in Manhattan but I've passed through it frequently and lingered enough to have an understanding of the layout and local amenities. Similarly, the woodcock alights in hospitable habitat along the flyway. Knowing where the woodcock stops for rest, relaxation and repast in the flyway is a key to a successful hunting.

The woodcock is not the quarry of the efficient nor the slothful. Nor is its pursuit appropriate for the pristine or the cowardly. This is *hunting*— taxing, dirty and painful. This facet of roughshooting is especially appreciated by the sellers of equipment, medicines and elixirs. In almost no time, new pants and shirts are in tatters. Copious amounts of cut salve and aspirin are consumed, and every evening the camp is host to those cheerful companions Jack Daniels, Johnny Walker or Mr. Stolichnya! Obviously, I enjoy woodcock hunting—it's tough, it's demanding, but it's rewarding for the persistent.

Although the woodcock was not an acquaintance in my youth, I have learned to love the pursuit of this bird from Maine to Minnesota. This pursuit started many years ago, in the far northeastern part of the United States, sometimes over my Springers and at other times over a friend's setters. Since then I've hunted woodcock in many places with many different partners and all manner of dogs. I've found that this bird really sorts out the hunters from the magazine readers. Some hunters seem to have an innate sense for where and how to find this bird. Success is usually the result of this knowledge and serious perseverance.

The woodcock is known as a pointing dog hunter's delight, and supposedly it holds tight for even the greenest dog. Unfortunately, where it holds is not where green dogs usually search because woodcock are generally found only in thick, tough cover. Rarely can you or your dog skirt the edges and find birds. In fact, just getting into birdie cover can be a challenge. I've walked logs to cross streams, crawled under hawthorn canopies and slogged through cattails to reach a birdie-looking piece of cover. Often these most difficult covers yield the most success because they tend to go unhunted.

Some dogs are said to disdain retrieving woodcock, but I've found most dogs to be enthusiastic about bringing back "timberdoodles." But the retrieving can be difficult at times when the birds fall into deep cover, are air washed, leaving little scent, or even hang up in a tree.

A GOOD WOODCOCK HUNTER HAS TO LEARN TO SLITHER

Boots Sylvester, my old hunting pal from Pennsylvania, would repeat the quote, "A good woodcock hunter has to learn to slither," from our late, lamented friend Ernie Mazzoni just before we launched off into some impenetrable tangle of tag alder, hawthorn or aspen in search of the woodcock flights. Ernie has been gone many years now, but his simple one-sentence maxims about the outdoor world of hunting live on with his friends. Although there is growing concern

Yes, Ernie, a woodcock hunter has to learn how to slither in order to negotiate the many stems of a new aspen stand. It is at this point that the young trees begin to hold birds.

about the future of woodcock populations in the eastern flyway, I don't think the problem results from hunter pressure. Most hunters are just too damned lazy to tackle the most appropriate woodcock cover. Pushing just fifty yards into a typical tangle makes a hunter sweat like a lineman going head-to-head with the Notre Dame front four—except here the adversary is a wall of young saplings, briars and tag alders.

Early season woodcock shooting when the sun is hot and the foliage is green can be exhausting work, as these two "hot-under-the-collar" Springers clearly reflect.

Woodcock love youthful growth, and rarely frequent tall woods. Most birds are found on the edges of the taller canopy, often in the new-growth haven that borders mature woods. Odds of a woodcock being in cover less than twenty-five feet tall are probably forty-to-one and the best cover is usually very dense. The Ruffed Grouse Society estimates that new-growth alder after a clear cut reaches forty thousand stems per acre in the early years before the density kills off the weaker saplings. With 43,560 square feet per acre, that equates to one sapling per square foot. Yes, Ernie, a woodcock hunter must learn to slither.

Once, in northern New Jersey, we parked the truck at 9A.M. in a roadside pull-off with the idea of hunting our way through an alder patch across the road. This favorite five- or six-acre patch had held at least a few birds on every trip for the last three or four years and had, on occasion, held a daily limit of birds if the flight was in full force. I let my old English Springer, Genny, out, attached a bell to her collar, then reached in for my old Lefever side-by-side. I didn't have the gun out of the case when she flushed the first woodcock. Two minutes later she was buzzing with excitement again and we were scrambling to be sure we had enough shells, glasses, gloves and other gear. After a frenzied search of the air currents for another thirty yards, she flushed a second bird.

Within the first hour, the two of us found, flushed and shot six woodcock and we had not yet reached the alder thicket that was our destination. Wildly entangled new growth, now only six or eight years old, was quickly filling in under a roadside power line after a clear-cut by the utility company. It had reached that undefinable stage that appeals to woodcock. Later, we tried the old familiar alder cover across the road that had been our original destination, but it was birdless. The trees were nearly twenty-five feet tall and the ground was filling in with weeds and grass. Apparently the birds on their normal north to south migration had checked into the new motel across the road, since the old hotel was getting a little long in the tooth.

THE WOODCOCK ISLANDS

"The islands" is a real place, a beautiful beige and red place that seems to run to the horizon, flat and wide. To the untrained eye the islands might not seem that beautiful, but to anyone who has made the effort at the right time, dragging and trudging through the sea of reeds, grass, hummocks and muck to get there, the islands are a haven for woodcock hunting. Though not technically islands, but more truly raised and semidry buttons of land surrounded by a vast plain of reeds, thick grasses and cattails, they offer fine woodcock cover.

A winding New England road lined with woodcock cover.

The first time I hunted the islands I was with Peter Casella from Pennsylvania and Tom Meyer from Minnesota—two friends of like mind when it comes to bird hunting. Peter is a runner, long-legged and strong, able to tackle tough spots, while Tom is lean and solid, a guy who works for a living. I looked the least physically able to try on the terrain but looks can be deceiving. This was the first day we hunted together and we eagerly raced to "get hunting." We each pulled a side-by-side out of its case. (Obviously we agreed on some of the important things in life.) It is rare that three people would choose to use the most traditional of all sporting guns, though these guns had little else in common. We had a 28-gauge Winchester 23, a Belgium 12-gauge guild gun and an English 16-gauge chambered for two and a half-inch shells.

Lunch break after a successful morning in the little patches of aspen shown in the background. This party consists of (left to right) Frank Sylvester, Dom Santarelli and Derek Sylvester.

As I recall, we had no intention of hunting the islands when we stopped. We'd been driving along a road with seemingly little prospect for appropriate cover when Pete said, "Oh, hell, let's jump in and push through this little patch of alder." No more than thirty yards in my English Springer, Ruffian, flushed a woodcock that rocketed off to the right. Soon another bird popped out to the right and flew away at top speed. Usually when hunting woodcock I carefully watch the flight of missed birds so we can follow up if the shooting is sparse. However, I missed seeing these, so I asked Pete if he'd seen where they went. "Yes, but you won't believe it! They both flew all the way over there to those islands in that marsh! Do you want to try to follow them?"

What a job! We waded and slogged to get there and we needed a rest after the trip. But what we found was worth the effort, an effort that no other hunters seemed willing to make. That day we hit a rare treasure trove of woodcock. Peter, in his orderly way, kept track of each bird on his flush counter. At the end of an hour and a half of hunting, we had each emptied the one box of shells we carried. We had flushed fifty-five woodcock (some, of course, two or three times), but *no* grouse! On this day the islands held only woodcock.

A few days later we returned to the islands and were disappointed to find only a few lingering woodcock. The main flights had apparently headed south. This time, however, we flushed five grouse on the islands. Grouse and woodcock do cohabitate, but maybe not on the same day.

WOODCOCK FALLS

The islands presented some severe retrieving difficulties for our dogs. Many of the woodcock winged out over the marsh and fell into the heavy grass and reeds—deep in the cover. Though woodcock falls are often short (less than twenty yards), retrieving the birds can be one of a dog's most challenging tasks in the heavy brush and tangles that obscure the view of the fall. A dog often sets off for the retrieve in the direction of the flight, but the bird often drastically alters its flight path. Some birds fall in the brush, others in the open and more than a few hang up in the trees. Woodcock also seem to leave very little scent as they fall to the earth. Some people say they are "air-washed" as they fold, leaving no telltale essence riding the air currents as they lay in the dense thicket. Letting the bird lay for a few minutes may provide the time needed to let a scent cloud develop.

Much has been made of some dogs' reluctance to retrieve woodcock but I've never experienced it with a spaniel or a retriever. I've seen some pointing dogs refuse to retrieve woodcock, but those same dogs often failed to retrieve grouse as well.

Most woodcock hunters keep a close eye to mark the fall well so they can direct their dog's attention to the exact fall area or pick up the bird themselves if they can see it. A dog that will "stay with the retrieve" until it is complete is a great asset, and careful training to teach the dog to ardently "hunt dead" is worth the effort. Harry Henriques, a professional bird hunt guide in Minnesota, believes that "hunt dead" training is an aspect of gun dog development that is too rarely ingrained to the fullest. He has developed a simple but effective procedure to enhance a dog's "hunt dead" skills, something that few professional trainers ever spend much time on.

THE EASTERN WOODCOCK CRISIS

I called on Dan Dessicker of the Ruffed Grouse Society to help me understand the obviously declining woodcock populations in the far eastern flyway. Dan thinks almost all of the decline is due to reduced habitat. He explained that lost habitat results from not only home and commercial construction in wooded areas but, more importantly, from habitat that has grown too old and therefore too large to support woodcock. Most aban-

Dan Dessecker of the Ruffed Grouse Society is shown banding a nine-day-old woodcock at the Moosehorn National Wildlife Refuge in Calais, Maine.

doned farmland in the East occurred during the 1950s and 1960s. When first abandoned, those farms produced fresh young growth that attracted woodcock nesting and migrating birds, commonly called "flight birds." Those farms are now long grown into thirty-year-old trees. Only a major change in land practices will reverse the loss of habitat for the woodcock.

WOODCOCK HUNTING STRATEGIES, TACTICS AND TIPS

Hunting woodcock in many ways mirrors grouse hunting except the woodcock is a migratory bird so its presence is less predictable. Most decent woodcock covers in the northernmost tier of the United States hold a few native birds and these birds can be hunted from opening day. However, the flight (migrating) birds come through at odd times for odd reasons. Maybe some shooters can predict the time of the calling that lures them south but I can't. Supposedly a full moon and a northern wind will blow the birds in from the North, but my experience is that it is just as likely to take them on further toward their Louisiana wintering grounds.

I can't describe woodcock cover but I can feel it when I'm in it. Once, my friend Erik Warren and I were hunting rather fruitlessly in northern Ontario. We weren't finding many birds, but suddenly I found myself standing in a spot that just felt right. I yelled over to Erik (he was out of sight of course), "Hey, Erik, bring that big setter over here, this is perfect woodcock—oops!" Bang! Bang! (I kicked up the bird.) I was right.

Woodcock hunters must watch the ground as well as the sky, for it is the soil that often holds the secret of the bird's location. Woodcock feed primarily on earthworms by boring their long thin bills into the ground to feed. Soil that is too dry, too hard, too wet or even too covered with trashy vegetation seldom attracts woodcock.

Long ago I read a book that stated that "Woodcock don't like to get their feet wet," but other ground conditions are just as critical to the birds' feeding. Once you can kick the ground and test for proper moisture and soil type you are a long way toward being a "compleat" woodcock hunter. As you learn, note the ground cover, density and soil moisture whenever you flush a bird and your woods lore will grow quickly.

When you hit a spot that "just feels right," start looking for "splash," white quarter-sized droppings on the forest floor. A significant flight will leave a "polka dot" carpet, even days after it has passed on south. When you do hit a spot, make your dog work it carefully, back and forth, for woodcock hold tight and seldom give off much scent.

When the birds flush, an open-choked gun will throw a large pattern at the swirly flyers. The best shots come just as the birds clear the treetops and pause before they rocket away. Some woodcock flutter out slowly, others rocket up and smoke away at a speed that would make a pheasant jealous.

The key to woodcock hunting is to cover likely ground until you find a spot, then work it thoroughly.

Woodcock hunting generally means lots of hard walking. Unless you luck into a flight of birds in the first spot you try, you'll be walking from spot to spot all day. Trekking is my word for a long-distance search for the hot spots. You walk long distances and hunt out each likely cover encountered, until you find the treasure. There are days, however, when for some reason the birds are widely scattered. On those days, you'll be forced to push through mile upon mile of cover to find the isolated singles, a bird here, a bird there, maybe ten or twelve flushes by day's end.

A real woodcock roughshooter never loses faith; some days you'll find birds early, on other days you'll find birds late. I've seen mornings go by without a flush, only to be rewarded by limits by two in the afternoon.

Tomorrow you can rehunt the same cover you scoured today fruitlessly or vice versa and find birds that were somewhere else yesterday. The woodcock are usually just visiting; they pass through and fly away.

WOODCOCK GUNS

On most days the grouse and woodcock covers were constantly interspersed, making it necessary to use one gun for both quarry. Were I

The American woodcock's range.

hunting only grouse I would probably shoot a 12 bore with one open choke and one modified choke. If I were hunting only woodcock I would probably carry a 20-gauge bored wide open in each barrel. As a compromise I now carry a 16-gauge gun with only a tiny hint of constriction in each barrel commonly referred to as skeet and skeet. Most importantly I carry a pocketful of different shells to vary how the gun shoots. Most mixed-bag hunters chamber either eights or nines in the first barrel, then back it up with seven and a halfs in the second barrel. Then after a bird flushes, most hunters switch to both barrels depending on the bird in pursuit, either both eights or nines for woodcock or both seven and a halfs for grouse. Though not naturally well organized, I have learned to keep the shells separated in my pockets to make loading easy: nines in the right vest pocket for the right barrel and seven and a halfs in the left vest pocket. That may sound like a useless bit of trivia, but when the shooting gets hot and fast, knowing that the two shells in the right pocket/right hand will load both barrels with number nines, is fast, simple and almost foolproof.

CHAPTER 5

A STUDY IN CONTRASTS: HUNTING GROUSE AND WOODCOCK WITH A SETTER, A SHORTHAIR AND A SPRINGER

This hunt took place many years ago, so I feel comfortable telling the story. One of the hunters is totally out of the sport, so he is unlikely to ever read this account. The other has switched his style of hunting and his dog allegiance, so he'd probably be the first to tell the story—except he was only there for half of it. The third is still a hunting buddy and we've discussed it many times.

It was October, in the midweeks when many of the leaves are down but the snow hasn't yet fallen. It was the best of times as we hunted in the beautiful auburn and gold woods of northern Minnesota during a strong upturn in the grouse population. We were fully blessed with good weather, good dogs, good friends and plenty of birds to hunt.

A mixed bag of grouse and woodcock is common during a day of hunting in Minnesota.

As usual I had two English Springers with me, which I alternated morning and afternoon, and we constantly rotated partners and dogs. Most of the dog types were covered: an English Setter, a Brittany, a German Short-haired Pointer and my two English Springers.

My partners were safe and solid hunters; not fanatics, but serious to the point of owning and training good dogs and pursuing the sport with a fervor ten to fourteen days per season. Dinner was always a reprise of the day's adventures, including the highlights, the misses and some good-natured barbs about the other fellows' dogs and shooting.

This group has always hunted by breaking off into two-man teams. Working together allows each hunter to give his dog a rest, morning and afternoon, and enjoy the camaraderie and the sharing of the day's experience. Such an arrangement also provides one with a very realistic assessment of the other fellow's dog, since you watch your own dog work for a while then switch to his dog for a session. This makes for a fairly direct comparison of how each dog handles the same birds, terrain, wind, scenting and cover.

Of course, we could have hunted with two dogs down at once except none of the pointing dogs were trained to back, so they'd have most likely run in to steal a point, a bad situation guaranteed to lessen each dog's staunchness. Secondly, none of the pointing dogs seemed to like each other. There is no way to work a pointer and a flushing dog together except when using the latter as a totally nonslip retriever—so we used the alternating dog method and it worked very well.

For the morning shift, Bob and I paired up and headed for an old favorite covert eight or ten miles northeast of the noon rendezvous point. Since I had two dogs with me, we decided to hunt a Springer first and then Bob's setter, and if either dog tired out, we'd hunt the other Springer before the lunch break.

As luck would have it we were barely into the woods when my little Springer Ruffy got birdie and flushed a grouse. Bob was still getting used to a new Remington 1100 Special in 20 gauge so he wasn't hitting as precisely as usual. We both missed. I've seen so many examples of a grouse flushing within a hundred yards of the vehicle early in the morning that I wonder about the connection. Random coincidence seems too unlikely. Probably the birds are by the roads to pick gravel and dust themselves. Anyway, Ruffy got really birdie on this first grouse and even after it had flown off, she continued to madly search the area. I had quite a hard time pulling her out of the old scent. No more than a hundred yards further into a stretch of damp alder cover, she again went crazy, only this time she flushed a pair of woodcock in rapid succession. Bang! from my 12-gauge Lefever; bang! from Bob's Remington, dog steady, two birds down, two birds quickly found and retrieved, two birds in the bag—seems almost routine. By 10 A.M. we were back to the truck with a grouse and three woodcock and we had missed long shots on three other birds. I assessed the scenting to be outstanding;

one of those days when the essence of scent hangs like a warm mist on the ground and the dog's nose hones in on a bird like a bee to the hive.

Now it was time for Bob's setter. This dog is the total opposite of my dogs. It is an eastern strain setter, one of the famous ones, bred and extensively advertised as a grouse specialist. It is a reliable dog and I've hunted over it several times, always with good success. But it is a big, heavy dog, probably seventy-five pounds and very methodical. The dog always works close and never needs hacking or screaming at.

The dog actually worked a smaller pattern than the Springers—close and methodical. As we followed the gentle tinkling of her bell, she was seldom out of sight, even in the thickest of cover. Soon she was on point, not a rock-hard, high-tail point, but more of a firm lean into the wind: tail level, gaze intense. Although we moved in quickly to flush the bird, no bird erupted. The dog began to move and soon we were off again following the dog. But in less than fifty feet she again locked up on point. Again, no bird. Bob said the bird was running in front of us. This happened five or six times before the bird finally flushed and Bob dropped it cleanly. From my vantage point I could see the bird fall to the ground and it lay in the open. The dog broke at the shot and ran to the fall area, but after sniffing the bird for a few seconds she turned her head to look for her master. When she saw he was on his way there to pick up the bird, she started off hunting again.

Her actions on the next two birds, both woodcock, were the same. But she was more intense on these points, with a hard body position and a higher tail—these birds flushed only six or eight yards in front of her nose. The downed birds she ignored completely, so we had to search a bit to find them in the thick brush. Bob related that even though she had been force broken to retrieve, her performance in that area was mediocre at best. She simply got no thrill from retrieving.

It was my opinion that the scenting was so good that she had been pointing the body scent the grouse left in the air as it was walking quickly away from us. Only after several points and move-ups did we get close enough to force it to flush. The setter showed more of a long-range nose than my Springer, but actually covered less ground. At no time did the setter make any indication of the path of the moving grouse, nor did she ever drop her head and follow the trail, even for an instant.

After a hood-top buffet of sandwiches on German black rye bread, crisp dill pickle wedges, bitingly sour three-bean salad, soft chocolate chip cookies and lots of hot, strong coffee, we set out for an afternoon of hunting.

This time Ted and I partnered up using his German Shorthair bitch, Gertie. Now Gertie is a real fräulein, an old-style German Shorthaired Pointer with no pretense of being modified to suit American hunting styles.

Gertie is a big-boned, leggy, dark-colored dog with a wide head and that steely Teutonic look in her eye. This is a no-nonsense German bitch with an attitude of "This is all business so let's get on with it."

Gertie was down first in the afternoon and set off at a long, easy lope, not the frenzied sprint of my Springers nor the laid-back amble of Bob's setter. The range was that of a gun ranger, and in the heavy cover at least 40 percent of the time she was out of sight. We tracked her by her bell and when the bell stopped ringing we found her where the bell had last tolled, off to the right in the heavy aspen, locked up solid and intense. Ted really detests electric beepers, so we had no blast of space-age wizardry to help us find the dog. To my way of thinking that's just as well, for the electronic beeping detracts greatly from the serenity of the woods. Gertie wasn't easy to find, but when we did, she was in a nose down pose, little more than three feet from the woodcock that Ted flushed from under her nose.

This woodcock towered and swirled before it fell to the earth at the first bark of Ted's old battered Merkel over-under, and Gertie was back with the bird in a flash. As we hunted on and further to the west, we crossed a marshy area of spongy ground where water was sometimes flowing through the roots of green moss-covered tag alders. Soon thereafter we scrambled up ten or twelve feet of slope to a higher level, drier ground, and continued west hunting an edge between a big forest and an overgrown field. It was mostly aspen whips, some birch, and a few golden yellow maples. A wind had begun to blow and here Gertie showed serious intellect by ranging out along the edge of the tall woods searching the likely cover with her nose, seeking scent on the wind coming from our left. She made several searching passes, at times reaching out as far as a hundred yards from us. We followed along readily as each section of cover was searched and discarded. Suddenly she wheeled in midstride and pointed rigidly, her nose like a knife into the wind. For a few seconds, maybe ten, maybe twenty, she pointed, then the point softened and she began to move forward.

"Lets move, she's trailing a grouse," Ted said, and we did. Sometimes slowly, sometimes stopped, sometimes quickly, we followed Gertie through a series of ten or twelve flash points. Finally she went rigid and held it. We moved forward sharply and the grouse thundered up. Ted's Merkel barked twice and the bird fell far out on the right. Gertie, again steady to wing but not to shot, was after the bird on the sound of the gun and brought it back willingly. Gertie found and pointed two other birds that managed to outfly our fire power. Later we hunted my Springers with solid success on woodcock in a stand of alder whips reaching to twenty feet high and totally bare of foliage. We hit a pocket of birds most probably newly arrived in the area from an overnight flight. We flushed six birds quickly, collected four and had a wide open view through the spiked maze of zinc-colored alder trunks, as the dog scented each bird, wheeled and followed the scent to the source.

It had been a wonderful day in a beautiful part of the world and each dog, with its own unique set of instincts and methods, had performed well and produced birds for the guns.

The three pointing dogs each had strengths and weaknesses. Each obviously pleased its owner greatly and as an interested bystander, I was able to assess each with a comparison of how it handled hunting conditions versus the actions of my own dogs.

The English Setter was by far the easiest to handle and the closest working. It required minimal whistle or voice handling, but it had a decidedly smaller range than the other dogs. Perhaps it was scenting conditions, but although the setter showed the most long-range nose on body scent, it showed little ability to track a moving grouse. Its retrieving was at best a perfunctory "point dead."

The German Shorthaired Pointer was a nice dog but very methodical. On occasion its independence got a bit frustrating. Due to its dark color it was hell to find on point. On the other hand, this dog could find birds and trail them to conclusion. The dog's nose was a compromise between the setter's and the Springers', a good nose for body scent but also able to trail a bird when needed. This old-style German Shorthaired Pointer was also a very reliable retriever.

The Brittany fell somewhere in between: good nose, fair range, a little harder to control, or maybe a bit more independent. She retrieved about half the time and held staunch every time, even if the bird moved off. She too was reliable, honest and capable.

The Springers were busy little dogs and worked harder and faster than any of the pointing dogs. But there wasn't much "get ready" signal in this thick cover except for the woodcock shot in the aspen whips when the dog was constantly visible and the flushes telegraphed by the dogs' birdiness and frenzy. Like the German Shorthaired Pointer, the English Springers retrieved with a high level of enthusiasm, and quickly found every bird shot.

This is what roughshooting is all about: good friends, fine dog work, pleasant old guns, birds to hunt, beautiful cover. It doesn't get any better than this.

CHAPTER 6
A CONVERSATION WITH HARRY HENRIQUES

HARRY HENRIQUES

Hunting and Fishing Outfitter
Orr, Minnesota

Harry Henriques is the kind of person many guys have thought about being at least a few times in their lives. At age fifty-five, he was owner/operator/president of a small book publishing company in New York City, had a comfortable lifestyle in Greenwich, Connecticut, was a member of the right clubs, and had two kids just out of college. Harry chucked it all and moved to the outreaches of Minnesota to start up a hunting lodge. Certainly it couldn't have been an easy choice; that's why most of us still show up on the job at 8A.M. every Monday.

But the timing and the circumstances must have been ripe for Harry's total life revolution. Today Harry, who looks ten years younger, now runs Wild Wings, a hunting and fishing outfitter based in Orr, Minnesota, population 315. Knowing Harry's background, it's not surprising that the brochure describing a few days at Wild Wings is thoughtfully written, not just normal ad hype. The reality of his life jumps into the picture when you call to make a reservation. The voice on the answering machine says, "Hi, this is Harry of Wild Wings. I live six miles from the phone so please leave a message and I'll get back to you." Six miles—doesn't that sound great! I can't seem to get six feet from a phone. Harry knows how to live.

You hunt almost every day of the season with a complete stranger. What do you do when you feel a hunter is unsafe in the way he or she is handling a firearm? How often does that happen?

Harry Henriques (right) with Mike Thompson, who has just shot his first woodcock.

HENRIQUES—All groups get a safety lecture upon arrival, even if they have been here many times before. We stress areas of safety and problems in the field. If an infraction happens in the field either the guide corrects it on the spot or it is mentioned to me that evening, upon which I take care of it either by speaking to the person or by my taking him/her in the field the next day where I can correct the problem. The most frequent problem is pointing a gun at a person while walking or shooting down the line.

What kind of dogs do you use at your lodge for people who don't bring their own dogs and is there a particular reason for this choice?

HENRIQUES—We use English Springer Spaniels for all guests who don't bring their own dogs, and most guests do not. Even when the guest has a dog we carry one of our springers as a backup. Our springers are very versatile dogs and are conditioned to the terrain and birds. Most times when we have to use a backup dog it is for finding a downed bird or when a guest's dog tires out. That happens pretty easily in this country of heavy slash and blowdowns.

How far out do your dogs range and how far out are the birds shot?

HENRIQUES—There was a year when I measured every downed bird (grouse, woodcocks and snipe). The average kill distance was seventeen yards. Our cover is extremely dense, thus our dogs must be at twenty yards maximum from the guns. With a downwind direction the dogs will punch out a little but they quickly turn at twenty-five to thirty yards, thus pushing birds back toward the gun.

Do you use any of the same dogs for duck hunting?

HENRIQUES—Yes, also for railbird shooting.

What kinds of dogs do your clients bring along and how well do they adapt to the local (woods type) game birds?

HENRIQUES—They bring Pointers, Setters, Vizslas, Labradors, Brittanies and Springers, and they all adapt to our extreme conditions (which I feel are the most difficult shooting anywhere) fairly well. Usually guest dogs run out of steam or get cut feet. I've seen some great performances and some not so great.

How good and how well trained are the client's dogs?

HENRIQUES—By and large I would say that most are well trained, but many are not very well handled.

Are the weaknesses in these dogs due to breeding or due to training, and what one thing would make the dogs a lot better?

HENRIQUES—The most common weakness I see is lack of conditioning in the dog. This is tough stuff up here. The other weakness is when the handler is not really reading his dog. Most all bring well-bred dogs, but proper conditioning would make the dogs better and more handling practice by the owners would make the teams more successful.

I've noticed that your lodge seems to attract a lot of southern hunters who are more used to quail hunting. Are those skills applicable to grouse and woodcock hunting?

HENRIQUES—We get hunters here from fifteen states and almost all do some quail hunting—not just the southerners. Quail hunting does help, because you must learn to handle the excitement of the covey flush (similar to a grouse exploding out) and then focus on one bird and above all, "instinct shoot."

What causes the most problems in the dogs you see?

HENRIQUES—They don't stay after a downed bird long enough to find it in the cover. We focus on finding *every* downed bird. Over the past seven years we have lost very few downed birds (grouse, woodcock or snipe) with our dogs. At least 50 percent of hunting is finding the birds you shoot.

Harry and Wild Wings Max watch the horizon for ducks.

Is there much difference in the hunting technique you recommend for grouse versus woodcock?

HENRIQUES—Yes and no. Basically we hunt for woodcock, knowing that we'll find grouse as well in many of the same coverts. If the weather changes drastically (freeze or snow) we change to pushing for grouse. The technique is the same but the coverts change.

Is there much difference in the habitat where you find grouse versus woodcock?

HENRIQUES—Yes and no. Young grouse will get into woodcock coverts that are eight-year-old growth and older. Grouse like edges while woodcock are in the real thick of it. But there are many edges within even the thickest stuff.

Is the shooting prowess of your clients in any way related to the type of gun they carry?

HENRIQUES—No! But I much prefer to see a side-by-side or over and under used—primarily for safety. Plus pumps and automatics must be plugged for three shells to hunt woodcock so the extra shots are minimized.

What's the best time to catch the woodcock flights through the far northern United States? Is it a one- or two-day event in your area or do they come through in waves?

HENRIQUES—The native birds are the first to bunch up and leave. The scattered birds are the flight birds. Our native birds leave around the last two weeks of September, but our best shooting is a little later on the migrating "flight" birds. They start to arrive as the natives leave and the flight birds linger until the last. Our very best shooting is when the flight birds begin to gather, which is usually around the middle of October. It lasts for about two weeks, but it all depends on the weather.

If we were to ask you about fairly sophisticated dog work such as full steadiness to wing and shot, the ability to "hunt dead" and the ability to take hand signals, willingness to swim to make a retrieve and honoring the work of a bracemate, could you give us your evaluation of their importance in real life, everyday hunting?

HENRIQUES—The steadiness to wing and shot helps give the gun an open shot without fear of hitting the dog, so from that standpoint it is of benefit. "Hunt dead" is vital; these are strictly wild birds, so they are a finite resource and true to our ethics, finding a dead bird is of the utmost importance. Hand signals are important on retrieves, and until a young dog learns good cover from bad, it is up to the hunter to direct the dog. Using hand signals is the way to do it. We usually only hunt one dog at a time, so honoring and backing are unimportant. Swimming to make retrieves happens fairly often, so it is of value.

If you had to do it again, would you leave New York City and move to the North Woods?

HENRIQUES—Yes, for a lot of reasons, but above all for the quality of life here.

HUNT DEAD

These are Harry Henriques's own words explaining how he teaches a dog to "hunt dead."

In the fall of 1991, I watched a woodcock drop from a fine shot. The dog "hupped" at the flush, was sitting over on the right, in a slight hollow of an alder patch. The bird had "dipsy-doodled" its way out of the alder, then through a stand of five-year-old aspen, and was streaking over a swamp of waist-high marsh grass tufts when it met its demise. As there was no possible way the dog could have marked the bird's flight, I called Sam (the dog) over, because both my friend and I had a good mark on the drop. Pointing the direction of the fall, Sam was told to, "Hunt dead." A half hour later, Sam produced the bird from under a dank swamp tuft with the grass growing down, as well as up, some five yards to the left of our mark. He had picked up scent, lost it, circled the area to find it again, came back to the original mark, and then snuffed under each tuft until he had success. How does one train for this? Only a perfectly trained dog will perform this "hunt dead" under such tough circumstances.

First a caution. Do not let your partner, or whomever made the shot, move. Keep them in place with their eye on the fall area and don't contaminate the fall area with a lot of human scent. Next, send the dog off in the correct direction, with the command, "Dead bird." As the dog hits the last known sight spot, command "Close, close," and repeat, "Dead bird." With proper training these two commands will make sense to the dog.

This is how I train the dog to hunt dead. Without the dog seeing it, I drop a dummy into a patch of grass or other cover, with the dummy being completely invisible. Next I call the dog back in toward me, then cast him off with a hand signal for direction and the command, "Dead bird." As he approaches the dummy, say, "Close, close." He should snatch up the dummy and bring it back to you. Do this once or twice a day, no more, but repeat the procedure in different places, day after day.

With the early sessions firmly instilled, make the dead bird situation more difficult. Little by little the skill grows. Change location of the exercise, do it at night, or at a different time in your training pattern. Always make it fun, always compliment him as though he were a world champion when the task is correctly accomplished. Use your simple commands, with excitement in your voice. Both you and the dog grow in confidence together. Do not overdo this exercise; practice a couple of minutes a day at most, until the dog is well experienced and is searching out plenty far enough.

Why go to all this trouble? Why have a dog search for an hour for a downed bird? Because it's a game bird. It is a finite resource that we should not squander. As hunters, we can not catch and release. Our act of hunting must be clean and professional. We have to show we care. We have our dogs for companionship, for the pure joy of watching great athletes perform, and above all, as a conserver of game.

CHAPTER 7
THE SOUTHERN TRADITIONS OF QUAIL HUNTING

Deep South quail hunting is steeped in tradition and has always been accomplished in a most luxurious and patrician manner. Mule wagons and horses once conveyed the shooters to the hunting grounds. There they would find big, hard-ribbed Pointers holding staunchly and awaiting the gentlemen's arrival. Today many of those animal-drawn conveyances have been replaced by customized shooting trucks or all-terrain vehicles (ATVs). Such unfettered splendor is enjoyable and most agreeable to the senses, but it could hardly be characterized as roughshooting. Roughshooting, where you march miles and miles over hill and dale through brush and briars to find the covey, may not be considered the most gentlemanly way to hunt quail, but it is great fun and a fair challenge as well.

The big-going, ridge-running, high-tailed Pointer is a part of the luxurious southern quail plantation hunting style.

Walking the woodsy ridges and creek bottoms of Missouri, Kentucky, Arkansas and Kansas for coveys is roughshooting in the truest sense and can rarely be successful using the all-out horizon running dogs of the Deep South and Texas. Here the properties are smaller, the roads nearby and fences many. The good foot hunter's dog must be a partner. Even as it reaches out aggressively a few hundred yards to search the most likely spots, it must also come around and check back frequently. When he finally locates a covey, the dog locks up staunchly and awaits your arrival—on foot. Bobwhite quail are the ultimate bird for the dedicated "bird dog" fan. Bobs are predictable and hold well for the staunch points that have given the bird dogs their stellar reputation.

Of all the featured game species, quail are by far the most predictable and reliable. I recall one day hunting with Glenn Hershberger at his farm in the Flint Hills of Kansas. "Well," he said, "there should be a covey over there along that woodsy fence line and another down by the creek bottom and another up on that ridge," and he was right in every case. True quail purists treasure the coveys and carefully study and protect the habitat, not unlike a grouse hunter or a pheasant hunter that studies the land and reinvests through practices that replenish the bird supply.

When Glenn cut loose, his muscular English Setter, Sam, stretched his legs over a good portion of the seven hundred acres in the first thirty min-

Sam, Glenn Hershburger's big English Setter, finds another covey.

utes, then he settled into a more purposeful effort. At times the dog was just a white streak along the creek bottom, but when he found the big covey up on the ridge, he held rigid as a statue for the ten minutes it took us to cross the creek and climb up there. A strong and healthy covey of thirty birds whirred off in every direction as Glenn walked it up. We marked the landing of several birds and followed up for some singles shooting, but Sam is primarily a covey dog. Although he found and held solid on several singles, he obviously would rather have been racing off to find another covey. The venerated covey dogs, big running, edge running, racing machines are beautiful to watch from afar if your nerves can handle the range.

Where the terrain and isolation allow the use of such a dog, they can cover vast amounts of ground very quickly with their wide open and far ranging style, even when dragging a thirty-foot check rope, which is often the rule of the day. Due to their range, these dogs must be solidly staunch when they lock up on point because the odds are that you won't arrive there for a while. A *covey dog* focuses its efforts on the most likely spots, using its experience to raise the odds. True covey dogs do not generally waste efforts on low-percentage property. There is little doubt that on the good days a covey of quail gives off a strong and forceful scent. Fine-nosed dogs that are used to running full blast along the cover edges questing for covey scent can hone in a full choke nose to locate a little circle of birds even at thirty miles per hour. A covey dog sliding to a halt or whipping around in midstride frozen in time is a thing of beauty to behold.

COVEY RISE

There may be no more exciting event in all of roughshooting than the explosive eruption of a large covey of quail. When you walk in to flush the birds, you know that the eruption is imminent and feel the rush of adrenaline. You have a lot to focus on during a covey rise—flushing the birds, keeping the dog steady, looking to see where the singles land and shooting. It's easy to understand why covey shooting is not always successful.

Much has been written about the missed shots of the rise, and the terms *covey shooting* and *flock shooting* have been coined to identify it. The natural tendency is to poke the gun in the general direction of the cloud of birds and pull the trigger. However, experienced shooters know that the only way to be successful is to pick one bird and shoot it, then aim purposefully at the next target and fire again.

SINGLES

Once the covey erupts, it can be followed for singles shooting. Some covey dogs will chop down their range to vacuum the area for the minimal scent of a lone quail; others won't and prefer to race off to look for the next covey. A few minutes' wait may improve the little scent cloud given off by the single, but that is not always the case. The ideal, of course, is two dogs working together, both reliable backers, but one a big runner to find the coveys and the other a careful worker to locate the singles. After the covey explodes and the singles and doubles buzz off to many new locations, the rules of the game change. The birds are no longer in predictable spots so the dog can no longer run the edges. Now the birds may be in open fields, Conservation Reserve Program (CRP) land, crop stubble, deeper into the woods or scattered in a fortress of hay bales. Under tough scenting conditions, single

Point! High on a hill.

Chad Betts finds "Ike" on point. In this cover it could be one pheasant or a covey.

birds may be missed by the dogs but inadvertently walked up by the hunters. Many quail purists decline to shoot any bird not pointed by a dog. It's a matter of honor, and for these enthusiasts the pleasure is in watching the dogs find birds—not in the shooting.

MULTIPLE BIRD AREAS

In many states the ranges of pheasants and quail overlap and the birds are often interspersed. The covers are worked differently depending on which birds you expect to find. In the wide vistas and open prairies of Kansas, I walked the prairie ridges with Chad Betts and Tony Woodward, letting the big dogs roll wide and fast in circling loops over the grassland ridges in search of prairie chickens. Then, as we dropped down the slopes into cropland, we checked the dogs in closer and directed them through the milo stubble and weed belts in search of pheasants. Finally, we moved into the woodsy edges along the streams where the same dogs ran flat out in search of coveys of quail in the deep weeds lining the brushy creek bottoms that drained the area. The experienced dogs like Blue, Chad's English Setter, and Misty, Tony's English Pointer, knew the game and adjusted their styles according to the terrain and the likely species. This was tough going, miles of ridges, clinging mud and some steep ravines. This was not the flat Kansas of legend; this was rolling prairie and roughshooting at its best—a sport for the dedicated.

QUAIL PREDICTABILITY

Quail habitat is so traditional that it seldom varies in its ability to attract birds. As long as the habitat (brooding protection) and food sources (usually milo, soybeans and weed seeds) are available, the quail will flourish, except for the ravages of frigid weather or predators. When I was a boy in Indiana I had my own secret little covey that always lived in the same corner of brush and weeds down by the farm auction barn. At that spot Whiskey Run Creek emptied into Blue River, and the habitat must have been perfect. The covey survived for years and even without a dog, I could go back there and walk around until I stumbled into the birds. I'd shoot a few and go home, leaving the covey to survive to another year.

When charting the location of coveys found during a season, most were found in the expected woodsy edges of food source crop fields. Generally the covey was pointed no more than twenty yards into the edge. This proximity accounts for the covey dog's tendency to race along the woods' edges, working the air for the essence of the little flock. Over time my own unscientific survey noted that 80 percent of the coveys were found in woods cover, 10 percent were found in CRP and the remaining 10 percent were found in harvested crop fields while feeding.

Interspersed patches of woods, weeds and crops provide ideal quail cover.

QUAIL CONSERVATION

Those individuals who own and nurture prime quail habitat generally have a strong but unwritten code of conduct for shooting:

Never shoot out the coveys—set a preseason harvest limit.

Roger Wells, a Quail Unlimited biologist based in Kansas, explained that the only way to keep from shooting out a covey is to know the early season quail population, then take no more than one-third of the birds. He used the example of a farm that holds three coveys of twenty birds each. If a covey size drops during the season due to hunting (below about eight birds), it may combine with another covey. If that combined covey is then shot down to eight or ten birds, it may also combine. Then only one tiny covey exists and it may not be strong enough to survive the winter and repopulate the area next spring. As before, he suggests analyzing the area and setting a preseason limit of approximately one-third of the known bird population. Hence, if you find sixty birds on opening weekend, plan to take no more than twenty from the area during the season.

QUAIL HABITAT

Quail thrive when the conditions are right and decline when they become poor. The hunter that recognizes perfect habitat is most likely to find birds consistently. Mr. Wells explained the factors that are believed to account for stable to rising quail populations in Kansas, Missouri, Arkansas and Texas while, simultaneously, quail populations continue to fall in the southeastern states. Both food and cover must be right for quail to prosper. Generally quail frequent the wooded edges that border weedy fields or grain fields. The woods provide protection from high-flying birds of prey while the weeds and grain feed the broods. Surprisingly, the highest energy food sources are not grains like milo, soybeans or corn, but the insects in summer (the highest energy source) and ragweed seeds of three varieties (the second-highest energy source). Clean, weedless edges hold few birds.

CRP ground has not been the boon to quail that it has to pheasants because it is neither an ideal nesting nor a feeding site. Wells believes that two factors are hurting quail populations in the Southeast. First and foremost, the woody fence rows so common in the era of sharecropping are being bulldozed away to allow big field farming on a much larger scale. This greatly reduces the amount of habitat available. Secondly, many formerly tilled fields have been planted for pasture with Bermuda grass or fescue, both of which are so thick and matted that they are not conducive to quail brooding and survival.

QUAIL LIKE IT HOT

Roger Wells (right) of Quail Unlimited and Larry Houf (left) examine a warm-season native grass planting as quail nesting cover on the White River Trace Wildlife Area in Missouri.

Quail like it hot. At least quail survive best where it is warm enough to ward off especially severe winter cold, so perhaps it would be more accurate to say that quail don't like it cold. However, truly blistering, sustained summer heat of over a hundred degrees day after day can be deadly for quail chicks. Most of the periodic swings in quail populations along the northern edge of the quail range are almost directly related to one or two really severe and long-lasting ice storms. The quail's natural covey mentality makes them especially vulnerable to being iced in or iced over. Their small size means that even a thin coating of ice on the ground and their food sources can be an impenetrable barrier to food consumption. Quail also have severe problems surviving deep snows, so generally their range is bounded by areas that frequently encounter such weather. Along the edges of the quail range, populations will gradually

The Bob White Quail range in North America.

increase during multiple-year periods of easy winters, only to plummet to near nothing after a hard winter. After the winter of 1982, the Iowa quail population hit bottom and after the winter of 1985, the Ohio quail population went to a drastically low level.

If you want consistently good quail shooting, the only answer is to go to the South. Georgia, Alabama, Tennessee, Mississippi, Louisiana and Texas are traditionally the big quail states, but Missouri, Arkansas, Oklahoma and Kansas are good quail states when they aren't at the bottom of a cold weather decline. Sometimes when we are pheasant hunting in the Midwest, we bust out a covey over a flushing dog that stands there totally unnerved by the eruption. When we flush a covey we carefully watch where they set down the follow-up for shooting. Hunting singles over a flushing dog, a spaniel or a retriever can be great fun as the birds blast out with little or no warning. This is snap shooting at its best; however, few quail ever fly more than shoulder high, so take care if the dog races after the flush.

Retrieving downed quail is a challenge for any dog. The dropped bird emits minimal scent and often falls in deep and heavy cover. Wounded birds can run like a miniature pheasant, and I have watched a tipped-wing bird run a hundred yards in a harvested soybean field while the confused dog pottered over its tiny little trail. Many birds can be lost, especially in heavy dense cover, if the dog isn't a conscientious and determined retriever.

CHAPTER 8

OTHER GAME BIRDS, OTHER TERRITORIES

Few places in the world support as wide and diverse a variety of game bird species as does the United States. Each has its own set of unique habits and habitat, often resulting in a restricted geographic range for given a species. Without extensive travel most roughshooters will only have a chance at two or three of the local species, so naturally most hunters' skills become well honed on the indigenous birds. Of necessity, *American Roughshooting*

On this spring morning, a desert quail sings while it sits in a tree near the Sedona red rock cliffs.

is focused on the birds having the widest geographic range, America's big four upland game birds: ring-neck pheasant, bobwhite quail, ruffed grouse and woodcock, but in some areas those birds are not normally found. Therefore, some roughshooters must adapt their style to the local varieties.

My far-flung hunting travels have convinced me that although the methods and tactics may vary slightly, a dedicated hunter with solid hunting skills, an honest dog and fair shooting ability can quickly learn how to pursue game bird varieties that may be new to him. In just days a veteran hunter will be cruising like a native because skilled hunters know that the key to successfully hunting any species is understanding its habits and habitat.

When I first moved to the West Coast I knew nothing of how to hunt California quail. I found my first covey by accident while getting my morning exercise riding my bike along an isolated road. After that I watched carefully and soon noted where and when I saw the coveys. I began to understand their habits and habitat and from there, hunting with dog and gun was a fairly simple next step. Make no mistake, it was brutal hunting, in the rock-strewn mountainsides, each sprinkled liberally with cactus, but it was doable, and it was the only native hunting near my home. By far the most outlandish upland shooting I have ever attempted was ptarmigan in Alaska. There, wearing waders, I slogged through marshy tundra in order to shoot at birds that lacked any fear of humans. On that day the mosquitoes were more of a challenge than the ptarmigan. The birds simply had no fear and refused to burst into flight.

Learning to find the holding cover and understanding the actions of the quarry is key to success. A few different rules hold true for each species, but in the end your success will be the result of your hunting, dog and shooting skills.

CHUKAR SKILLS

Chris Christensen is one of the few people wise enough to enjoy life while he is still physically able. Now in his early sixties, he has sold his medical practice and retired to hunt and fish worldwide, full time. Still trim and muscled, Chris tackles the mountain ridges of eastern Oregon on a section of leased property that holds chukars. The birds are especially vulnerable to weather

Pick the right dog and it can do double duty as a productive companion for duck or goose hunting

and while one season brings a bounty, the next can result in a dearth. Chris grew up in Michigan, hunting pheasants and grouse, but transferred his allegiance to western species more than thirty years ago. High on the rocky ridges, the birds can only find shelter under sparse vegetation and usually congregate in steep draws near water. This arid country is a hostile habitat that only a few hearty species could call home.

Transferring hunting skills to a new species requires an understanding of their habits. This can be gleaned from books, observation or hunting partners. As Chris tells it, he goes after chukar based on these rules:

1. The birds run uphill, then fly down.

2. The birds are usually found near vegetation (overhead cover) and a water source.

3. The birds will covey up in a good spot if not pushed too hard by a big-running dog.

4. The birds hold best for cautious pointing dogs.

5. Shooting is fast and difficult because gravity adds speed as the birds fly downhill. Be sure to take enough gun (sufficient firepower).

6. This is rugged, grueling hunting. Wear good boots and get in shape.

Based on those six principles, Chris has devised a system to hunt chukars and has effectively transferred his Midwest pheasant hunting skills to the rocky ridges of Oregon.

PRESERVE HUNTING

Many avid hunters add months of preserve hunting to their wild bird pursuits in order to extend their season. In many places open season on wild birds lasts only a few weeks, and without preserves the good dogs and great guns would get very little use during the year. Here in Michigan our preserve season runs from September through April and adds at least five months to the hunting year.

Most preserves stock just four varieties: ring-neck pheasant, chukar, bobwhite quail and Hungarian partridge. Those four are easily raised and if properly acclimatized they can prove to be almost as exciting as wild birds.

The hunting and gunning is often nearly as challenging as wild bird shooting, but only well-controlled dogs can pass the test for preserve shooting. The reasons are fairly simple: The dog must work your assigned piece of ground, maybe eighty acres. If the dog insists on hunting next door, you won't be very popular. In addition, the dog must be absolutely staunch, for it is bound to see a few birds on the ground, and nothing tempts a dog to creep like a full view of a walking bird. Preserve hunting is great fun, but it brings a slightly different set of rules.

PART II
DOGS

CHAPTER 9

THE DOG'S PART IN ROUGHSHOOTING

Roughshooting is at its best when the birds are found and retrieved by a high-quality, high-performance bird dog, and the personal satisfaction is greater when the dog doing the work belongs to you. Naturally, most dedicated shooters aspire to own a top-quality dog, but how they go about selecting, training and caring for a top-notch bird finder is subject to widely divergent viewpoints. This section is devoted to a factual review of the various types of dogs, and candid interviews with some of America's top hunting dog trainers about what it takes to own a top-quality gun dog.

This is not a "how-to" training manual. A variety of very good dog training books are already on the market, so I have steered this text away from tactical training advice and more toward a focused discussion of realistic dog actions, expectations and pitfalls. By focusing on the end use of the dog, the owner can better decide what skills and talents are most important to select the best dog and then use the other available literature to complete the training.

In many ways a hunting dog can be compared to a car. Some cars are unexciting and unpretentious, but they start every morning, run reasonably well and despite occasional required maintenance, provide an honest level of reliable transportation in line with the price paid for them. Some bird dogs match this description pretty closely.

Other cars are exciting, high performance, almost all-out race cars. But they tend to be temperamental, less reliable, prone to breakage, expensive and sometimes aggravating. They are extremely exhilarating but best suited to sporadic thrill seekers. Some bird dogs are like that.

Some cars have no redeeming virtues. They are overpriced, always breaking, dull performing and unreliable. Some dogs are like that, and both cars and dogs of this ilk are nuisances that deserve to be discarded in the former instance and put to some other use in the latter.

Then there are those classics—cars that provide a consistently high level of performance, excitement and reliability, all at a reasonable price. Cars like that are a pleasure to own and drive. Dogs like that exist as well, and more frequently than you might expect. A little luck mixed with some common sense and consistent basic training can increase your chances of owning such a dog.

Over the years I've hunted many places, over many different dogs, some great and some awful. Generally, the most productive and enjoyable hunts were with average dogs that were very good at the basics. The most memorable dogs simply found birds in a way that allowed our shooting to connect. Surprisingly, most of those dogs needed to do only three or four things well to be of great value.

Some of the so-called "superdogs" I hunted over were such a constant hassle that they took the pleasure out of the hunt. What good is a dog that is gone for hours at a time? I have also hunted over more than a few dogs that were so lacking in basic desire and intensity that they had no real value. They just went for a nice jog in the sun. Somewhere in between those two extremes are many reliable and productive hunting dogs.

I'm convinced that an honest dog with instinctive talents, one that works with you and finds birds for you is what it is all about, but finding such a dog may not be as easy as it sounds.

The average hunter has a limited opportunity to observe first-hand how the various breeds and types of bird dogs function. Some of the classic dog literature bears no relationship to the reality of how the dogs actually work in the field. The dog selection process is further complicated by the need to match hunting needs with the everyday realities of integrating a dog into a busy life. That's why a hunter should go see the dogs work, hunting, in hunting tests and in field trials to actually see the various types of dogs in action. The dog trainers that acted as consultants on this book have a combined total of several hundred years of dog experience. In just a year they see and train more dogs than the average hunter sees in a lifetime, and because they have minimal emotional ties to an individual dog, they are able to evaluate it with an unbiased openness as few hunters are able to do.

All of the trainers agree that if you acquire a dog with the proper mix of natural talent, bird instincts and range tendencies, the job of training the dog and keeping it under control will be much easier. The key to proper dog selection is to cast the dog in an appropriate role, a role that matches the style, talents and instincts of the character the dog is expected to play. Dogs fit some roles better than others. The most satisfied roughshooters are those that have selected the right dog for the part.

I have also come to believe that many breed aficionados, or people who have been totally focused on only one breed for many years, are often neither qualified nor objective enough to evaluate "their" breed versus other breeds. Take your time! Your dog will be with you for many years and you owe it to your family to do a thorough search for the perfect dog to match your situation. Where possible, I have interviewed trainers with multibreed and even multitype experience, so their broad backgrounds and their candid answers will shed light on the talents of all the most popular breeds. But we all have different expectations. A breed weakness that might frustrate me to the point of getting rid of the dog might be only a minor annoyance to you. So understanding the implications is important, too. Detailed discussions of the personalities and hunting styles of both pointing dogs and flushing dogs will follow.

Most of my training experience relates to English Springer Spaniels, a breed I thoroughly enjoy due to its natural talent and broad versatility. However, I have been fortunate enough to hunt over numerous dogs of many breeds and I hope to share my own experiences throughout.

NOSE

The reason you take a dog along in the first place is so it can find birds with its keen scenting ability or nose. But nose is hard to quantify in picking a puppy. If the parents have good noses, odds are the puppy will, too, but even littermates will vary. There are different types of noses, too. Some dogs have a nose that is adept at finding body scent. Pointers and setters have a nose for body scent. Some can find birds at long distances in the right wind conditions. The late Chuck Goodall, a celebrated dog writer from the 1950s, cautioned against trying to teach a spaniel to point, because Goodall didn't think the spaniel had the right kind of nose to find sitting birds at long distances. It is obvious when you watch the different dogs work that many pointing dogs of English background don't have the kind of nose needed to trail moving birds, but most Continental breeds can trail. In the end, the nose comes with the dog. With experience, all dogs will use their noses better, but the basic nose and its innate talents is inherited.

HONEST TALK ABOUT DOGS

The dog section is the most difficult to put on paper because it is so personal and so emotional. Most of us can take a bit of good-natured ribbing about our guns or our shooting or choice of covers or our woods lore, but say something unkind about our dogs and we get offended quickly. One of my biggest concerns is that my honest discussion of dog work will be easily recognized by some of my old hunting cronies and wound their memories. A man's dog, like his family, is often seen through rose-colored glasses, and there is little point in tarnishing any old dog's image. But I have an obligation to tell it honestly and although you may not agree with my viewpoints, I won't hide them.

BIRD DOGS, CONTINENTALS, SPANIELS & RETRIEVERS

So many of the terms in this game are defined only by the practitioners of the sport. These terms aren't found in Webster's Dictionary—just in our vocabulary. I've never held firm to convention, but obviously the real hard-core traditional southern hunting folks call only English Pointers and English Setters "bird dogs." Based on that very narrow definition, the remaining breeds must be called something else. No one is quite sure how the term *bird dog* came into usage, especially when continentals, spaniels and retrievers are also commonly used for bird hunting! I've always called my spaniels bird dogs. But some people look at me askance when I do that. When someone says, "Yeah, I own a couple of bird dogs—a pair of Brittanys," it sounds OK to me, but not to the purist and the traditionalist. Based on tradition, I'll try to stick to convention throughout the book. I'll try to call them: Continentals for continentals or versatiles; Spaniels are spaniels; Retrievers are retrievers; Hounds are hounds; Only Pointers and setters are "bird dogs."

But it won't be easy. It's certainly not worth losing much sleep over.

POINTING DOGS

The pointing dog chapters are devoted to those wonderful dogs that lock up solid as classic statues and await the arrival of the hunter. Pointing dogs come in two very distinct varieties: those that originated in England and those from the rest of the European continent. British dogs have been in the United States far longer than the Continental

Four beautiful rock-ribbed, high-tailed English Pointers lock up solid when they find the essence of their existence, the scent of quail. Of all the sporting breeds, the Pointer may display the most instinctive bird-finding ability, but that hard-going nature brings with it the promise of far horizons. Every hunting dog has its attributes. Some will match the needs of the average roughshooter, while others will stretch his patience to the limit. None of the sporting breeds can outperform the Pointer under certain circumstances, but what circumstances? David Jones

breeds, and as you will read later, are now so truly Americanized that few exist in England. The Americanized English dogs are very focused; they are specialized to do only a few things, but they do those few things very well.

The Continental dogs (often called versatile breeds) have come to this country much more recently (the German Wirehaired Pointer as recently as 1960), and breeding stock still occasionally flows in from overseas. These dogs are supposed to exhibit a very broad set of skills. That is why they are called versatile, because they were expected to fill a wider variety of (seven or eight) roles fairly well. They may not perform some functions as well as the English dogs, but they are expected to be jacks-of-all-trades.

The roughshooter, seeking to find an appropriate pointing dog to match his needs, has to sort through a wide group of alternatives. Ten breeds of sporting dogs point game and each has its own unique style, instincts and personality.

A POINTING DOG'S TRAINED ATTRIBUTES

In the everyday roughshooting situation, the Big Four basic attributes—range, control, staunchness and retrieving—spell out the difference between solid, pleasurable, productive hunting and a long, brisk walk in the country.

Range—Acceptable range is always a criterion decided by the hunter, and as long as the hunter and dog are not grossly mismatched the day can be a success. A detailed discussion of range is included in chapter 19.

Control and responsiveness—These attributes allow the hunter to direct the day's activities. On occasion, a productive day will result from just following the dog wherever it decides to go, but generally, unless the dog will hunt at your direction, many productive covers will be missed and some potentially dangerous situations can occur. If the dog is totally unresponsive, you will spend your days hunting the dog, not the birds. Each of the pointing dog experts discusses control in detail.

Staunchness—Once the dog finds birds and locks up on a solid point, it must hold staunch until you get there to shoot. If it creeps in or busts the birds before you get there, the effort was meaningless. Rock solid staunchness is an absolute expectation in any pointing dog.

Retrieving—Finding the birds you shoot is the ultimate goal and the dog's olfactory talents should be put to use to assist in this effort. Whether in a point dead or a full retrieving situation, the dog should be a working partner to find the birds you shoot. Over the last twenty years the natural retrieving instinct of most pointing dogs has declined. The experts explain why.

Note that I have not mentioned style (either pointing style or running style) or nose. Many dog people today are so focused on style that they totally miss the solidly productive bird work that makes roughshooting successful. Stylish dogs are great, but only if that style is in addition to reliable and productive bird-finding ability and a reasonable display of the four key elements. Bird finding is a result of nose and bird sense. Nose is inherited, although it can be honed with experience, and "bird sense" is something good dogs learn with exposure.

OTHER ATTRIBUTES

Backing—If you plan to hunt much with more than one dog, it is a nice refinement if your dog will back the other dog's points. By locking up staunchly whenever it sees the other dog on point, it avoids the delicate situation where one dog steals another dog's find, or worse yet bumps the birds into the air. Backing is considered unimportant by hunters who always hunt alone or those that only hunt one dog at a time.

Steady to wing—Steady to wing can save your dog's life. A dog that chases after birds will often be in the line of fire, and especially when hunting low-flying birds like quail. Most everyday shooting dogs should be "broke," meaning steady to wing.

Steady to shot—Many dogs that are steady to wing are allowed to break and chase at the sound of the shot. Some of the best hunting dog trainers feel that this increases the chances of retrieving the bird while minimizing the chances of the dog being in the line of fire. The level of steadiness a hunter expects should be one of the early agreements reached between the trainer and owner.

FLUSHING DOGS

The flushing dog chapters of this book are devoted to the selection, training and everyday usage of the marvelous breeds of hunting dogs that "find 'em, flush 'em and fetch 'em" for the roughshooter.

In recent decades, Americans have become increasingly active and vigorous people. As healthy and involved enthusiasts, they hike, mountain

Flushing spaniels, like pointing dogs, also operate on instinct, but will also try to catch the bird on the ground, or even in the air, as this bold English Springer Spaniel is attempting. Flushing spaniels are ideal for game that tends to run away from the hunter and will stay after it until it flies to flee. In today's smaller covers, more physically active hunters are, in many cases, opting for close-working but boldly aggressive flushing dogs that find 'em , flush 'em and fetch 'em. John Friend

bike, backpack, hunt, fly fish, swim, play tennis and ski well into their late seventies. The style of dogs they hunt has also changed to reflect a more physically active hunter. Both flushing dogs and close-working continental pointing dogs, which require a more active and involved role from the hunter, have become increasingly popular. The changes in game habitat, farming practices and road traffic have also changed the type of dog we can turn loose. On small, more confined properties, a more controlled, closer-working dog is almost mandatory. Finally, many hunters are just plain tired of spending their days in the field hunting for their dog when they would rather be hunting for birds.

The flushing dogs, both spaniels and retrievers, exhibit a wide spectrum of speed and effort. Some are extremely fast, wide-running and intense, while others are more deliberate, laid back and easily controlled. But all flushing dogs must work within gun range to be of value. Even the fastest, most intense flushing dogs seldom range more than forty yards from the hunter. I find that hunters who choose flushing dogs tend to be more consistently involved, both physically and mentally, as the day of hunting unfolds.

As the late Richard Wolters pointed out in his book *Game Dog,* the methods used to train a dog of a retriever breed for upland hunting are very similar to those used to train a spaniel. Originally, I planned two separate sections for spaniels and retrievers, but as I completed the research for this book and interviewed the "experts," it was obvious that covering many aspects of retrievers and spaniels for upland hunting would be redundant. The expectations and modes of hunting for both dog types are quite similar; although each has strengths and weaknesses, their training process and the end result are quite similar. Therefore, I recommend that retriever and spaniel hunters read the entire flushing dog section of this book.

The reason the training methods and expectations for both breeds are similar is the fact that they hunt the same way: (1) quarter and quest, searching for game within gun range; (2) track moving birds and push them until they flush; and (3) mark the fall of shot birds and retrieve them to hand. Simply put, the dogs "find 'em, flush 'em and fetch 'em." You will come across that phrase often in this book.

You should recognize, however, that some portions of the training will be easier for the spaniels, while others will be easier for retrievers. For example, it is easier to get a spaniel to quarter and quest for game than to get the same performance from a retriever, but generally retrievers are more reliable markers and easier to control than spaniels. I also caution you to guard against classifying any training method as either a "spaniel method" or a "retriever method." If a training routine works well to achieve a desired result, by all means use it, regardless of its origins. Every dog is an individual, and where the training difficulties will arise is unique with each dog and each breed.

CHAPTER 10
TRADITIONAL BIRD DOGS

ENGLISH SETTERS

Although the English Setter is the classic pointing dog of hunting literature, it comes in a variety of performance variations, many of which are very specialized. When someone says English Setter, the next question is, what kind of English Setter? As Dale Jarvis put it, "When someone calls to arrange for me to train his setter, I never know what kind of dog will get out of their truck."

If I were to total up all the days I have spent hunting over English Setters in the last twenty years, the number would be second only to the many days I spent hunting over my own English Springers. These setters came in every size, shape, color and style. Some were marvelously intense, stylish dogs, with stamina, talent and brains, but others were just dogs. Anyone who seriously watches a group of setters work will soon realize that the breed has been fragmented into numerous subgroups, each with a very different range, intensity, running style, pointing style, level of independence and size. It is ironic that the dog most likely to come to mind as a hunting dog, most likely to be photographed in a grouse setting and most likely to be bought by a traditionalist is also the least predictable. The dyed-in-the-wool traditionalist roughshooter, intent upon owning a fine English Setter to accompany him into the coverts, has a lot of homework to do before he plunks down his cash for the "type" of setter to match his needs. To me, the measure of a dog is whether, after watching it for a day, I want to take it home with me. Some setters I've yearned to own, others I'd have gotten rid of in a minute, were they mine.

I've seen some folks err pretty badly in the picking. Often the dogs they picked were marvelous animals, just inappropriate for the owner's hunting style. A close friend, a consummate and intense grouse and woodcock hunter, owns one of the most talented setters I've ever seen—strong, stylish, all-day stamina, good nose, straight-up tail, nice manners—but this dog came from prairie stock and his natural range is about three hundred yards. He is like a ghost, because he is seldom seen in the grouse woods. I'd love to own that dog if I were hunting quail down south. But on northern birds in heavy cover it takes a considerable amount of continuous training effort, a strong handler and a frequent dose of electricity to hack the dog down to a woods range.

Another friend, Chad Betts of Kansas, owns a similar setter—a nice little bitch named Blue that

This is "Sam," Glenn Hershberger's big white English Setter, a big-going covey dog. Sam found this covey as he raced along the edge where a wheat field abutted a woodsy fence row.

Later as we hunted singles, Chad Betts's dog "Blue" found the birds and "Sam" backed. Here the bird had dropped into an edge between the woods and the milo stubble.

has the same style and bionic stamina as the North Woods dog. I'd like to own Blue, too, but I'd choose to hunt her right there in Kansas. She, too, is a big-running, all-day dog with a nose that can really find birds, so she is perfectly matched to the rolling Kansas prairies.

Some strains of setters seem inherently adjusted to their circumstances. Frank Sylvester of Pennsylvania has owned and tested more than a dozen setters of many different strains. He has of late become devoted to a North Woods type of hunting setter that is tall, lean and physically athletic, yet does not exhibit the clod-throwing gallop of the plains setters. Their trotting speed and lower intensity is more in keeping with their surroundings. They cover a lot of ground, but I doubt that they would ever open up to the race-over-the-ridge speed of the true plains dogs.

One of the most unique varieties of setter is the huge and deliberate northeast strain of woodcock dogs. They are as big as a small pony, but they work very slowly and very carefully, and their range is usually quite limited. They find birds, but I like more fire and intensity and a lot more ground-covering capability in a dog of any breed.

Some setters exhibit intense, high-tailed points. However, the spectrum extends to dogs so soft on point that a few slowly sink to the ground in the style of the ancient dogs. If you decide to hunt with a traditional bird dog, a Pointer or an English Setter, accept the fact that these are the most independent of all the sporting dogs. They operate mostly on instinct and inherent urges. Most are fast, stylish and intense, but they are also somewhat disconnected. The setter's independent streak must have been selectively bred into the dogs, for the responsive spaniels and the aloof setters all come from the same roots back in eighteenth-century England.

Both the Pointers and setters I have hunted over have shown a level of independence that keeps them from responding directly to commands. They may acknowledge your presence, and most will eventually turn in your direction, but they will do so in their own good time. They will seldom respond immediately to your turn commands like the other breeds seem willing to do. Over the last twenty years I think the independent streak of the dogs has gotten worse, not better, as most hunters have come to rely on an electric collar rather than the dog's inherent biddability to hone their training.

ENGLISH POINTERS

The English Pointer, a natural talent at finding birds.

No sporting breed exhibits more natural talent to find birds than an English Pointer. When this awesome natural nose is carried through the fields in a powerful athletic body, capable of hours and miles of ground-eating strides, the combination is awesome! Add the high level of grace and classic style inherent in the Pointer, and the triad of nose, style and stride makes the English Pointer the most respected pointing dog in the world.

The English Pointer has long been acknowledged as the premier southern quail dog—the ideal dog for the wide open spaces of five-thousand-acre plantations. The dog's leanness and short, smooth coat suit the blazing summer heat and mild winters of the South. Their pace and stamina suit the wide open spaces.

But as David Jones states so eloquently, "Many Pointers are like little Indy 500 race cars, single-purpose machines singularly suited to the formidable task of big range bird hunting." Unfortunately, most people aren't capable of coping with an Indy racer on a daily basis, nor do they have access to the kind of grounds appropriate for such an awesome racing machine of a dog. As much as every one respects the talents of the English Pointer, the average American roughshooter is generally unable to use the almost unbridled power of these Indy 500 canine super-athletes.

Most Pointer and setter owners are not great fans of the ring-neck plains. Pointers and setters are the least likely of the pointing breeds to handle a skulking, moving, runaway quarry. While the nose of these dogs seems ideally suited to find even the slightest whiff of a bird's body scent, genetic selection has resulted in a nose that is somewhat unsuited to follow foot scent or to trail body scent hanging on the cover.

Here on the Texas plains, two of the speedy English Pointers, trained by David Jones for the Gaffney Ranch, find and back and await the arrival of the hunter.

Over the years a few Pointers have found their way into the North Woods and these dogs, with naturally smaller range and a more responsive nature can be good dogs in heavy cover. But in general, the Pointer is a relatively rare dog in the alder thickets, where its range is simply too big for the conditions.

A limited gene pool of less than ten thousand dogs per year produces almost all of the big-going southern quail dogs and Open All-Age winners. Hence, in this breed, conservatively 50 to 75 percent of the top breeding stock is from horseback trial champions. By definition, a horseback dog is mismatched to the task of roughshooting.

GORDON SETTERS

The Gordon's stated attributes are its close-working style and narrow range. The true Gordon is a foot hunter's dog of easily controlled nature. However, its dark color makes it hard to see in the deep woods and its beauty seems to be leading it into the showring. Gordies are so unusual that I'd demand to see proven field performance before I'd write a check to buy any Gordon Setter.

Unfortunately, the Gordon seems susceptible to the "beautiful dog" curse that literally destroyed the Irish Setter. This dog, too, has a unique style and grace, and it has caught the eye of an avid group of show breeders. In fact, a recent all-breed Detroit dog show attracted an entry of fifty-one Gordon Setters. With only 1,393 Gordons registered for the entire year by the American Kennel Club, it is obvious that a large portion of the Gordon Setter fans are focusing on beauty and coat. However, in the last ten years an increased emphasis has been directed toward retaining the field qualities of the dogs, even those in the showring. You can find a Gordon that will hunt, but I would demand to see it proven in the field.

WILL POINTERS & SETTERS RETRIEVE?

Some Pointers and setters will retrieve and some won't, and even the most drastic force training methods are not 100 percent reliable. During the past year I have personally shot birds that were retrieved by both breeds. On several occasions the Pointers of David Jones and the setters handled by Chad Betts searched out and brought back birds, then laid them in David or Chad's hand, just like a retriever would. Derek Sylvester's setters "pointed dead" but wouldn't retrieve. One afternoon his big stylish grouse woods setter found two grouse that I had knocked down but could not find without the dog's help. Unfortunately, only about half of the dogs of these breeds will consistently show that level of performance.

CHAPTER 11
A CONVERSATION WITH DAVID JONES

DAVID JONES

Gaffney Ranch
Victoria, Texas

Talk about life's contrasts! David Jones, born in Wales, was raised among the cold, green, rain-washed crags and valleys of the Welsh countryside. At age eighteen he signed on as an apprentice gamekeeper at Carrog Shoot, working driven shoots and training dogs.

There, as a spindly youth, he worked the old stone house kennels, training dogs in the rabbit pens, learning all the ways and nuances of the English style of training shooting dogs. Then after ten years of work as a gamekeeper, he was lured to the United States by a pair of Texas sportspersons looking for an honest, personable gamekeeper and dog trainer. Who better than this cheerful, outgoing young man from Wales?

But did David realize that he would be moving from the cool, green dampness of his home near the Irish Sea to the blazing, hot vastness of the south Texas plains? As fast as a jet will whisk you around the world, David was transplanted

David Jones, born in Wales, now trains dogs, mostly English Pointers, on the coastal plains of southern Texas. He has obviously adopted the jeans and boots of the local custom.

77

to a large Texas ranch on the coastal plain as a chief gamekeeper, hunt director and dog trainer. Obviously, this is quail country, and David soon acquired a significant respect for the big-running Pointers of the American South.

Now, fifteen years after David came to the United States, he is still with the same employer, overseeing and training a kennel populated by twenty Pointers, six spaniels, three Labrador Retrievers and about forty Greyhounds. The spaniels and Labs are used for dove and duck hunting in September, October and November, then as pick-up dogs during the December, January and February quail hunts. The Pointers are used for quail hunting on the ranch and a few local foot hunting trials in the area. The Greyhounds are trained in the basics on the ranch, then shipped off to trainers in Corpus Christi or Houston for racing.

You grew up with spaniels and retrievers; close-working, obedient flushing dogs. Now you train and handle big running Pointers. How difficult was the transition?

JONES—It took some getting used to, but it grows on you. There are natural differences in the instincts of the dogs that make them perform differently. The flushing dogs are much more obedient than the Pointers, but even so, our Pointers do respond to direction and I am able to use some of the same basic training methods. Most of it was a mental adjustment on my part to get used to having a dog running out so far. I also carefully selected a strain of Pointers that are very responsive and biddable.

As David walks in to flush the bird, the dog holds a staunch, high-tailed point.

How did you select your line of Pointers and are they difficult to train?

JONES—No, they are not difficult to train, most probably because I studied the lines before I bought. I wanted shooting dogs, so I stayed away from the open all-age breeding, which are very tough, hard-running dogs that take a lot of handling. I don't have anything against those dogs, but they're bred for different purposes. You can look at it like those dogs are Indy racers and you don't buy an Indy car to go four-wheel driving. The kind of dogs I want are four-wheel drives. Too many people look in the *American Field Magazine* and see that so-and-so is a nine-time champion and they decide they want a pup out of him because he is a nine-time champion. Well, he is a nine-time champion Indy car and he is going to throw you little Indy cars that go two hundred miles per hour and unless they are bred to the right bitches, they're not geared to ever be more biddable and responsive. That's just the way it is. I wanted dogs that I could work with and dogs that would work for me.

How do you develop a strong response in such an intense line of pointing dogs?

JONES—What I do is very similar to the yard work I use with a spaniel or a retriever. I use a check cord in the yard and I use a consistent whistle command for all our dogs, regardless of breed. There is no need to have different commands for different breeds. I use a double toot to mean turn. Some people will also incorporate the electric collar training with the check cord. They give the command, then they turn the dog with the check cord and they will give a low stimulation shock to get its attention. Over time the yard work, day after day, is the key to responsiveness in a pointing dog.

Over the years I have heard people suggest that you can just leave a Pointer in the kennel for the first year, don't do anything with it, then just turn it loose and let it run on its own instincts.

JONES—And that is why the Pointer gets a reputation of being a crazy, wild, uncontrollable hunting machine. That little Pointer bitch in our kennel was in the house as a pet with a little girl for only a few weeks, but she has never forgotten it. She is a more affectionate dog because of it. A lot of her personality developed in those few weeks. If a dog has been left in a kennel run for twelve months without any socialization or yard work, then it is taken out and let to run, it is not going to respond to you then or maybe ever.

So you basically socialize your Pointers just like you would socialize a Springer or a Lab?

JONES—Yes, absolutely. All of our pups start outside here in our yard in a pen and if we have enough time and enough room, they go into a travel crate right here on the front porch by our front door. I almost always have a few puppies living in crates outside the door here. I let them out five or six times a day and they run around the house with me as I do chores. You have to make a personal time commitment to do it right, but it pays off in the end.

If you were taking in a dog to train at a year old, and you had your choice of a dog that had been in a kennel or a dog that had been raised as a pet around kids, which one would you pick?

JONES—Without a doubt, I'd pick the one that had been with the kids. There is something special about a kid raising a puppy.

Do you find that your Pointers have a basic retrieving instinct as young dogs or do you have to start from zero and force break them?

JONES—I've found that the Pointers I have in my kennel do have a basic retrieving instinct. But you have to be very careful. Any little mistake can

All the dogs at the ranch are expected to back reliably.

turn off that instinct a lot easier than with a Labrador or an English Springer Spaniel. With all these young Pointers, you can throw something for them and they will run out and pick it up and you can usually entice them to bring it back to you. But when they get older, they are just more sensitive. I don't think the retrieving instinct is as strong as in the retrieving breeds, so any little mistake, any little show of annoyance from you, and that dog won't come back to you when it's got something in its mouth. You can switch it off very easily.

When you say young, six months?

JONES—No, no, much younger than that. By eight weeks I like to have them retrieving something. The program I use on the Pointer pups is no different than the program I use on the Spaniel or Lab puppies. I use retrieving dummies and get down on the ground and pet them on the head when they come back. But I will tell you, with the Pointers there does seem to be more of an inclination to hard mouth. Especially when we first switch from a dummy to a bird.

Do you force break the dogs later on?

JONES—If they're really good retrievers I just force break them to "hold" the bird for delivery, but if there is any kind of serious retrieving problem, then I go ahead and do the complete force breaking.

If you go out for a day and you shoot twenty quail, how many of those will the Pointers retrieve?

JONES—Just a rough estimate: fifteen. I generally keep a Springer at heel to go get the birds with the broken wings that can hit the ground and run really fast. On average, a Pointer just doesn't seem to be able to trail those birds as well, although a rare one can. I understand why a person who is out hunting may let his dog break to the shot because there is a higher possibility that the Pointer is going to catch that wounded bird and retrieve it.

How natural is it for these dogs to lock up on point and when do they begin? Three months or six months?

JONES—Very early! You can get them to point at six or eight weeks old with a wing on the end of a cane pole. Play around with that cane pole a couple of minutes a day and it will really bring that pointing instinct on. That helps a lot when they find their first bird. I usually let them find their first wild birds early just to see how they are going to handle it and to see what kind of a dog I have coming along. The first time they smell a bird they usually flash point it and then take it out and chase it as it flies. Later, the more birds they point the longer the pointing time will last. The first time it might be a half a second, but by the tenth or eleventh bird it might be five seconds, and as long as you see this time duration increasing, it's fine. During this period I absolutely do not want the dog to catch a bird. I am very careful about using pen-raised birds because when that time duration is increasing and you're getting a five-second point, then a ten-second point, if the dog jumps in and captures some weak and lazy old pigeon— oops! Then you're back to square one and he is only going to flash point the next time before he races in to catch that bird.

These are big-running dogs that work out a long distance from you. How long do they need to be staunch in order for you to get there to shoot?

JONES—I like dogs to adjust their range distance to the cover. Usually that comes with time and experience. It usually takes between five to ten minutes before we can get to them and they have to be absolutely staunch. This is fairly open country so we can find the dogs fairly quickly even when they are quite a distance away. We never allow them to creep in to flush the birds. Usually by eighteen months they are solidly staunch.

I know some guys who hunt in heavy woods who allow their dogs to creep in to help make the flush.

JONES—Yes, I know some hunters who will command the dogs to flush. But when the dog flushes the bird it almost always chases after the bird and that can lead to many situations where you can't shoot or it is a dangerous shot over the dog's head. I feel the dog should be at least steady until the shot is fired.

You obviously understand why some hunters allow their dogs to break at the shot. But still, your dogs are all steady to wing and shot! Why?

JONES—That's because we sometimes run them in shooting dog stakes and your dog must be fully steady to wing and shot. Also because I am not just hunting by myself. I have a lot of different people coming here to the ranch to hunt, and if our dogs are not steady there is a higher chance that the dog could get shot. About once a season I hear about somebody's dog that got shot. Most hunters are concentrating only on shooting birds and quail don't always fly very high, so there is a lot less chance the dog will get shot if he is *not* chasing after a bird.

Any other tips on dog safety?

JONES—Yes, if I am hunting with a bunch of people, three or four guns that I don't know well, I hunt only a single dog. What happens is in their enthusiasm sometimes the gunners will not give the second dog time to come in and back the pointing dog. So, the first dog will point and the gunners will start walking in to flush the birds. If the birds get up and fly toward the second dog you've got a problem. I went down to the King Ranch on the "Mariposa" and helped on a commercial hunt. The organizers ran all single dogs and when I asked why this was done, *safety* was the reply. But I love to run braces and when I am out hunting with known, safe hunters who are well-disciplined gunners, we always run braces.

I have heard it said that a pointing dog with a decent nose needs to do only four things: 1. It needs to work at a reasonable range; 2. It needs to follow your direction so that it hunts where you are going; 3. It needs to hold point until you arrive; 4. When you shoot a bird, it needs to help you find it.

Does that make sense?

JONES—Yes, generally, but that second point could be a little misleading. I don't worry when I see that dog heading to a patch of briars a long distance away, even if it is not in the direction I am going. I just don't worry about it. I let him work that patch of ground and then work another patch of ground on his way back to me. He may cover a complete area without me ever having to go over there. But if I want to hunt north and the dog just independently is heading south, I will force him to hunt with me and go north. I definitely won't follow him south.

You often hunt two dogs at the same time; do you teach all of your dogs to back? How difficult is it to train?

JONES—All our dogs back, but I don't think it is difficult to train. I've found that if you start early enough and teach them to back, it becomes natural. I try not to make a big deal out of it. I use a lot of repetition to teach them to back and I use both a live dog and a silhouette. A silhouette works sometimes, but I have had more luck using a live dog. That takes a solidly staunch dog, because while that dog is on point, you're behind it concentrating totally on the other dog that you are teaching to back. Right now I have only one dog in the kennel that I can use for backing training. He is completely staunch and he will stay staunch even if I start messing around with a backing dog trying to rectify some problem. He will not get nervous and lose his intensity or get upset. It takes a special kind of dog to be a training dog.

CHAPTER 12
THE CONTINENTAL BREEDS

Every sporting dog breed was developed or evolved with a purpose and a style. Read the Howell breed books on the various sporting breeds and you will learn how, in each case, an individual or a group of fanciers worked to perfect their own ideal dog. Virtually every sporting breed found in the United States today came as a finished product; defined, stylized, patterned and typed. When the Brittany came from France, the German Pointers—Shorthaired and Wirehaired—and the Weimaraner from Germany, the Vizsla from Hungary and the Wirehaired Pointing Griffon from Holland, each had a distinct style and manner that appealed to the importers and was expected to fill a void among dog breeds available in America. To the greatest extent, dogs of the six Continental breeds were expected to be all-rounders, *pointing* dogs that were close-working, biddable, able to trail game and naturally strong retrievers.

This example of an older-style German Shorthaired Pointer is Wilkinson's Willoway's Mike-he owned by Harry Wilkinson, Pentwater, Michigan.

From what I can gather from talking to the old-timers, the original dogs fulfilled that niche very well. Many serious, hard-going foot hunters enjoyed many successful days walking and shooting over these "old-style" Continental dogs. The dogs were a bit methodical and journeyman-like in the way they went about their tasks, but they were productive! Sure, they often lacked the fire, flash and style of traditional American bird dogs—the Pointers and English Setters—but their importers felt that what they lacked in *pizzazz*, they made up in utility.

But Americans are competitive by nature, and soon a group of owners were field trialing their dogs. In order to stand out and win, they began to breed in more flash, more fire, more run and more range. Then a second group of breeders, the backyard breeders, added thousands of dogs to the gene pool, many that were not quite up to the original standards. Then a third group of breeders focused on the "show" dog strains within the Continental breeds, dogs that were bred to look great and maybe work a little on occasion. By now the breeds were getting pretty diluted.

Rumors abound that some breeders have also crossed several Continental breeds with English Pointers to put more Americanized style and run into the dogs. The most common place where the Pointer cross is rumored is in the German Shorthaired Pointer (GSP) because the size and build of the breeds were similar. Some people think a lot of white in the coat of the shorthair is the tell-tale sign of outcrossing, although historically some white was natural in both breeds. The results have not been

The newer-style German Shorthaired Pointer. This is Voglein's Billy of Sundance, owned by John and Irene Voglein of Zion, Illinois.

catastrophic, but several old-line breeders I've talked to think outcrossing has adversely affected the GSP's range, trailing and retrieving ability over the last twenty years as the dogs developed a more wide-ranging and flashier Americanized style.

As a consequence of their breeding for different traits, breed alone does not guarantee the hunting traits you might expect. If you are a foot hunter who is looking for a close working, easy handling, *pointing* dog, you should look long and hard to find a dog to suit your tastes, and *before* you buy, you should see the parents work to be sure the dog's style matches your expectations.

THE CONTINENTAL BREEDS

Recently I had the pleasure of watching a beautifully athletic, fifteen-month-old Brittany bitch come of age while hunting pheasants in the rolling Iowa prairies. Over the four days of the hunt, the little dog's

"Penny," Wil Avril's Brittany, comes from a hunting family.

experience, self-confidence and natural instincts grew a giant step toward maturity as she became a near-perfect dog for the average American roughshooter.

Brittanys are found in many styles and sizes, from horseback horizon runners to shoe polishers. This dog exhibited a natural range that should please the physically aggressive roughshooter. At the outside edge she reached out 150 yards but generally was within seventy-five or eighty yards of the hunter. Depending on the cover, she was sometimes only twenty to forty yards away. She quickly learned to adapt her range to the situation.

But this young bitch's level of performance was no accident. Starting even before the dog was whelped, Wil Avril made several wise and unemotional choices, each after carefully considering the facts. The *first* and most important choice was his selection of a puppy. Here he consulted Dale Jarvis, a reputable professional trainer that Wil trusted to steer him to a high-potential litter. Dale was not the seller of the puppies so he had no vested interest in the sale. However, Dale was confident enough of the breeding to purchase a puppy from the same litter for another client. This puppy was also from a repeat breeding, therefore, Wil could not only assess the parents' work in the field, he could also see siblings from the previous litters in action.

Second, Wil raised Penny as a house pet. The youngster slept in the den and was truly loved and nurtured by the whole family. Her breeding and subsequent nurturing resulted in a self-assured little hunter with a level of self-confidence seldom seen in kennel dogs of the same age.

Third, at a carefully considered age (twelve months in this case), the dog was turned over to Dale Jarvis, the professional trainer who had recommended the puppy. Now, at fifteen months of age, after a few months of basic training, the very birdie little bitch was aggressively searching for game, responding well to voice and whistle commands and pointing staunchly. She was showing the results of three months of professional training and so far only one glitch had surfaced. For some reason, her retrieving was weak.

On Penny's first day in Iowa she was a bit tentative. Unaccustomed to such unrestricted freedom, she constantly checked back to Wil for reassurance. Wil was a bit uneasy, too, and whistled for her whenever she reached out beyond his comfort zone. He naturally worried that she might become lost. But by the time we headed home, Penny ranged out independently and Wil let her freely search for birds.

Moving pheasants baffled Penny at first, but with experience, she learned to follow their trail with assurance. By day four Wil would say, "She's trailing a bird, let's go!" While many of the running birds flushed out ahead of the dog before she had a chance to point them, a few held still long enough for her to lock up on solid points. The overjoyed owner scored a solid hit on one of the first roosters that held tight for one of her rock solid points. He tucked that big Iowa cock bird into his game bag and his memory.

In retrospect, this dog seems naturally bred to please this roughshooter. Her lean, leggy and athletic physical structure allows her to run for hours at a quick but reserved pace. She is a "many hours a day dog," a valuable asset to the one-dog hunter like Wil. She has the temperament to be a lovable and obedient house pet, yet she is a smart little dog that learned over the four days to handle fence rows, sloughs and Conservation Reserve Program ground with equal ease.

The success of this dog/hunter team resulted from proper breeding, well-considered socialization and an effective training program.

The German Wirehaired Pointer, this is SRG Dirty Laundry owned by Bill and Gail Richardson, Metamora, Michigan. Bill Richardson

CALM AND EASY TEAMWORK

I like a dog that goes about its work with a minimum of direction and hacking. The grouse woods and the big prairies can be a quiet and peaceful setting if the sounds of nature are not constantly rent by a roughshooter's thundering voice and screaming whistle. Make no mistake, I make my own good share of noise when hunting, and perhaps that is why I appreciate quiet handling. The closer working Continental breeds are prime prospects for quiet hunting, and if properly conditioned to respond to the hunter they can be some of the most peaceful hunting partners

A wirehair in the woods, SRG Silent Running, M.H. owned by Bill and Gail Richardson of Metamora, Michigan. Jim Basham

available. Some of the better dogs I've hunted over needed almost no direction—no yelling, no hacking and very little whistling. A few actually worked better when the handler just backed off the whistle and let them come around naturally. Much of the yelling often results from early season nervousness. Some time on the ground for both dog and hunter calms the situation and lets them settle into a quiet routine.

Some Continental breed dogs really don't get out a whole lot farther than a flushing dog but they generally work much differently. The flushing dogs tend to work a set pattern like a windshield wiper and they usually respond quickly to a sharp whistle command. Continentals tend to run lines to birdie spots and then "come round" in their own good time. The tuned-in dog will, at the end of its reach almost naturally turn back toward the hunter. When the dog/hunter telepathy reaches its zenith, they can stay in touch with a minimal amount of verbal commands. As this confidence level grows, it allows the team to tackle more risky properties. There are many places in Iowa where prime hunting territory runs close to busy highways. In the big north country of Minnesota and Ontario, a dog that disappears for an hour may be gone forever. The Continental breeds are far more likely to be attuned to the hunter in a way that will allow him to hunt his dog on these marginal properties.

STYLE AND CLASS

Over the years the Continental breeds have taken a lot of flack from the bird dog purists for their lack of style and intensity. The bird dog purists fault the Continentals in three areas. First, they say the Continentals do not run with intensity and abandon. Then, they add that the dogs "feel" their way into a point, tiptoeing and mincing until they are sure of themselves. Finally, they criticize the points—too soft, too limp—not the high-tailed statue points seen on the cover of *The American Field*.

These complaints have some basis in truth. However, these dogs are expected to perform multiple tasks, to be versatile and generally, the broader the range of expectations, the less likely the dog is to be perfect in any one area. The reduced drive when questing for game usually results from the breed's closer-working nature. The dogs' reduced intensity on point occurs because they tend to check out a point for a few steps, making dead sure that the bird is sitting tight, not moving.

The original importers of the Continental breeds achieved their objective for a responsive, close-working, versatile dog. They never envisioned dogs that would have the range and style to challenge the English Pointers and English Setters.

C H A P T E R 1 3
CONVERSATIONS WITH LEE SEINKOWSKI AND DALE JARVIS

LEE SEINKOWSKI

Sundance Kennels
Versatile Breed Dog Trainer
Bristol, Wisconsin

Lee came to dog training naturally; he followed his father's footsteps. Bristol is on the Illinois/Wisconsin border, smack between Chicago and Milwaukee and within a day's drive of some of America's best wild bird hunting. For years Lee drove a truck and trailer across the nation running Continental Pointers in field trials and in the process, collected eight national championships, all with German Shorthaired Pointers. But a growing business, a wife, four children and an eager clientele of hunters pulled Lee off the field trial circuit and into the shooting dog world. Having personally witnessed the evolution of the Continental breeds, competed at field trials on a national level and now having trained hundreds of personal hunting dogs, Lee is the perfect "expert" to ask about the versatile dogs. His common sense, easy-to-understand concepts are enlightening in a world often littered with undefinable superlatives like "stylish." I think you will enjoy his directness and understand his ideas.

Have you been in the sport long enough to see the Continental breeds, especially the German Shorthaired Pointer, evolve to what they are today?

SEINKOWSKI—Definitely. When I first got into the game there were a lot of the old-style German Shorthairs around. They were a jack-of-all-trades, but a master-of-none breed. On the up side they were better retrievers, much better water dogs and closer working. But what has happened over the years is that the shorthair has been transformed into a pure bird dog, at least from a field trial standpoint. The dogs today are more along the lines of an English Pointer. Where the breed has suffered is in the retrieving instinct; it is not there as naturally anymore and the dogs are a little less manageable, for the average foot hunter. Today's shorthair will really get out and *rock and roll*—it is a stylish, classy, hard-going bird finder— a true bird dog.

Then these are not the old versatile dogs that will do a little of everything?

SEINKOWSKI—Absolutely not. There has been a lot of give-and-take and the hunter has suffered. The field trial dogs are really classy dogs that I like to hunt over, but I'm a dog handler by profession. I can deal with the really high-powered dog. But the average hunter, when he turns one of these dogs loose, he has his hands full.

Are any of the old-style shorthairs still around?

SEINKOWSKI—There are fewer and fewer as the years go by. A very few of the North American Versatile Hunting Dog Association people still breed them, but when people call me for the old-style Shorthairs I really don't know where to send them. A lot of the old fellows who originally brought them over from Europe are dying off. Apparently a few dogs of that style are still available in Europe and I train some dogs for people from Argentina that are of the old style.

Are there now widely divergent strains in all the Continental breeds?

SEINKOWSKI—Well, it's certainly true in most breeds. There are field trial dogs, show dogs and just a ton of backyard dogs. With the backyard dogs the performance is all over the map. An exception, and a breed that has progressed a lot, is the Vizsla. They used to be ultraclose-working dogs, not very stylish, slow foot speed and very soft. But today they are hard driving with a good medium range. They still have a lot of natural retrieving instinct and they are very trainable. That breed has come a long way in the last ten years and I'm recommending Vizslas to a lot of people who are afraid of the range of a German Shorthair. The Vizsla is my second choice in a Continental hunting dog.

As for Brittanies, their field trials in my mind have hurt the dog. So much run, run, run has been bred into the trial dogs that the pointing instinct has suffered. You almost have to teach those big-running dogs how to point. But I see Brittanies out of hunting stock that are excellent, just great all-around dogs. Nice, close-working dogs that point hard. Most Brittanies are very soft and delicate to train. With several different strains in the breed, you have to be careful of your selection.

The wirehairs haven't changed much over the years. They are now a little more stylish, a little less heavy-coated, but the honest retrieving instinct is still there. They are a solid hunting bird dog but they are very, very soft. Wirehairs are sort of hard to train because they are both soft and stubborn. Stubborn in that they want to do it their way, soft in that when you try to make them do it your way they may want to quit on you. The wirehair trainer has to tread lightly. But they are nice dogs and they have retained a lot of their natural style. They haven't changed a lot.

Do you train the different breeds differently?

SEINKOWSKI—Not really. We train them all using the same methods, but we tailor the pace to the individual dog. There is a big difference in how hard you can come down on them. Every dog has a breaking point and you want the dog's natural bird desire and intensity to overcome its fear of the unknown; for example, fear of gun noise.

At the top of the scale is the English Pointer, which has so much natural bird desire and intensity that it just bounces back from any stressful situation. At the other end of the scale, the Brittany is often so soft that if you look at one cross-eyed, it may roll over and urinate. A Brittany may get real nervous about the gun and if the dog is without a strong bird intensity, you need to be very, very careful. For example, if I put on too much pressure in the steadying process, a Brittany may start to blink-off birds.

The soft breeds are Brittanies, Vizslas and wirehairs. You have to go along at the dog's pace so it takes longer. We actually adjust the pace of the training to the individual dog's temperament.

How do you train a dog to work at a range that suits the hunter?

SEINKOWSKI—I always tell people that you cannot change a dog's natural range and pattern. But what you can do is get the dog to *respond* to your commands. I train the dog to respond to my whistle blast. I *force* the dog to check back to me. You need to be able to get him to come back from wherever he is. Some dogs are only twenty yards away and out of control,

Lee Seinkowski

while another dog may be two hundred yards away and in perfect control! I personally like a high-powered dog and being out several hundred yards doesn't bother me, but when he goes on point, he darn sure better hold it and wait until I get there. If the dog holds point at two hundred yards until I get there, he is more in control than the dog that is twenty yards away knocking birds and not responding. But the big-running dogs are not for everyone. Many hunters are uncomfortable with them, because they can't work them in small covers. They can be a handful, and if such a dog makes you nervous get a dog from closer-working stock.

Is there much difference between a grouse dog and a pheasant dog in your opinion?

SEINKOWSKI—You bet. For grouse you need a dog that walks on eggs. If not, he'll bump a lot of the birds. He can't be a bull in a china shop, he must be light on his feet and cautious, with a long-range nose.

For pheasants you need a dog that will range out a ways and work the objectives and be able to track a moving bird. The shorthairs are really good at that. They can work a bird until they pin it down where it has to flush.

What about some of the finer points. Do you train hunting dogs to back, or to be steady to wing and shot?

SEINKOWSKI—The answer is yes and no. We do train some dogs to back and it is fairly easy to do, but most hunters don't need it and very few of them ask for it. As for steadiness, we train a lot of dogs to be steady to wing. That is a safety measure to keep the dog out of the line of fire, but most hunters want the dog to break at the shot to go get the retrieve. It is fairly easy to keep a dog steady to wing, but beyond that, most will not stay steady to wing, shot and drop (fall of the bird) without a lot of constant training, and the complete steadying is not all that valuable to the hunter.

How can a busy executive or a businessman who has to travel a lot keep a high-quality dog and keep it trained properly?

SEINKOWSKI—Let me give you some examples. Every summer we have a refresher course for dogs. The focus is to reinstall range control, staunch them back up after a long layoff and generally get the dog to listen again and remember what it was taught. With today's high-powered dogs, especially on shooting preserves, control is very critical. Actually a dog for preserves is harder to train than a dog for wild birds because control is so much more important. The dog has to work on your piece of ground.

Wild birds also tend to train a dog, because if the dog creeps in too much the birds fly off, so the dog becomes more cautious. But on preserves sometimes a dog can creep in and catch a bird. If the dog catches four or five birds, you can turn a pointing dog into a Springer Spaniel in a day!

To keep a good dog really performing well, the owner has a choice. He can either work the dog every two weeks and stay on top of him or he can turn it over to a pro to be sure it is done while the owner is busy. We also do sessions with the owner and the dog where we work together to train the dog and teach the owner how he should read and control the dog.

Some hunters are hesitant to work with a pro. I fly fish a lot and I always hire a guide when I'm in a strange place. I don't think a dog owner should ever be uncomfortable asking a pro for assistance.

Let's say a hunter bought a well-bred dog based on your recommendation, then took it home and socialized it with the family. At what point do you want it here for basic bird training?

SEINKOWSKI—This will surprise you, but I want a well-bred dog with lots of known bird interest at five months. If it was an unknown, from backyard breeding, I might wait until it was eight or nine months old. But as soon as a dog's birdie instincts come to the surface, training should start. The precocious well-bred dogs come on real strong, very early. Socialization is also very important. Get them trained to collar and lead very early, then they are ready for bird work.

DALE JARVIS

Dog Trainer
The Hunter's Creek Club
Metamora, Michigan

Dale Jarvis is a quiet individual who graduated from Michigan State University with a degree in parks

Dale Jarvis

management. But more than twenty years ago he decided that his first love was dog training, so he became a full-time employee of the Hunter's Creek Club to pursue his chosen pastime. His focus is on pointing dogs, which he trains with a quiet, unassuming style. When you ask Dale a question you get a slow and thoughtful answer; reserved, simple and to the point. You come to realize that he had thought it through long before you asked the question. Once you get to know Dale there is a depth of knowledge and vision in his experience. He does not and has not trained field trial dogs, but some of the dogs he has trained have been used in AKC-approved trials and those of various other shooting dog associations. His focus and goal is to train high-quality shooting dogs and good companions for busy American roughshooters.

You have been training dogs in the same place for a long time. Do you see many changes in the way breeds perform today versus twenty years ago?

JARVIS—Sure, for example, the old-style German Shorthair was kind of a plodder, a close-working, methodical dog. Now we are seeing German Shorthairs that really get out there cutting it up, like all-age dogs. Right now I have an example from a client who brought in his two German Shorthairs. One is the old style that points hard and works right in front of you and retrieves well, while the other one is out there criss-crossing and racing around like crazy. He's impressive as hell to look at but not a true shorthair and not all that productive either. Some of the new-style German Shorthairs must have a little Pointer blood in them because they are beginning to range pretty big.

Speaking of range, how far do you think the average dog should reach out?

JARVIS—When we talk about range in Michigan we are usually getting dogs ready to hunt grouse in the woods or pheasants on farmland. The owners don't want a dog to range out a half mile. We don't have ground like that and if you have dogs that run that big in Michigan, they are going to get hit by a truck and killed. The close-ranging dogs are out about a hundred yards or less, while the big-ranging dogs push the limit at a couple of hundred yards.

After you train a dog, then turn it over to the owner, if the dog misbehaves is the owner usually too harsh or too lenient in his handling?

JARVIS—Neither one. Usually he's just not consistent, or else he may not read his dog very well. He may come down on the dog hard for something

I would think nothing of or he may go lenient on the dog for something that I would really come down hard on. Truly, the owner and the trainer need to agree up front what is expected and what is important and then work the dog consistently.

You train mainly pointing dogs. I have always thought a pointing dog hunter is a person who tends to be fairly relaxed and laid-back. Do you agree with that?

JARVIS—Yes, that's why I like pointing dogs because that's my personality. Actually, a good pointing dog lives right on the edge of being out of control compared to a Labrador, but a Lab has to be much more regimented by the hunter, whereas a pointing dog must have the freedom to hunt. You can almost think of it as having a little bit of a harness on a wild dog. You have to relax and let the dog's hunting instinct work. Maybe it's about 60 percent out of control and 40 percent in control. If you're lucky it's half and half, but if you make a pointing dog too regimented, if it is thinking too much about you, it's not out there doing its job finding birds! A more laid-back person can relax and let the dog have its freedom.

One of my biggest frustrations is the hunter who is screaming and yelling almost constantly and all the while the dog is out there doing what it's supposed to be doing. These owners are yelling at a dog that isn't programmed instinctively to respond to them. The only result of all that hollering is that it orients the dog to the hunter's location. But it all goes back to range; people start to yell when the dog gets beyond what they (the people) think is proper range.

Suppose you had three puppies, same breed but totally different breeding, and you didn't know anything about their ancestry. One was from big-running, all-age trial stock; one was from middle-range breeding; and one was from a very close-working strain of grouse dogs. If you trained them the same way, not knowing their backgrounds, would the range in them come out naturally?

JARVIS—Absolutely, they will tend to range like their parents. Range is almost always instinctive. But remember, you can always reduce range. You can't always slow them down, but we can bring them in. You can put a rope on a dog and bring it in, but you can't put a rope on a dog and push it out. Normally, the big-running dogs don't slow down, but we can make them work closer. It may not be easy, and it takes a firm handler, but they can be pulled in closer.

Now almost everybody trains pointing dogs with an electric collar. Is that really helpful in controlling range?

JARVIS—It just extends the length of your rope. It's a great invention, but it isn't a cure-all for all dog problems. A dog has to know why it's getting buzzed. It has to be prepped and I prep them on a rope long before I ever introduce the collar. When they get that shock I want them to know why they're getting the shock. A lot of dogs are ruined because they get shocked and they don't know why. Consequently, it inhibits their desire to hunt.

Recently I have seen some so-called "close-working" dogs that I think were so close because they were so clumsy they couldn't get out of their own way.

JARVIS—Yes, I definitely see that and what comes to my mind is some of the eastern English Setters bred to be close-working. They are close-working, but they don't cover much ground even working in close.

Do the English Setters you train retrieve naturally?

JARVIS—In my experience in a litter of ten setters, even if the mother and father were both retrievers, probably five of those pups will be natural retrievers and five won't. I used to get upset when I had a setter that wouldn't retrieve, but I have come to the conclusion that some do and some don't—it's just that simple. I've learned to put my emphasis on responsiveness and staunchness when holding a classy point. If they naturally retrieve a bird, I consider it a bonus.

Of the Continental breeds, what percentage are solid retrievers?

JARVIS—It's unusual to find one that doesn't and I expect them all to. They were bred not only to point but to retrieve, even so, a few of them don't naturally retrieve.

Does force breaking really work to improve retrieving?

JARVIS—It does, but you have to be ready to take your time. Force breaking is a negative experience for any dog. Most of them will require a recovery period. Mentally you take them down pretty low during the force training and then you have to bring their spirits and enthusiasm back up and get them going again. It might take a whole season of hunting to get them back up to where they were in their desire to find birds.

Has the retrieving in the Continental breeds gotten better or worse over the last twenty years?

JARVIS—Probably worse, but that's because breeding has gotten a little more spread out. As any breed gets older, you get more backyard breeders' dogs out there that aren't the top of the line.

Let's talk about absolute staunchness. In your opinion, how long does the dog have to hold point to be considered really solidly staunch?

JARVIS—That goes back to range. They have to hold at least as long as it takes for you to get up to the point. If that dog is half a mile out on point, he has to hold it a long time. If he is fifty feet away, he only has to hold solid until you get up there. It's the time element. That's the bottom line and you will usually need to see harder points in the setters and the Pointers than you do in the Continental breeds because they range out further.

Is it more difficult to teach a Brittany or a shorthair to be really staunch?

JARVIS—It's tougher because you can't be as physical with them. It's a rare Brittany that you can jerk around like you can a setter or a Pointer. With most Brittanys, if you shake them they will turn around and worry about you. Setters and Pointers get into a trance and you can pick them up and turn them around and they won't even know it. Brittanys usually aren't that hard on point but that doesn't mean that they can't be staunch. They may hold there for a long time, but they don't go into a trance. Many wirehairs have a real intense point. They are one of the harder-pointing Continental breeds.

In your opinion, what is the most common dog problem that reduces a hunter's success or increases his frustration?

JARVIS—There are two common problems and I don't know which is worse. Number one is range. Number two is not holding point staunchly, creeping in and flushing birds out of range. The two kind of go hand in hand.

Do you get many guys who say to you, "Okay, Dale, now that you've trained the dog, now train me"?

JARVIS—Yes, a lot of guys understand that and they do ask, but learning how to handle a dog takes experience and follow-through. A lot of people who have very good intentions, don't have the time. They are high-powered executives—they work long hours, they travel, they're tired. We work with them on tune-up classes and it works out pretty well.

I'm always pleasantly surprised at what ten minutes in the yard with my dogs will accomplish. Is that also true with pointing breeds?

JARVIS—Yes, it's true with any dog. If you can give a dog a consistent time block, regardless of how long it is and just do a few basic things, you will get results. Put a leash on the dog and take it out and walk it around, make it heel, sit, stay. You'll be surprised how far this goes just to remind the dog who is boss.

Can the dog switch from the trainer to the owner without a problem?

JARVIS—Most of them can. That's why when I send a dog home, I tell the owner to work the dog on the leash in the backyard. Get the bond re-established. It's frustrating when the client takes the dog right from here to a hunt and then he calls me up the next day and says, "How come my dog didn't mind me?" Hell, the dog didn't know who he was! That dog needed a day or two to rebond with the owner.

Do most hunters carefully research their puppy purchase or do they just show up with a dog they bought on an impulse?

JARVIS—Unfortunately, most of them buy on impulse. They generally don't research the breeding and they have never seen either the father or the mother hunt. People should go out and see the parents work before they buy, but I bet only one out of a thousand people does it. Let me emphasize, you don't have to go to some big-name breeder to buy a dog. If you have a friend whose dog hunts the way you think you want your dog to hunt, then it's okay to get a puppy from him. Every aspect of picking out a puppy is a bit of a gamble, but you want to try to get the edge on all the factors when you are gambling. Knowing the pedigree and the parents is a way to get that little edge.

CHAPTER 14
RETRIEVERS FOR ROUGHSHOOTING

There is probably no way to know how, where or when retrievers became accepted as full-fledged seek, find, flush and fetch bird dogs. But the people I've talked to see it as a relatively recent phenomenon, probably most prevalent in the last twenty years. It seems logical that as the waterfowl population declined and easily accessible blinds became extinct, the gunner would try to find another use for old Rover.

Couple declining duck hunting with a strong pheasant population in duck fly-way states like Michigan, Wisconsin, western New York, Pennsylvania and Illinois and it's easy to see how some Labradors found their way into the pheasant fields. Back then the abundant pheasants could be walked up even without a dog. Having a retriever along to puzzle out and bring back the cripples and occasionally flush out a skulking rooster was a big plus. Soon that dog was known as a

Many people think of the retriever breeds only as "bring it back" dogs, and many fit that description. This Irish-bred Labrador, Seanbaile Sari, owned and handled by Clare de Burgh of Naas, County Kildare, Ireland, had just won the ViVi Mahan Perpetual Cup when this photo was taken.

pretty fair pheasant dog. Later, as the pheasant population crashed, retrievers were expected to pitch in and help find the scarce birds. A few successful trips to the grouse woods, a bagged woodcock or two and imperceptibly, retrievers took on a wide variety of upland roughshooting chores.

However, retrievers were not always expected to exhibit such versatility, at least not in the sense of formal breed expectations. The archives of dog literature reveal little or no reference to the use of retrievers for the job of seeking out and forcing upland game into flight. Indeed, as late as 1942, William F. Brown, then editor of *American Field*, wrote the book *How to Train Hunting Dogs*. Mr. Brown, a well-known and extremely knowledgeable bird dog man, stated that "the function of a retriever on upland game (fur or feather) is to walk at heel or remain on the line until ordered to fetch dead or crippled game... thus while the retriever has nothing at all to do with the actual finding of live game... he is called upon to mark where the killed or crippled game falls." Brown continued, "Any retriever would be immediately condemned if he romped (about) like some of the other gun dog breeds."

Frankly, no one knows for sure when or where the retriever breeds became accepted as upland game dogs because the transition of a breed is not the kind of story that is documented in the daily newspapers. We do know that the expectations and popularity of retriever breeds for roughshooting are now at an all-time high.

Considering the current popularity of retrievers for roughshooting, it is surprising that as late as 1964 when Richard Wolters wrote his fast-selling classic *Water Dog*, he only briefly mentioned using the retriever for anything beyond strict nonslip retrieving. Indeed, the term *nonslip*, used so frequently in that era, signifies an intense level of control that kept the dog closely at heel or sitting resolutely in its spot until commanded to retrieve. Nonslip means that the dog does not attempt to *slip away* to hunt up game. But the use of retrievers was rapidly changing and in 1983 Wolters was ready to write another book, *Game Dog*. That book marked a major change in direction by acknowledging the retriever's transition from a fetch-only dog to a full-blown game finder. When you read Wolters's *Game Dog* you will note that the suggested training methods resemble those used in spaniel and Continental breed pattern and range training.

I witnessed the potential of well-trained and -handled retrievers in the exceptional performance of a pair of Labradors in the 1991 edition of the Ruffed Grouse Society's "National Grouse and Woodcock Hunt" held in northern Minnesota. Tim Kurtzman and Sam McQuale handled their own dogs during a real-life hunting test on wild native birds and against more than thirty all-breed teams of hunters. The two-day formal competition included some very prestigious teams using top-quality dogs of both pointing and spaniel breeds. In validated competition the Labradors found, flushed and retrieved the most wild birds, a performance that proved to me and a lot of others that properly trained and conditioned retrievers could do an outstanding job on upland birds at any level of expectation.

BREED POPULARITY

The Labrador Retriever and the Golden Retriever both reached the American Kennel Club's "top-ten list" in breed popularity during the 1980s. In 1993 they retained these extremely high levels of popularity: the Labrador Retriever ranked number one with 126,393 registrations and the Golden Retriever ranked number four with 64,322 dogs registered. Contrast that to 5,198 Chesapeakes, 17,404 English Springer Spaniels or 14,154 German Shorthaired Pointers.

This is Jim Kurtzman's Labrador Retriever, "Buck."
Each fall these two hunt far, wide and successfully.
Kurtzman

A retriever used for upland game must reach and
quest for game so early nonslip training should be
avoided. Kurtzman

But beware! Unfortunately, both the Labrador and the golden suffer from the popularity curse just like the little American Cocker, the Poodle and the German Shepherd Dog did before them. Great popularity attracts inexperienced and profit-motivated breeders who then generate thousands of "backyard" breedings with little or no concern for or understanding of the traits, style and type of the breed with which they are working. A June

Buck with a grouse, of course! Kurtzman

1994 article in *Gun Dog* magazine discussing Golden Retrievers related that when five very knowledgeable Golden Retriever breeders were queried about the breed, they identified four distinctly different and specialized strains: show, obedience, pet and hunting. They also observed that the hunting strains comprise only a minor percentage of the registered dogs and have two distinct subdivisions: field trial stock and gun dog stock.

The Labrador suffers from exactly the same situation, and today hundreds of thousands of Labs in this country have not seen a bird in three to five generations. Today's Lab puppy buyer must honestly ask, "What is this puppy's innate level of bird hunting skills and instincts?" All too often the answer is, "Who knows?" For sadly, many dogs have not been tested for generations!

This puts a great burden on the hunter seeking a really capable hunting dog. You must search out and select a dog of talent and potential. Given the relatively small percentage of all Labradors and Goldens that have *proven* their ability in recent generations, you have no small task ahead of you.

A RETRIEVER AS A PET

A hunting retriever with solid journeyman's skills is like a big woolly bear of a hunting pal, loping through the woods in an intentional but controlled way. You want a dog sufficiently birdie and interested in finding game to be on a mission, but calm enough to control its emotions and be guided by your directives. I think the retrievers make the most consistently warm and controlled house pets. Of all the hunting breeds, many people (mostly non-hunters) choose Labradors and Goldens as pets for their pleasant nature and cuddly presence and that accounts for their extreme popularity. In short, Labradors and Goldens make fine family dogs. Although the Chesapeake Bay Retriever can be a bit aloof and slow maturing, they are also reliable family dogs under the proper conditions.

WHAT KIND OF A HUNTER MOST APPRECIATES THE RETRIEVER'S STYLE?

Most people can visualize a Lab or a Chessie hunkered down in a blind searching the horizon for the approach of ducks or geese. Many people can also visualize the Lab owner as an English sporting gentleman, with Barbour coat, "wellies" and tweed cap. He leans on a shooting stick by his shooting butt waiting for driven game. In a scene straight out of *Shooting Times* magazine, he has his well-made side-by-side open and cradled across his forearm, and a well-mannered Lab of English type sitting at heel, obedient and quiet.

However, the Lab used for roughshooting is much more active and best appreciated by the "athletically comfortable" hunter. This hunter is alert, interested and involved. Because these biddable dogs work for the hunter, the normal hunting sojourn is a steady and purposeful trek afield. Although hunting with a retriever may lack the driving intensity of spaniel hunting or the disconnected style associated with the most wide-ranging pointer breeds, it is aggressive. Retriever hunters tend to be the relaxed, athletic types.

CHAPTER 15

USING A RETRIEVER IN THE WOODS AND FIELDS: INTERVIEWS WITH JERRY CACCHIO AND CHARLIE MANN

I posed a number of both general and specific questions to two widely known retriever training experts, Jerry Cacchio and Charlie Mann, who work day in and day out with retriever breed dogs for upland hunting. Both train "gun dogs" and neither trains dogs for all-out field trial competition. In my view, all-age retriever trials generally focus on a very different set of skills than those needed in an upland hunting situation. Although retriever all-age trials are interesting, roughshooting dogs need to be trained differently.

JERRY CACCHIO

Pondview Kennels
Staatsburg, New York

Jerry Cacchio is a bit of an enigma, a street savvy New Yorker of Italian heritage with a deep-seated love for English tradition. Jerry is an anglophile who spends each January on a shooting preserve in Wales and each August at the race track at Saratoga. He built his first career as a big corporation soldier with IBM for several years, but he chucked it all when IBM began to retrench. He opted for an early buyout in order to train dogs full time, a difficult but rewarding choice.

Jerry (his real name is Ray) is shy with strangers, but very direct with old friends. Once he gets to know you, if he feels that you are wasting time on a dud dog, he will tell you with complete candor. In my opinion, his clients get their best work after he gets to know them and understands their real expectations. Unlike some trainers who train dogs only for competition, Jerry seems to understand the differences between gun dogs and trial dogs, and can readily adjust the training schedule to the different levels of need and expectation.

Now in his early fifties, Jerry has reached that point in life when he is his own man. He has a comfortable home, a solid business and a wealth of respect in his chosen field. It seems unlikely that even substantial dollars could sidetrack his lifestyle. He started in English Springer Spaniel field trials in the late 1960s and frankly remembers that he wasn't all that welcome in the field trial community as a brash kid with a passion for good dogs, fast cars and pretty girls. But his talent, his dogs and his polish matured over time, and by the late 1980s he had won two Springer national championships and made numerous English Springer Spaniel field champions. By 1985 he had come into his own in the sport. Though still one of the most respected trainers in spaniels, he also trains retrievers for roughshooting. Retriever owners have very basic expectations; they want to use their dogs to seek out game and flush it before their guns, then they expect the dogs to retrieve what they shoot. The clients pay Jerry to train their retrievers to hunt like spaniels.

Jerry Cacchio holds a ring-necked pheasant that was just found, flushed and retrieved in this corn stubble field by this Labrador Retriever trained to work as an upland game dog.

I've known you for many years as a top-notch Spaniel trainer. How did you get into training retriever breeds for upland work and what percentage of your business is focused on that now?

CACCHIO—I got started in retriever training about fifteen years ago because of the high demand. In my local area there are a lot more Labradors than spaniels and the Lab owners just kind of forced me into this situation. They wanted their dogs to hunt like spaniels. Now I train three times as many retrievers as spaniels.

Are they all labradors? No Goldens? No Chessies?

CACCHIO—Oh, sure I train Goldens and a rare Chessie. Most Goldens have a great nose, but you have to go easy with Goldens, believe it or not. They don't take heavy pressure well and can get a bit snippy if you push them a little too hard. Very few people use Chessies for upland hunting around here.

Do you see major differences between the basic natural talent and basic natural instinct of a retriever versus a spaniel?

CACCHIO—I believe a spaniel thinks a little faster than a retriever and the spaniels mature faster so they figure things out quicker. The spaniels want to quest naturally so they tend to be a little more wild-eyed birdie. The retrievers are calmer and Labradors, especially, can take whatever training you give them and just keep going. The Labrador is a dog that readily accepts tough situations and keeps trying whereas with a spaniel, you have to be careful. If you push a spaniel too hard it may quit on you. Maybe that's why Labradors are willing to go into ice water. They have so much drive and power and perhaps they think if they just keep going it will all work out okay.

Do you find most retriever breeds to be naturally birdie?

CACCHIO—Birdiness varies widely. Today you watched me train the Labs. The first Lab we worked was a nice birdie dog from day one, very intense and very natural, but she was an exception. The second dog we trained was more normal, a bit more laid-back. It took time and experience to make her birdie. Unfortunately, a very few retrievers are not birdie at all and that creates a real problem for both me and the owner. I believe that one of the reasons retrievers are easier to control than other sporting breeds is they often lack the wild-eyed birdiness that takes them over the edge and out of control. So the lower intensity is both a blessing and a curse.

Are there things that retrievers do naturally better than spaniels?

CACCHIO—Yes, they are better markers of retrieves in general. Obviously, they handle big water and cold water better and they are naturally easier to control. They don't have the off-the-edge intensity of some spaniels. A lab will seldom get out of gun range. Apparently, some people think they are easier to handle as a pet, too.

What about expected basic retriever breed instincts: natural willingness to retrieve or to pick up a bird?

CACCHIO—Most of the dogs are pretty good natural retrievers, but did you know that in retriever field trial training almost every dog is force trained to retrieve? So if you send your Labrador to a field trial trainer, the first thing he is going to do with your dog is put him on a table and force break him to retrieve. So is that a natural retriever? Unfortunately, that means that a lot of dogs that are not really natural retrievers go on to be bred. Some Labs from field trial breeding can be pretty sloppy on retrieves unless they are force trained.

Why do you have concern about force training a dog to retrieve?

CACCHIO—I really hate to see these trainers put every dog on the force retrieving table because they are only fixing basic problems. Later, if that dog wins, then that dog will get bred, then the next generation will have the same problem or worse. With me the table is a last resort and I do it only when a hunter really wants to save the dog because his family is already attached to it. Then we make a special effort to make it into a satisfactory hunting dog.

But are there still some natural retrievers?

To build their enthusiasm, the young dogs are allowed to find birds with their nose as they hunt and then chase wildly as the bird flies. Very young dogs are best worked in light cover where they can run easily. Heavier cover can come later when the dog is stronger and more enthusiastic.

CACCHIO—Oh sure. What I like for upland hunting is the mixture of a show and field trial breeding. It just takes a little edge off their intensity. They still have plenty of drive to hunt and lot of natural birdiness but they also want to please you. Some are quite natural as all-around bird dogs.

Has the Labrador Retriever changed over time?

CACCHIO—I think so. I have a friend who is an old-time Labrador Retriever trainer and he stops by here to use my pond once in a while to train his dogs and they are all nonslip retrievers. He is a believer that the only thing a retriever is supposed to do is retrieve—period. He does not believe that they are supposed to search for game by quartering and hunting. Obviously, I am looking for a different dog with different talents than he is. Both strains exist within the breed so the buyer needs to select the type he wants—nonslip or quester.

How would you buy a retriever puppy?

CACCHIO—Regardless of the breed, the best way to buy a pup is to watch the parents hunt. If you like what you see in the parents, then that is the way to go. Unfortunately, most people buy dogs out of a cardboard box and they have never seen the parents and they have no idea if the dog will have instincts to hunt or not.

Do many of your clients choose a retriever breed as a compromise dog, a combination pet and hunting dog? Do you consider them good pets?

CACCHIO—Yes. Frankly, retrievers are a bit less active than spaniels, nice big cuddly bears of a dog that can still get out and be great hunting partners. But part of it is also keeping up with the Joneses. If somebody calls me up and says they're coming up with a Labrador to be trained, it is often the Black Labrador in a silver Mercedes situation. Labs are very socially acceptable in the Northeast these days.

Do you ever run into any mouth problems in the retriever breeds?

CACCHIO—Hardly ever in the Labs, but I see it a bit more often in the Goldens. You have to be very careful when using an electric collar. If you put too much pressure on the dog when training with a collar, the dog's only release is to crunch birds. An electric collar improperly used can create mouth problems.

I have always been kind of anticollar. But I'm seeing some trainers I really respect getting into the new method of electric training. How do you feel about that?

CACCHIO—I agree. I was always against collars, too, except in carefully considered circumstances. But with the new methods of collar training, it does work very well, but only after the trainer has been carefully trained himself.

How do you feel about the new strains of "pointing" Labs?

CACCHIO—I'm not a fan of the advertised pointing Labs. I think that is a meaningless modification of a good breed. If you want a pointing dog, buy one from one of the recognized breeds. I still see Labs as flushing dogs and most have great talent to do it. A few Labs flash point naturally then go ahead and flush the bird for the gunner; that's okay.

So, in general, you train a retriever using virtually the same spaniel training methods?

CACCHIO—Right. They are flushing dogs so you want them to quarter and hunt in gun range, aggressively flush the birds they find and retrieve what you shoot. It's as simple as that.

The quartering doesn't come as natural to the retriever breeds but over time they learn it and they are easy to keep in gun range and under control.

If a pheasant runs, they can track it out and make it flush and with experience, the retriever breeds will find, track out and flush birds with enthusiasm.

As for retrieving, they were bred for it; they mark well, almost naturally, so they get to the fall area quickly to bring the bird back.

No breed will satisfy everyone, but these are darn talented dogs and for the right style of hunter, they are very fine hunting and family dogs.

What, in order of importance, are the three things that qualify the Lab as a first-class hunting dog?

CACCHIO—Retrieving is number one, they do that very well.

Stamina is number two; you can hunt them day after day after day and they're tough. They're powerful dogs. They don't get hurt. They keep going.

And three, you can keep them under control. Probably about half of all the hunting dogs in America, of any breed, are out of control because the owners haven't trained the dog. That is probably a pretty good reason why so many people want a dog that is always *in control.* The Lab probably comes as close to that as anything.

CHARLIE MANN

Dog Trainer
Hunter's Creek Club
Metamora, Michigan

Charlie Mann is the son of Preston Mann, the long-time operator of Hunter's Creek, a prestigious shooting preserve and hunting club about sixty miles north of Detroit. As Preston phased into retirement, his younger son, Charlie, took over the daily management of the club along with training dogs. Charlie is a graduate of Michigan State University and has been working at the club all his life. He became a full-time dog trainer and part-time club manager upon graduating from college and then assumed full-time club management as his father retired.

Charlie now tends to focus on training retrievers while Dale Jarvis trains the pointing dogs. Retrievers are very popular in Michigan, especially for the avid waterfowlers in the Great Lakes flyway. But many of the retrievers Charlie trains are used for roughshooting, and retrievers are also a common sight around the shooting preserve at Hunter's Creek. Charlie inherited his father's wry wit and way with words and is always there with a quick smile, a wink, a good joke and a laugh. Charlie is equal parts dog trainer, outdoorsman, raconteur and entertaining companion.

Charlie Mann sees more and more retriever breed dogs being used for upland game in his Michigan home base. He trains and works the dogs aggressively in the fields at Hunters Creek Club, but also builds their enthusiasm for the game by throwing dummies and letting them chase after the bucks.

What is your number-one selection criterion for a retriever?

MANN—Number one is a combination of natural retrieving and natural birdiness. When we run into trouble is when the dog doesn't have enough natural desire to retrieve or when it is not naturally birdie, or a combination of both. If the dog doesn't have natural birdiness and a desire to retrieve, we will spend the first months of training just trying to get the dog enthused and turned on. We can't do much obedience work without birdiness because it dampens the dog's enthusiasm and sets you back. The naturally birdie dog is much easier to train.

Let's talk about teaching a retriever to quarter. How many of the retriever breeds will naturally quarter and hunt as opposed to tending to want to walk at heel most of the time?

MANN—Most all of them will quarter a little naturally. But if you have trained the dog to be nonslip as a puppy, then you may have a hard time getting him to reach out and quarter because he was trained to stay at your side. There are a few retrievers that seem to be almost natural heelers. If that's the case, the dog may never quarter very well and once in a while we encounter a dog that has an instinct to stay in place until you send it out on a line to retrieve.

The owner must be realistic. If he wants to teach a dog to take a long, straight line to a retrieve like in a retriever trial, then we can't start out teaching the dog to quarter and hunt upland and then change its whole life and try to send it on three hundred-yard straight-line retrieves. You have to make the choice early in the dog's life.

What you are basically saying is that you can't have it both ways?

MANN—If you're really going to make an upland game hunting dog out of a retriever, then you don't want to instill that absolute line steadiness, the nonslip part, because you are going to have a hard time getting the dog out of that. I don't think you can have both.

Do retriever breeds naturally run patterns or do you have to teach them to do it?

MANN—It's more of a training process. First you get them birdie. Then once they are birdie and running like crazy and chasing and racing around all over the place looking for birds, just hook a rope to them and teach them to quarter for two or three weeks. The next thing you know, the dog is in such a habit of quartering that the pattern is ingrained. If you really want to teach it to quarter you must train it until that quartering becomes a habit.

Do you see any mouth problems in the retriever breeds?

MANN—Sure, we see a few hard-mouth dogs, but it is usually something that was man-made. Many owners make a young dog hard-mouthed by playing tug-of-war with it and yanking toys out of the dog's mouth. I have never had a dog so hard-mouthed that I couldn't hunt it.

Where should I buy a retriever puppy?

MANN—I think you should buy a dog from field trial breeding even for upland hunting, because those dogs have to be birdie to compete, they display an infallible desire to retrieve and the trainability is inherent. Trainability, birdiness and desire to retrieve; what more could you want in an upland hunting retriever? My training partner, Dale, would disagree a little. He likes a pup of mixed field trial and show dog breeding, but I think if a dog has a lot of proven field trial blood in its pedigree, it is potentially the best bet to become a good upland hunting retriever.

Do you see a different kind of hunter using retrievers than the hunter running pointing dogs?

MANN—I think younger guys run Labs, because the hunter has to expend more energy and work harder himself. These are athletic guys who jog and ski and work out. If the Lab gets hot following a bird, the young guys are not afraid to hot foot it a little bit to keep up. Here, in the Midwest, the Lab hunter we see is a less traditional hunter and is usually going to be a more physically aggressive type of hunter.

CHAPTER 16
HUNTING WITH A RETRIEVER

The retriever breeds obviously excel at the task of finding downed birds, and in generations past the trait of returning promptly with anything shot was taken for granted. That is not as true today as it was thirty years ago, but most retrievers of *proven* hunting breeding are reliable fetchers. On a positive note, perhaps of all hunting dogs, a retriever's style is easiest to control. Naturally close-working and responsive to direction, few retrievers are ever lost because of any wild, out of control range. More often hunters have trouble getting the dog *Out!* to quest for game aggressively.

If the retriever makes a good pet, retrieves solidly, stays controlled and in gun range, what could be its drawback? There are two.

First, these dogs don't point, and second, to a great extent they don't flush aggressively. The retriever's main drawbacks are its lackadaisical bird finding and relatively passive questing style. On a scale of one to ten, even the best retrievers are about a five for intensity of bird finding and aggressiveness when questing. This same lack of intensity carries over into the retriever's tracking style, which is slower and more methodical than that of a spaniel. Less intense questing is not much of a problem on woodcock or quail, but on running pheasants or grouse, only aggressive tracking forces the bird into the air.

Today, pointing Labradors are advertised in several hunting magazines. This is not surprising, since many Labs flash point naturally when very close upon strong bird scent. The question is whether the Lab naturally possesses a nose of sufficient range to point birds without bumping them into flight. The fact that most knowledgeable dog trainers don't have much faith in the potential of the pointing Labrador provides a straightforward answer to that question.

In the end, the selection of a retriever breed for roughshooting is a good choice if:

1. The dog will be expected to tackle a wide range of tasks, from duck hunting to grouse hunting.

2. Losing a shot bird bothers you badly and you want a dog that will stay after a retrieve until it is complete.

3. You have an energetic and athletic "walk up" hunting style that makes you and the dog a team, together in the brush, pushing out birds.

4. You enjoy snap shooting with little warning except the dog's animated body language.

5. You hate the idea of a dog you can't see or find; you want the dog to work close and stay in touch with you at all times.

6. Companionship and family acceptance are high on your list of necessary qualifications.

WHAT TO TRAIN FOR?

There are many fine books available that go into great detail on the how-to's of dog training. Unfortunately, few segregate the training by priority. Some aspects of the dog's training are absolutely essential if the dog is going to be useful in the field. Others are nice, pleasant or add polish, but you can have great success without them. They are not essential. An example would be "steady to wing and shot." A dog

This big South Dakota retriever, a cross between a Labrador and a Golden, hunted aggressively all day mile after mile, usually well within gun range, flushing many birds and helping with the "work" of the day.

that is "steady" is a real pleasure to hunt over, but it is not essential. Quartering within range on the other hand *is essential.*

TRAINING CHECKLIST

If you plan to train a retriever for upland hunting you will need to focus on these three aspects of the dog's development:

1. *Retrieving.* Any retriever should first and foremost bring back everything you shoot. Don't assume that one of these dogs is automatically a great retriever. Plan to hone the natural talent of any retriever into prompt and exacting response when a bird is downed.

2. *Bird finding.* The dog must learn to enjoy finding game and to do so, it must quest through the cover, searching for game scent and then must pursue that game to force it into flight. Some retrievers possess these talents naturally, but many others grow slowly into birdiness. It is the job of the trainer to continually nurture and increase the level of birdiness and bird-finding talent. Deciding how to go about this requires astute observation and planning on the part of the trainer.

3. *Range and control.* Most retrievers are a pleasure to hunt and you shouldn't have to spend the day whistling, yelling and cursing to keep the dog where you want him or to get him to respond to your commands. Generally, the difficulty is not keeping the dog within range or under control, but encouraging the dog to reach out and search to the edges of gun range. In those rare instances where a retriever with birdiness and enthusiasm begins to reach out and hunt beyond gun range, the best solutions are the same as those commonly used to control range in any breed; train for quick response to the turn command, build a working bond with the dog and try to ingrain a tendency for the dog to work in a natural zigzag path that returns the dog to the handler's path frequently.

The methods most frequently used by spaniel trainers are very applicable to training a retriever for upland roughshooting. I recommend theses books that focus on how to use a flushing dog for upland hunting: *Game Dog; The New Complete English Springer Spaniel; HUP* (Howell Book House, New York); *Expert Advice on Gun Dogs.* All are listed in Chapter 33, "Books to Read."

RETRIEVER TRAINING ADVICE: GENERAL & PRELIMINARY TRAINING

BONDING

The earliest efforts at training a retriever should involve building a bond with the owner early in the dog's life. The better the relationship between the owner and the dog, the more likely the dog is to show enthusiasm, work with the hunter, and stay under control throughout its life. Socialization in a wide variety of situations is important and play time is essential. These big dogs mature rather slowly, so try not to get overanxious in the training regimen. Over the first year your retriever will need a solid foundation of basic obedience in order to be a pleasant companion and a reasonably controllable hunting dog. Obedience to the Come!, Sit!, Stay! and No! commands is essential.

Dave Maynard of Sonoita, Arizona, works his Labrador on the ice in the cattails of an Upstate New York shooting preserve, with obvious success.

A WORD OF CAUTION ON THE HEEL COMMAND

Retrievers almost always learn to heel naturally and easily. The more you reinforce this instinct early in the dog's life, the more difficult it will be to teach the dog to quest and quarter at one year of age. Were it my dog, I'd forego any heeling at all and I'd use the lead sparingly and only if absolutely needed. If you can find a large, confined area where the youngster can learn to run, hunt and play as you walk along, so much the better. Retrievers rarely run away. Mostly they need to be allowed to romp about you freely in about a thirty-yard circle, so that over time they become less constrained by their natural instincts to heel.

RETRIEVING

The first nine months of the dog's life is the time for fun, puppy-style retrieving. This should be started in a way that minimizes any ingraining of bad habits. Most young retrievers have natural instincts to pick up and carry objects and most will return to you with these objects if encouraged to do so. The old game of playing fetch in a long hall gives the dog little alternative but to return to you. The more enthusiasm you can build for retrieving, the easier it will be to switch over to bringing back shot birds in the field. Try to get to the point of throwing three to five retrieves for the dog every day and let it chase after these flying objects. Letting your pup race after the thrown retrieving buck is a great way to build enthusiasm. Any attempt to line steady the dog should be delayed, for at this young age it could cause a serious decline in retrieving enthusiasm. Also, try not to encourage any bad habits that will be hard to overcome later. For example, never play tug-of-war with any object. Always encourage the dog to return the object to your hand (rather than laying it down, or worse yet, laying down with it and mouthing it).

Once the dog is retrieving consistently you can introduce the "cap pistol" to simulate very low-volume gunfire when the dog goes to make a retrieve. Over time the noise level can be increased if the dog shows no adverse reaction.

GUNFIRE

The introduction to real gunfire should be very slowly and very carefully considered, for once a mistake is made, undoing that mistake is slow and has a low probability of success. There is absolutely no reason to rush into the cap pistol training until the dog is six months old. Remember, even though the dog is big and strong physically, mentally it is still very immature.

PATTERN

At seven or eight months of age, start teaching the dog to run freely in a windshield wiper pattern. You can encourage this by walking a zigzag path whenever you and the dog are out for a walk in the country.

LIVE BIRDS

The introduction to birds should be approached with care. Start first by throwing freshly killed, small-sized game birds (pigeons or quail) in the dog's *normal retrieving area*—same place in the yard, same commands, same everything. If the dog responds positively you can move on carefully to fully taped, winged, live birds. If that is successful you can move up to flutterers: birds with only one wing taped. All these actions should gradually build on the confidence of the dog and result in a heightened level of enthusiasm for birds.

Once the dog is enthusiastically retrieving taped wing birds, it is time to let the dog find a few in the field as it romps with you on a country walk. Soon the dog will put two-and-two together and begin to hunt around to find the birds. Gradually it will begin to use its nose rather than its eyes. At this point the preliminary training is complete. The dog works in range, finds birds and retrieves what it finds. Most professional trainers would love to be given a one-year-old dog with such a solidly laid foundation.

Now it is time for a decision: Will you continue to train the dog yourself or turn it over to a professional trainer? Both avenues are rewarding and effective. If you have the time, talent and facilities, you can tackle the job yourself. If not, you should feel very comfortable turning your dog over to a well-qualified and carefully selected professional for the next steps.

A retriever (or flushing dog) that will find 'em (*within gun range* and at your direction), flush 'em (boldly and aggressively, pushing runners into the air) and fetch 'em (bring back the birds you shoot) displays all the basic attributes necessary to be called a solid roughshooter's dog.

CHAPTER 17

HUNTING WITH SPANIELS

Some very knowledgeable people believe a spaniel will put more game in the air, before the gun, than any other dog of any breed. Those who espouse this view do so for two reasons. First, a spaniel covers the ground very thoroughly, seldom leaving any major gaps in the cover, so every bird on the course should be found. Second, a spaniel will actively pursue moving birds, a running rooster or a moving grouse, usually forcing all birds encountered into the air. That does not mean, however, that the spaniel will always provide easy or nearby shots; just that a spaniel won't bypass many birds and that it will usually get that game into the air.

SPANIELS: FOR WHOM?

This typical field-bred English Springer Spaniel is "Cruise," owned by Jack Williams of Peterborough, Ontario.

The hunting style of any spaniel is best suited to an active hunter who is physically able to walk in the cover and keep up with the dog on a continual basis. The most intense spaniels are dogs for the physically aggressive. Since the dogs flush birds for the gun with only body action as a bird indicator, the hunter who hangs back and dawdles will be constantly shooting birds at the edge of gun range. This does not mean that the hunter needs to chase after the dog, but he will need to move aggressively. Although a spaniel will not usually "point" the birds before they flush, it will go into intense spasms of excitement, and one would have to be in a coma to miss it when a keen spaniel gets birdie.

WILD AND WOOLLY SHOOTING

When you are really into the birds, you'll have no shooting as fast and as challenging as what can be had over a quick and birdie English Springer Spaniel. Even some of the most talented and experienced Pointer and setter trainers in North America will confide that getting a birdie spaniel into a score of quail singles in a brushy creek bottom or a flight of woodcock in a young alder thicket or a group of fast-moving pheasants in an Iowa drainage slough is a thrilling rush of snap shooting excitement seldom matched in any other hunting situation.

Spaniels are at their very best when cover is concentrated, the birds are flying strong and the shooting is quick. Classic literature always details how the spaniels' lively tail action and animated body gyrations send a strong signal to the shooter that the arrival of game birds is imminent, and that is true. But it's not the locked down, get set, creep-in-on-the-quarry game of shooting over pointing dogs. Often as a spaniel churns into a birdie frenzy, the bird erupts from cover five, ten, even fifteen yards away. The same animated spaniel action that excites the hunter makes birds flush by creating a nervousness that results in flight to escape. For the hunter, the only reaction that suffices is to turn, look, snap the gun into place, point and fire. Shooting over spaniels is an acquired taste and a day of success can hook a roughshooter forever.

POINTING DOG BIAS AGAINST FLUSHING DOGS

Sadly, many accomplished and experienced hunters have never had the pleasure of hunting over a really well-trained flushing dog. These people have a built-in bias for pointing dogs and refuse to acknowledge the truly outstanding potential for success that flushing dogs can provide in the field. I recall with amusement the reaction of an elderly Iowan, a close friend, who trained and field trialed high-powered Pointers. Upon learning that I had acquired a spaniel, he gave me his opinion. "Son," he said, "as bird dogs go, those spaniels make mighty nice pets." His bird dog vision was purely for high-tailed Pointers.

But my first spaniel served me well and provided many wonderful hours of pheasant hunting. Later, when we moved to New Jersey, he adapted quickly to woodcock shooting and we had a great time in the eastern thickets.

THE SPANIEL NATURE

The spaniel's method of finding game does not appeal to everyone, and I've partnered with gunners who never really got tuned into the flow of the dog. To them, the dog was constantly birdie, and this kept the gunner from being able to relax and enjoy the ambiance of the hunt. Although a spaniel constantly covers the ground near the hunter, searching for game to flush, it rarely offers shooting for the partners as good as it is for the dog handler. This is in contrast to hunting over pointing dogs where the shooting for handler and guest is usually about equal as they both walk in to flush the bird. Reading a spaniel is easy for most people, yet difficult for a few. I try to handle this by coaching my guests, "Get ready, she's birdie." That alerts them to the pending flush of the bird.

RANGE

The range of a spaniel is a function of three factors: natural athletic ability, birdiness and training. An extremely athletic and intensely birdie spaniel with little or no training will bubble over and begin to hunt outside of gun range. However, when this athletic talent and birdiness are channeled through careful and consistent training, that same dog can become a dynamo of bird-finding excitement always well within gun range. The range and intensity of the dog is generally based in its genetic make-up, so selecting a spaniel to match your own personality is important.

FLUSHING BIRDS

A spaniel will by nature attempt to catch the bird. This driving effort forces the birds into the air and the dog's ability to trail skulking pheasants and grouse is one of its main appeals. It is this tracking attribute that has rightfully earned the English Springer its reputation as the premier pheasant dog.

RETRIEVING

Most field-bred Springer Spaniels are quite natural in their retrieving instincts. Indeed, most young spaniels become hooked on the retrieving game quickly and will race to and fro, returning with a thrown retrieving dummy time after time. This yard retrieving transfers quickly to real hunting, and in the field most spaniels are quite adept on any of the game birds: pheasants, grouse, woodcock and quail.

English Springers are famous as pheasant specialists, and, as I recall, my old Genny dog handled the find and retrieve of this bird in a fairly routine way in a little field in eastern Pennsylvania.

All in all, a spaniel of journeyman's retrieving skills will, in an upland setting, retrieve birds one-for-one with most retrievers.

In heavy cover, many times a spaniel will be down in the cover searching for the bird when it flushes and is shot. In these cases, it is most helpful if the dog will obey the hunter, take hand signals and search the area of the fall for the downed bird. This skill is easily taught and soon "hunt dead" will become a valued part of the dog's natural skills retinue.

If one hunts upland game more than a few times, a retrieve into or across water will occur. Most spaniels and retrievers will finish the retrieving job from water—be it a creek, river, pond or lake, or even if it involves swimming across a stream finding a downed bird on the other side and swimming back.

STEADY TO WING AND SHOT

True spaniel field trial aficionados demand complete steadiness to wing and shot from their dogs, but most hunters do not expect this level of performance. Steady means that when the bird is in the air (on the wing) or when the gun goes off (the shot) the dog instantly sits (or hups, in spaniel language). The spaniel then waits until the handler or hunter commands it to "Fetch!" before it goes out to make the retrieve. If the bird is missed, the dog is commanded to return to the handler, where it is then cast off again to hunt close and carry on.

If an unsteady dog chases after a missed bird and further down the field flushes another bird and chases it, that dog can be gone for a long time, flushing many birds out of gun range. Many hunters train for something in-between called a controlled chase, where the dog chases the bird only twenty or thirty yards and then returns to the handler if the bird is not found. Today it is quite common for retriever breed upland dogs to be steady to wing and shot just like a flushing spaniel.

SPANIEL EXPECTATIONS

The spaniel, of good breeding with natural talent and some basic training, is a very versatile hunting partner for all manner of upland bird species. I have also seen them used in England for some fast and furious rabbit and hare shooting. They will retrieve feathers or fur with equal enthusiasm.

I have personally shot fourteen different species of game birds over my spaniels including pheasant, ruffed grouse, bobwhite quail, woodcock, doves, valley quail, sharptails, Hungarian partridge, spruce grouse, chukar and snipe, as well as ducks, geese and rail birds.

Rewards of Barney, a field trial champion and a busy dog during every fall hunting pheasants in Michigan, Iowa and the Dakotas. Barney belongs to George Wilson and proves that some competitive formats are relevant to a day of hunting.

In order to fully enjoy using a spaniel, several basic steps are involved:

1. Start with a dog from good *field breeding*. Every popular spaniel breed is split between show dogs and field dogs. In some spaniel breeds 99 percent are show dogs and only 1 percent have serious field instincts.

2. Hone the dog's natural talents! Most spaniels of good breeding naturally retrieve, naturally hunt for game and naturally work to the hunter. Some even quarter naturally. A good trainer spends most of his time polishing and molding the dog's natural instincts. If the dog shows a serious deficiency in any of these areas, you may have the wrong dog.

3. Develop a strong range control mechanism through consistent obedience training. The dog's intensity and birdiness can take it out of range. You'll need to get a firm grip on the situation. A spaniel that is out of gun range is useless. A dog that turns on the whistle and naturally works for you and with you is a great pleasure.

4. Consider training the dog for the higher levels of performance such as steady to wing and shot, hunt dead and taking hand signals to downed birds. A keen dog will be eager to learn throughout its life, and some of these skills can best be taught at age three or four years.

5. Make water retrieving a normal part of the dog's work. Spaniels will even handle some very intense and heavy-duty duck retrieving with the proper training. So a grouse retrieve across a creek should be a piece of cake.

6. Don't overlook the spaniel's value as a house pet and family dog. It can really increase the human/dog bond so valued in a hunting situation.

TRAINING A SPANIEL (OR OTHER FLUSHING DOG) IN A PHONE BOOTH

One of the real advantages of training either a spaniel or a retriever is that much of the routine daily dog training can be done in a relatively small amount of cover. You can accomplish a great deal, even in a little, hidden away corner of cover as small as two or three acres. Since you are simply trying to teach the dog to quarter the ground, find birds, try to catch them (flush them) and retrieve the birds, you can often make great accomplishments toward your training goals without ever firing a gun. Although you cannot finish the training of a spaniel or a retriever without a significant amount of shooting over the dog, many of the dog's basic skills can be honed in on nonflying birds. This training is easier to accomplish with a spaniel or a retriever since a flushing dog is less likely to run out of control than a pointing dog. Instant response to commands is, after all, the key to success with a dog that must always work and flush birds within gun range.

Once, when I lived in New Jersey, I was able to lease five acres of "right-of-way" underneath a power line. It was covered with weeds and trashy growth, but it gave me a perfect starting place for young dogs. One of the dogs that I started on that property learned how to quarter, respond to my commands, find fluttering, taped-wing pigeons that juiced up her bird enthusiasm, catch those birds and retrieve them quickly. Additionally, I used a retriever trainer to simulate the gun going off, the flight of the bird and the marking of long retrieves into the heavy cover. In that small patch of cover I was able to lay the basic training foundation in a dog that went on to place second in the English Springer Spaniel National Open All-Age Championship.

Even a spot of weeds and brush as small as a hundred feet square can be used to teach the dog how to use its nose and find birds in cover. When you throw long retrieves into this heavy cover, the dog learns to search with its nose, not just it's eyes.

This ability to keep a dog well trained while living in an urban or suburban setting has significant appeal to many roughshooters who work in a city environment.

HUNTING AN UNSTEADY (CHASING) SPANIEL

In the process of writing this book I decided that after fifteen years of hunting almost exclusively with dogs that were steady to wind and shot, I would back up, so to speak, and hunt an entire season with a dog that was totally unsteady. At the end of the season I would compile my observations and record them in this book.

The season brought both joy and disappointment, but the disappointments were relatively minor, so the ups far outweighed the downs.

The unsteady dog I chose to hunt was a two-year-old Springer of good breeding that simply lacked the speed, fire and burning desire to be a field trial dog. It was as if his transmission only had three gears, not five; he never shifted into high gear and his tendency to flash point ended any hope for a field trial career. However, he was naturally obedient, had a great nose, could track birds and loved to retrieve. He was such an easy dog to hunt that he often looked to me for direction and would generally hunt off in the direction where I waved my hand. He was the opposite of the out of control spaniel. Still, he reached out to hunt aggressively and covered a sizable bit of ground.

In retrospect, this dog might not have been the best example of the *unsteady spaniel revisited,* for he just naturally limited his chasing. If a bird flew far and fast after the guns fired, he broke off the chase after fifty yards or so and returned to my side. So from that perspective I didn't have to venture into the next county to search for the dog after he'd chased a pheasant out of the territory.

All in all the hunting was quite productive, and after hunting high-powered field trial spaniels for several years, this was like rocking chair hunting. To most people, this springer would have been ideal; to me he was a bit too laid-back for the kind of hunting I like to do.

However, he did produce many birds for me, almost all easily in gun range. We mixed his time on the ground with the dogs of my hunting partners and he always found and retrieved his share of birds. In many ways it was like going back to my roots, for he echoed many of the traits and attributes of my very first spaniel, a dog that was naturally easy to hunt productively.

Easygoing, naturally talented, instinctive dogs exist in every breed and if that matches your need, the key is to select carefully to match your preferences.

ON-THE-EDGE SPANIELS

My favorite kind of a spaniel for hunting is a fast and flashy dog that is just on the edge of control and flies through the cover. I know a dog like this turns off many hunters, but for me a dog of this intensity lifts my spirits with its unbridled enthusiasm. In the big pheasant covers of the Midwest, a big-running spaniel will find and flush far more birds than any close-working, easily controlled dog.

Most people, when hunting with me and my spaniels, at first feel that the dogs are running too wide and reaching out too far from the guns. But soon they mentally adjust to the dog's range and find it perfectly acceptable. The most aggressive spaniel hunters have learned that despite the dog's big range, few birds are lost due to being flushed beyond gun range. A surprisingly high percentage of the birds that are flushed out at the edge of gun range fly back toward the gunner, giving him a decent shot.

FLUSHING DOG RANGE AND STYLE

Some spaniels and retrievers naturally work very close to the gunner; they tend to be slower and more methodical and they seldom push a bird out of range before it flushes. Such a dog is especially suited to the hunter that doesn't have a lot of time to reinforce control and handling. This is the kind of dog that is very productive, week after week, without intense remedial training. Dogs that are more naturally intense require a consistently firm hand.

Whether you choose the wild and intense, big-running spaniel that I like, or the careful and methodical dog preferred by many other hunters, rest assured that both types have advantages and disadvantages. The slow, close-working dog is easier to control and it will generally flush birds within gun range, but it will leave some birds unfound at the edges of its range. The big-running, wide-ranging dog will almost always find more birds, but some of the shots will be very difficult and a few will be flushed out of gun range, and those big-running dogs require more constant attention. Life is always a series of choices.

WOODCOCK SPANIELS

The name Cocker Spaniel comes as a contraction of "woodcock" spaniel. These little dogs were intended to buzz and burrow through, under and around the thickest tangles of cover to find and flush these elusive little birds. The small dog's range is fairly restricted in order to keep the flushes close to the gunner in the dense, tangled thicket of brush and thorns the woodcock calls home. When the dog and gunner happen into a pocket of flight birds, the little dog and handler work together to hunt out the cover meticulously until all the birds are found. The intensity and bravery of a good cocker in tough cover is a sight to behold, and such a dog can provide some of the fastest and most sporting shooting in the world.

Cockers can be marvelous grouse dogs, too, as they tackle woods cover. Some people are surprised to learn that these merry little hunters are fully capable in the Iowa sloughs where they can find and retrieve wild pheasants hour after hour.

SELECT PROVEN FIELD-BRED STOCK

Usually well-bred spaniels exhibit a great deal of natural birdiness at an early age and few ever need to be "hyped up" for the task if introduced to birds properly. Unfortunately, not all spaniels are natural bird dogs. Hence, some cute and cuddly spaniel breeds have succumbed to the "pet market" curse, and the saddest example of a working dog that has lost its way is the American Cocker Spaniel. Although more than sixty thousand American Cockers were registered by the American Kennel Club in 1994, it is doubtful that even 1 percent of the total Cocker population is ever used in the

This is my longtime friend and hunting mentor, Leon Vaughn, one of the best and most dedicated pheasant hunters I ever hunted with. Leon is hunting a fence row on his own farm, outside the little city where he lives in Southern Iowa, in the heart of bird country.

field. Hunting strains of the American Cocker Spaniel (a totally separate breed from the English Cocker Spaniel) are very rare indeed and one must demand absolute proof of hunting prowess before purchasing a hunting dog of this breed.

The English Springer Spaniel is by far the most popular spaniel breed in the field and thousands are bred each year specifically for field use. But one must also be very careful when purchasing an English Springer Spaniel, for there are two very distinct strains within the breed: show dogs and field dogs. The field dogs are more naturally birdie and usually one can rely on their possessing the necessary talents to be good hunting partners. On the other hand, show dogs run the gamut and while some are pretty good natural bird dogs, others simply show no interest in game—a sad state of affairs for a dog from a sporting breed. In any spaniel breed, your chances of success are greatly enhanced if you start with proven field stock.

As in every breed, some of the most intense field trial dogs are a handful for the average hunter. However, in each litter there will be individuals that show extremely intense behavioral tendencies, while some of their littermates will be more laid-back and, therefore, more easily controlled.

The *English* Cocker has both a show strain and a strong, growing field strain. English Cockers of field breeding are frequently imported to the United States from England

This English Cocker, Lockridge Lucy, is a tiny but effective flushing spaniel belonging to Jim Karlovec from near Cleveland, Ohio. Even though she weighs just 20 pounds, she can retrieve pheasants and has placed in field trials.

at present, although some field strains of the breed have been in America for many generations. As is true with Springers, English Cockers of field breeding are quite separate from the show strains, in talent and natural hunting instincts, and the best hunting dogs of this merry little breed are quite exceptional in ability.

Except for the breeds just discussed, all the other spaniel breeds are quite rare and their ability in the field is truly a mixed bag. Several books are available that describe the expected differences in size, style and hunting methods of the rare spaniel breeds. But if I were looking for any spaniel other than an English Springer or an English Cocker, I would demand a hunting demonstration from both parents before the purchase. Unfortunately, many of the lesser-known spaniel breeds have gone unhunted for so many generations that the genetic instincts necessary for hunting may have been allowed to lapse.

SPANIELS THAT FLASH POINT

Some spaniels have an inherent tendency to flash point just before flushing the bird. This is not all that surprising, considering that the root stock of flushing spaniels and pointing setters is thought to be the same. Both are believed to have developed in England from the same spaniel roots in the sixteenth and seventeenth centuries. But over time, they were very selectively bred to intensify their tendencies to either boldly flush birds or staunchly point birds. Having hunted over several spaniels that flash pointed birds before they raced in to flush them, and an equal number of setters that locked up tight on point then slowly crouched and crept until the bird flushed, it is obvious that mixed genes still lurk, though repressed, in the heredity of some of these dogs.

In the field-trial spaniel world, flash pointing is a serious fault that will result in severe penalty points. As a result, dogs that flash point are routinely dropped from competition quickly and unceremoniously. Frankly, most spaniel field trial dropouts are then sold off to hunters who make them into fine hunting companions.

For the hunter, the tendency of a spaniel to flash point for just an instant before it begins to work at flushing out the game is not of serious concern. Let me caution you, however, that as Charles Goodall, the well-known spaniel writer wrote years ago, the spaniel's nose is a very different nose than the setter's nose. Spaniels in general do not find birds from the distances commonly achieved by pointing dogs. A spaniel has the unique type of nose that can track birds that move or walk about on the ground, a talent that almost no pointing dog could ever match. In summary, the spaniel that flash points on the way to do its true job of flushing the birds presents little concern for its habit. However, the flushing spaniel that points so staunchly that it refuses to flush its own game is of doubtful value. The really knowledgeable trainers I have talked to feel the same way about retriever breed dogs that point; retrievers are and should be flushing dogs, fully able to trail a skulking rooster pheasant until it flies.

THE LITTLE PLEASURES OF DOG WORK

Some of the less frequently mentioned dog responses will yield some of the greatest pleasure in a day's hunting.

Hand signals is an example: Over time most of my dogs learn to hunt at my direction, usually through hand signals. If I point left, they usually head that way; if I gesture to an aspen clump they will usually give it a loop. I'm not sure it yields many birds, but it makes me feel better that the dog covers the areas that look birdie to me.

Hunt dead is a fairly simple skill that most dogs are never trained to develop until it is needed. Harry Henriques has a simple but precise method of training that must work, because he loses very few birds. But until you've stood at the spot of a fall and yelled "Hunt dead!" while your dog was off hunting for new game a hundred yards away, you don't understand the psychic value of this skill.

CHAPTER 18
A CONVERSATION WITH DEAN BRUNN

DEAN BRUNN

Spaniel Trainer
Milltown, Indiana

Dean Brunn and a springer pupil after a training session where the dog successfully found, flushed and retrieved several birds.

Dean Brunn, whom I first met about fifteen years ago, is a professional dog trainer who specializes primarily in English Springer Spaniels for field trial competition. This is not surprising, since his father, the late Don Brunn Sr., was a springer trainer of note. Dean epitomizes a no-nonsense kind of dog trainer who communicates very well with dogs but can be abrupt with people. He has a sometimes overactive sense of personal pride that prevents him from "schmoozing the client." If he thinks a dog has no talent and further training would be a waste of time, Dean will probably say so, quickly and directly, even if it might not be what a client hopes to hear. That's just his way and he says he can sleep soundly knowing he earned his pay and told the truth. This directness

129

Shooting is generally a part of flushing dog training. Here after the dog has flushed the bird, it hups (sits) and remains steady to wing and shot until commanded to retrieve.

The dog retrieves to hand. Note the cover is similar to CRP cover, where pheasants are usually found. The birds being used for training are guinea fowl, which will normally run very aggressively. This natural tendency teaches young dogs how to track and flush birds boldly, a positive asset for their future as useful gun dogs.

can hurt clients' feelings, but it generally saves them money that might be spent on pointless training efforts.

Over the years Dean has trained some top spaniels, including two national champions and numerous other field champions. He maintains very high standards for the dogs he trains, since many are headed for the highest levels of competition. Many of the dogs that are initially trained for spaniel field trials fail to measure up as the training progresses, and those dogs usually end up as someone's high-class gun dog. Hence, Dean has trained many gun dogs over the years.

Of the eight land spaniel breeds, how many do you train?

BRUNN—I train mostly English Springers and English Cockers. Both are used regularly with hunters, but many more Springers are hunted than Cockers. Even though Cockers are gaining in popularity, Springers still comprise the vast majority of all hunting spaniels. All the other spaniel breeds are fairly rare in the field.

Do all breeds of spaniels work the same and are they trained basically the same?

BRUNN—Yes, although their style, speed and intensity will vary, I would train a Welsh or a Clumber or a Boykin in the same way and to do the same things. The result you are trying to achieve is the same: to teach the dog to find 'em, flush 'em and fetch 'em!

Is that the focus of training for spaniels?

BRUNN—Yes. But not only for all spaniels, but for any upland hunting dog of a flushing breed, even if it was a Labrador or a Golden Retriever. Basically, because you can train a Lab or any of the retrieving breeds to do the same job on game birds as a spaniel, and you train it with the same methods that you would use on a spaniel. Even when you are training a retriever to quest for game and run a pattern, you should use basically the same training methods.

Dean waits in place for the dog to return with the shot bird.

In your experience, what's the retriever breeds' response to the spaniel type of training methods?

BRUNN—They respond well to it. Generally the retrieving breeds are a little tougher. They can take a more intense training program. It seems to me that they have a little less nose and maybe a little less tracking instinct, but they are quite good as upland flushing dogs for pheasant and grouse.

Do they tend to run as big as the spaniels do naturally?

BRUNN—They tend to work on about the same level as a spaniel that has been trained as a gun dog, but not as big-running as a spaniel that's been trained for field trials. For field trials we train the dogs to run bigger, wider and a little flashier and more to the edge of gun range. The Labs work about the same as a regular hunting Springer.

If you were going to prioritize these eight things, how would you put them in order: Tracking game; Staying in gun range; Finding game; Retrieving; Using the wind well; Water retrieving; Steadiness to wing and shot; A bold flush?

BRUNN—The first priority for any gun dog is finding birds. So you want a dog that has the instincts to get out and look for birds and use the wind and quest through the cover, and spaniels must do that within gun range. Marking the fall and bringing the retrieve to hand is important, too, and any good gun dog has to do that. So the three top priorities are finding birds, working within gun range and then bringing birds back.

Being steady to wing and shot is nice, but not really necessary. What is necessary, however, is to have a dog that hunts while under control, and in many cases that requires steadying the dog. Many hunters now are hunting on preserves, and you can't afford to have a dog chasing a missed bird down the field and flushing the next three or four birds in that field. So it is important that the dog stays under control, and in many cases that requires being steady.

As for flushing birds boldly and taking runners, in a hunting situation flushing birds boldly is not as necessary or as big a priority as in trials, but what is a high priority is that the dog stays after the bird until it forces it into the air. That's not very important on tight setting birds, but on a hot runner, if the dog is messing around while the bird runs away he may never force that bird into the air. The dog's job is to make the bird so nervous that it wants to fly away. The same is true for a retriever used for upland hunting.

Using the wind comes under the heading of finding birds, and a dog with good, natural instincts and experience soon learns how to use the wind. Tracking is part of finding birds, and most spaniels will retrieve in water with a little experience.

Do you think most hunters fully take into account how a spaniel (or any dog) has to work in order to find birds using the wind?

BRUNN—Probably not. I think most guys don't fully understand that a dog needs to get downwind of a bird in order to smell it and when tracking, the dog picks up the scent by working across the scent. Whenever the dog gets upwind of the bird he loses the scent, and I am not sure that most hunters understand that. With experience a hunter can read the dog and see it pick up the scent on a setting bird or follow the track of a moving bird. Reading the dog well adds a thrill to the hunting experience.

What do you consider the ideal hunting range and is that hard to achieve?

BRUNN—No, it's not hard to do, but it takes some training. A lot of it depends on the individual dog. Some dogs have an instinct to work close, while others tend to range out more. What's important is deciding the ideal range for the conditions that you are hunting under and getting the dog to do that. In fairly open country, hunting pheasants, you need a dog that gets out and covers as much ground as possible, even to the edge of gun range, which might be forty or forty-five yards from you. But, if you're hunting in thick, heavy cover like tag alders for woodcock or thickets for grouse, you need a dog that works close, and it's important that the dog continually checks back to you on its own. Most dogs will learn to adjust to the conditions. When the cover gets heavy, most dogs tighten up and work a little closer and when the cover is light, they open up and cover more ground.

Some hunters see no need for a dog to be steady to wing and shot or limit its chasing. Do you?

BRUNN—Yes, because it adds an air of class and control to the dog's performance. In most cases, teaching a dog to limit its chasing is going to take almost as much effort as steadying the dog. When I was young I had a Springer that could stop on a runner with just the peep of a whistle. Even when he was hot on a hot runner I could peep the whistle and he would sit right down. I never steadied him to flush because when he would flush a bird he would never chase it more than fifteen or twenty yards if it didn't come down. I never found it necessary to steady him. But if you have a dog that you have to scream and holler at and it takes fifteen minutes to get him back from a missed bird, that dog needs to be steadied to be under control. That kind of dog can ruin your day. Training for a controlled chase takes a lot of work and you may as well just go ahead and steady the dog.

How about spaniels for retrieving?

BRUNN—Fortunately, most spaniels retrieve naturally. If a dog doesn't have any instinct to retrieve at all, I don't waste much time with it. However, if the dog brings back a bird but sets it down maybe fifteen feet from me, or if the dog has the natural instinct to pick up and carry birds around, I will force train it to finish the process. But I would say that probably about 95 percent of all well-bred spaniels are birdie, and usually if they are birdie they're going to have an instinct to pick up birds and carry them around. The percentages drop lower with show-bred spaniels where only about 50 percent are really interested in birds. But I have had some exceptional ones. I trained a show Springer years ago that I ran in some field trial puppy stakes and he took three firsts and a fourth. He turned out to be an exceptional gun dog.

Are spaniel field trials relevant to hunting, and can field trial stock be adapted to everyday hunting situations?

BRUNN—Yes, unquestionably. Spaniel trials are very relevant to hunting. That's where our dogs are proven, and even a dog that's been competitive in field trials will make a superior gun dog. What the trial dog has to learn is that in field trials it runs for twenty minutes at all-out top speed, but in actual hunting it will work for eight-hour intervals, so spaniels soon learn to pace themselves. In spaniels, unlike some breeds, the field trial stock is really the same as the hunting stock. It's just that we train our field trial dogs to give everything they have for a short burst of time and run to the edge of gun range. The blue ribbons often are won out on the edge of gun range.

How much of the average spaniel's work effort is hereditary?

BRUNN—Generally, for field trials I think it's probably about fifty-fifty. However, a gun dog is probably more like seventy-five–twenty-five, with about 75 percent being natural instinct. A well-bred spaniel operating just on good, natural instincts to find, flush and fetch can really be a pretty darn good hunting dog so long as it is *under control.*

Are spaniels good water dogs?

BRUNN—I have hunted ducks and geese with spaniels since I was a kid, sometimes in the middle of November, up on the Mississippi in Wisconsin where we were breaking ice. The only real drawback to a spaniel is that he doesn't have a coat like a retriever. If you want to train them to that level, you can train them to do anything that a retriever will do, but the really cold water is hard on them.

Do you ever use an electronic collar?

BRUNN—Yes, I have been using an electronic collar off and on for about five or ten years. It's just a handy training tool. There is nothing you can do with a collar that you can't do with legwork, but using a collar can often make it easier. Over the last five years I have probably used it on about 50 percent of the dogs at one time or another. But you have to be careful. If improperly used you can ruin any dog in about one second. It's possible to ruin a dog instantly, but you'd need to do something stupid.

CHAPTER 19
PICKING THE RIGHT DOG FOR YOU

Before you can realistically select the right roughshooting dog for you, you must consider several important factors. These include your own style and needs, including how and where you hunt, the birds you will pursue, your own physical effort, investment and the dog's living arrangements. Every professional trainer interviewed in this book said that the toughest problem they face is dealing with a sincere client who has purchased a puppy of the wrong breed (doesn't match the style of the hunter) or the wrong breeding (either poor potential or wrong strain within the breed). Then after the puppy has become an emotional part of the family, it is very difficult to rectify the situation. I asked Bob West, a man who sees almost every breed in action sometime during a year, to give us his impressions of how to select the right breed for the hunting one has in mind.

A CONVERSATION WITH
BOB WEST

Gun Dog Consultant
LeClaire, Iowa

Bob West has an enviable lifestyle. Handsome, articulate and infinitely likable, he gets paid for hunting

Bob West is shown here working with a Labrador puppy on the basics of retrieving. As a consultant to Ralston-Purina, Bob attends competitive hunting and field trial performance events for many different breeds and probably sees more dogs work in competition than anyone else I know.

and dog-related activities year-round. For years, Bob was a full-time professional dog trainer who gradually began to share his knowledge by writing for periodicals such as *Gun Dog* and for the Ruffed Grouse Society. After his reputation for unbiased dog advice became recognized, the Ralston-Purina Company asked Bob to work as a full-time field consultant to the sporting dog industry. Although West no longer trains dogs on a daily basis, he probably sees more dogs of every sporting breed perform in the field than anyone else in the United States. Because of his wide exposure and insights into how all these breeds work, I asked for his views on how a roughshooter should go about picking a dog.

How would you help a hunter pick out and find the dog that is best for him?

WEST—The hunter has to make a real honest assessment of his own hunting needs, how he is going to keep the dog and how the dog is expected to interact with the family. There *are* some very good hunting dogs that also make good pets. *First,* do you want a house pet or a kennel dog? *Second,* what is the real focus of your hunting? For example, most of the Labrador Retrievers and Golden Retrievers that are registered in America are mainly kept as pets. So if you must have a dog that you can keep in the house as a family pet, and if most of your hunting is waterfowling plus a few days of pheasant hunting or a little bit of grouse hunting, then one of the retriever breeds would be great for you. On the other hand, if your main interest is hunting down south on big quail plantations or out in the big open country for pheasants, then you're probably going to want a dog that works out wider and farther in its search for birds. In general, the more far-ranging and intense the dog, the less likely it is to be a great house pet. The more intense, big-going dogs, like the Pointers, are seldom kept in the house as everyday pets. Now I know somebody will say that they keep their Pointers in the house as pets and that's true, but not generally speaking.

You mention intensity. Are you saying that dogs that are less intense are generally easier for the foot hunter, the roughshooter, to handle?

WEST—No, not at all. I think for any dog to be a really good hunting dog it has to have desire, it has to have intensity, it has to be very serious when it goes about its business, but it may do so in a less far-ranging and more biddable manner. Some breeds of dogs are able to keep their intensity while still maintaining their communication link with their owners. Other dogs are very intense but also aloof and distant. Hunters want dogs that are working and communicating, whatever the range.

How would you differentiate Pointers from English Setters in terms of natural intent and most common usage?

WEST—There are exceptions to every rule, but the Pointers tend to be open cover dogs, which tends to make them very strong on quail and they can be very good in big, open pheasant country or up in Montana on sharptails. Some varieties of setters tend to be a little closer dog and you will see more setters in the grouse woods and the woodcock thickets than anyplace else, probably because the dogs tend on average to hunt a little more cooperatively. There are a lot of open cover setters mainly used for quail. Open cover dogs tend to work out a couple of hundred yards or more in order to be effective, whereas woods cover dogs should work closer.

Let's talk about the group of dogs referred to as Continental breeds. This includes the Brittany (which used to be called the Brittany Spaniel), the German Shorthaired Pointer and the German Wirehaired Pointer. Can you explain your own opinion of the difference between the three?

WEST—Sure, let's start with the German Wirehaired Pointer and let's put the Wirehaired Pointing Griffon in the same category because the two breeds are very similar. These two breeds were developed in Europe basically for the one-dog hunter who wanted to hunt fur and feathers and do some waterfowling as well. All of the Continental-type dogs will do that to some extent, but the German Wirehair and the Pointing Griffon are the best of the group when it comes to hunting fur (rabbits), tracking and water work. At the opposite end of the scale is the Brittany, which is generally the least adept at water work but maybe the best in cover. The German Shorthaired Pointer falls somewhere in between. So, again, it goes back to the hunter making a decision on what his own style is going to be and what mix of hunting he is going to do.

Bob, where would you put the Vizsla and the Weimaraner in this line-up?

WEST—Neither the Vizsla nor the Weimaraner are as popular in the field as the Brittany or the two German Pointers. In terms of ability, the breeders strive to go versatile, kind of in the middle, a reasonable mix of bird dog, duck dog, fur retriever and tracking dog. They should also be pretty good all-around dogs as are most Continental or versatile breeds.

How would these Continental breeds stack up as house pets?

WEST—In my experience, that depends a great deal on the individual dog. Some of them make great house pets, but as in other breeds some tend to be either a little bit aloof or a little hyper. I think you just have to select the right individual dog and the best way to find out is to spend some time with the parents if at all possible. It is really important to try to understand the basic traits and instincts of the individual dog you are buying.

What about a Gordon Setter?

WEST—It is my experience that the Gordon is a little easier going and significantly more close working than the English Setter. The true Gordon tends to work close and easy.

So summarizing, when an individual is picking a dog, how would you recommend he go about it?

WEST—The first is a real honest assessment of your own hunting style and what you really like and what thrills you. If you love to watch a dog stand like a statue on a staunch point, then you ought to have a setter or a Pointer that will perform really classic points. If you hate to have the dog out of sight, pick a close working strain of a Continental breed. If the real thrill to you is a strong, aggressive flush to see birds in the air, and fast and furious action, then maybe you would be happy with an English Springer. If making long, difficult water retrieves gives you a thrill and never losing a duck for the game bag is absolutely paramount to you, you have got to be sure that you pick one of the retrieving breeds.

You also have to really assess your own physical and mental characteristics. For the guy who wants to get out and hunt aggressively and doesn't mind tearing his clothes on the brush, a spaniel is a perfect companion. On the other hand, somebody a little older, a little less physically active or someone who just wants the dog to do more of the work might feel more comfortable with a pointing dog so he doesn't have to be in the brush himself. Of course, the family situation and taking care of the dog is a big factor. I have a couple of puppies at home right now, two Labs and two English Setters, and it's obvious that the Labs seem to be more "personable," but all require a lot of contact.

Most importantly, before you buy any dog, do a bit of homework. Most people do a lot better job of buying their second dog than they do their first. The first dog is often an emotional purchase. With the second dog, they usually do their homework first. Don't ever be afraid to ask a lot of questions. Understand, too, that within each litter there is going to be a range of puppies. It is a little bit of a roll of the dice, but the more homework you do ahead of time the better your chances of ending up with a dog that really meets your desires. The more you like the parents, size, attitude and style of hunting, the more likely you'll be satisfied with your new pup.

RANGE

Anyone in the process of picking a puppy must consider range carefully because it is the one instinctive dog trait that is most likely to match or mismatch you and your dog. Just listen to hunting dog owners talk and range will be involved in 50 percent of all the negative comments. Make no mistake, range is strongly hereditary and if the dog you select is in conflict with your hunting style, the partnership will probably never completely click.

No topic of hunting dog discussion generates more heated debate than range, and certainly no action on the part of the dog causes more frustration, training, punishment and vocal exercise than range. The equipment manufacturers love range because excessive range sells long-distance electronic training collars, drag ropes, slo-balls, harnesses, beeper collars and other related paraphernalia. Professional dog trainers spend more time on range control than any other training task. Range cannot be overcome with training; it can only be modified with consistent and forceful controls.

Virtually all of the dog people I respect have voiced the belief that range is a function of the dog's genetic inheritance and is only modified slightly by the dog's individual personality. A dog's inherent predisposition to a specific range is due in part to physical size, length of leg, athletic ability, inherent stamina, lung capacity and length of stride. However, it is mainly influenced by the dog's mental make-up including its desire to run, independence, biddability and predisposition to reach out. Within each litter, siblings display some variance in range, but the basic genetic predisposition is inherited.

FOUR CATEGORIES OF RANGE

All hunting dogs, whether pointing or flushing types, fall into four basic categories of range. I call them: *horizon runners; ridge runners; gun rangers;* and *boot polishers.*

Horizon runners are a small but exciting core of extremely high-performance pointing dogs that reach out far beyond the needs (or practicality) of the foot hunter. These magnificent flying dogs are truly only suitable for horseback, truck or ATV hunting in the wide open country— places like Texas, the Florida panhandle or big southern quail plantations. It is not unusual for a dog of this bent to range out a half-mile. They truly become specks on the horizon and although they are awesome hunting machines they are of little value to the foot hunter. Some people say that these dogs "adjust" their range to match a hunter on foot. I haven't found that to be the case.

Ridge runners are the medium-range pointing dogs that while reaching out a few hundred yards, still maintain a relationship with the hunter. Their range in open country is usually much bigger than in heavy cover where they adjust to more realistic distances to match the sight lines. A dog like this makes some hunters nervous when it sometimes disappears for more than a few minutes.

Ridge runners must, by definition, be pointing dogs, for a flushing dog that ranges beyond forty or fifty yards is useless. For a ridge running dog to be of value it must check back to the hunter frequently and must inherently maintain an awareness of the hunter's location, presence and direction. Ridge runners often run as fast and as purposefully as the horizon runners, just not as far. If you frequently hunt the big plains or the quail bottoms, these are great dogs that provide big-time thrills.

If a dog of this range turns well on the whistle and especially if the dog will automatically adjust its range to the density of the cover, the ridge runner will work well in all but the biggest quail covers and the tightest grouse and woodcock covers.

Gun rangers seldom reach out much beyond gun range, which extends to about fifty yards. Several breeds of pointing dogs, and the most aggressive styles of flushing dogs, work at this range. Gun ranger dogs, of either pointing or flushing breeds, can be solid bird finders. Although the horseback crowd may find them boring, most hunters can find rangers to be very exciting when they hunt with intensity and find birds with style! The mere fact that the hunter can always find the dog makes this type quite appealing, and you seldom waste the morning looking for your dog.

On a recent trip to Kansas, we hunted several large and productive properties, a few of which bordered highly traveled, paved roads. These close-to-the-traffic tracts were always worked by the gun rangers, since no one wanted to risk losing a ridge runner to the bumper of an eighteen-wheeler. Many of the most productive roughshooting dogs fall into the gun ranger category.

The fourth category of dogs I call *boot polishers*, but certainly not in a derogatory way. Just because they seldom range more than thirty yards from the hunter, whether pointing dogs or flushing dogs, does not reduce their effectiveness. There are many circumstances when this is by far the most productive dog. When tackling small woodcock coverts or when hunting extremely spooky pheasants in fence rows, a boot polisher will generally produce the most realistic shooting opportunities. Some breeds and some strains of popular breeds, are far more likely to fall into this category than others. Some strains of Brittanys, Gordons and Vizslas, plus most Cockers, the rarer spaniels and many Golden Retrievers fall into this category. If you doubt that hunting over a boot polisher can be exciting, let me know your feelings after a dog like this has found six or eight pheasants virtually underfoot or helped fill your bag with woodcock flushed from a tiny patch of wet-footed tag alders.

Dogs with this very close type of range appeal generally to hunters who work small, dense or restrictive covers, and some of the most celebrated and photographed grouse dogs fall into this category. People who quickly become frustrated when searching for a dog that is out of sight for even a few minutes should focus on finding a talented dog of this natural range.

RANGE POTENTIAL BY BREED

	Horizon Hunters	Ridge Runners	Gun Rangers	Boot Polishers
Pointers	X	X		
English Setters	X	X	X	X
Continentals	X	X	X	X
Gordon Setters			X	X
Spaniels		X	X	X
Retrievers		X	X	X

THE GREAT RANGE DEBATE

There is a great debate raging in the pointing dog community as this book goes to press concerning the extreme range of the open all-age dogs in both the Field Dog Stud Book and the AKC field trials.

Even some well-respected and dedicated field trialers have chimed in with the opinion that some of the events are no longer relevant to everyday hunting situations and that some of the winning dogs could be more easily classified as runaways; totally unwilling to connect with the handler, or in any way respond to the handler's direction. That is a shame, because the highest levels of competition should be the proving ground for the breeding stock that sets the tone for the mainstream needs of any breed. Fortunately other stakes and types of competition and testing do exist, such as the shooting dog stakes, grouse or woodcock cover trials, and the AKC hunting tests and pheasant championships, which all focus on and reward a more realistic working range and more biddable pointing dogs.

Despite the trends toward dogs of extreme range in open all-age events, a few kennels have built an esteemed position in their dog community by breeding biddable, responsive dogs that can be hunted. The Elhew

Pointers are consistently mentioned by professional trainers I respect as an example that biddability does indeed still exist in even the most potent strains of the high-performance breeds.

The vast majority of all puppies are bought out of the whelping box without the buyer ever getting a chance to see either parent work in the field. That is a high-risk way to select a dog you expect to own for the next fifteen years. The very best way to select a dog for roughshooting is to buy a puppy from a dog you have enjoyed hunting over.

The puppy buyer needs to seek out a breeder that carefully produces the type of dog to match the hunter's needs.

PET DOGS

If a primary part of your dog's existence requires it to function as a pet, be realistic in your selection. Some breeds, notably spaniels and retrievers, are very people-oriented and it is their nature to form very close bonds with their owners, but that does not mean that they are always calm, quiet lap dogs and sleep by the fire. Some are quite boisterous and rowdy and a few are truly hyper. However, many spaniel and retriever field trial champions are everyday house dogs even during their competitive years. Some of the very best gun dogs of these breeds are consistently raised as house pets.

Many of the Continental breeds are also routinely kept as pets by a variety of hunters and nonhunters and although these dogs may require some specific control measures, such as a fenced yard and consistent restraint when running free, they can make great pets when properly managed.

At the far end of the spectrum are the all-out horizon runners. It is not that these dogs are antipeople; to the contrary, they can be most affectionate and friendly. However, they require huge amounts of exercise and can be very destructive in the house as the tail of such a dog can easily wreak havoc in close quarters. These dogs also tend to disappear the first time a crack appears at the door, so constant restraint is a necessity. I have a close friend who owns, hunts and trials one of the big-running strains of pointing dogs. His dogs sleep in the house every night, but in his own words, "The dogs cannot be trusted to come home like a spaniel and so they are *never* turned loose to run free. They are always on a lead, dragging a check cord or wearing an electric collar, except when in all-age competition."

THE ODDBALLS

Some people take great pleasure in owning a unique or "oddball" breed of dog. This can be great fun as people ask questions and ooh and ahh over your unusual companion, but it is not without some risk. Usually the very rare breeds, like Spinonis, Muensterlanders and the like are far less proven in the field, so you are taking a major gamble. Even some of the less famil- iar AKC breeds like Irish Water Spaniels (a retriever breed), Wirehaired Pointing Griffons and Welsh Springer Spaniels are a bit of a roll of the dice. There are so many fine and proven breeds available that buying a dog just for its uniqueness seems to be a bit risky and a time-consuming way to generate conversation.

SHOW DOGS

At the opposite end of the spectrum far removed from the field are the show breeders who are so focused on looks and the physical attributes of their breed standard that they have ignored the hunting talents of their dogs. Yes, there are a few dual (show and field) champions in some sport- ing breeds, but in many sporting breeds, including Labradors, Gold- ens, Springers, Brittanies, Gordons, German Shorthairs and Weimaran- ers, a large and influential group of show breeders are so focused on appearance that they are diverting these hunting breeds away from the field attributes inherent in the orig-

It is so easy to fall in love with a puppy. They are all so cute. But take your time, do your homework and select carefully.

inal dogs. The more popular the breed, the more likely it is to have an avid show following and a separate show strain.

BUYING FROM CHAMPION STOCK

There is a tendency in all of us to demand the best. We've learned over the years that it only costs a little bit more to go first class. So we think, "What the heck, why not buy the best champion-bred puppy available?" The problem comes in defining *best*. There are many different championship and testing formats, each varying by breed type, so you must carefully investigate the testing procedures to be sure the achievements in the dog's pedigree relate to your style of hunting. You need to be sure, *before you buy*, that the dog's inherited winning ways match your needs and expectations. Frankly, money will seldom stop you from buying a "best dog," because even the most expensive puppies or finished dogs are not all that expensive when compared to boats, race horses or country club memberships.

But the way some people pick a dog is by counting the number of field champions in its pedigree, a valid selection method *only if* the championship format exactly matches what you want in a dog. Some of the newer hunting tests and hunting championships were designed to reward the dog's working ability under conditions that closely resemble real hunting.

A PUPPY OR A FINISHED DOG?

There are pros and cons to either raising a puppy or buying a finished dog and a list of the advantages and disadvantages to each alternative follows. Most people believe there are huge cost savings in raising a puppy. However, they almost always overlook the ongoing cumulative expenses of the first two years of ownership. When you total up the vet bills, food and training trips during the first two years of the puppy's life, you add a large amount to the original puppy investment. If you train the dog yourself you will have a major time investment. If you send it out to a pro you will have a major dollar investment. Either way, by the time you have a trained, two-year-old dog, which you raised from a puppy, your total investment in time and money will probably be two or three times the original puppy price. However, it does allow you to spend the money over a longer time period, sort of like payments.

On the positive side, there can be great personal satisfaction in raising and training a puppy and often a deep emotional bond is formed between the dog and the trainer (and the trainer's family). But herein lies a dilemma; if the dog does not work out as a hunting dog, the emotional bonds are so strong that the family can seldom bear to part with the dog. So you are saddled with a poor hunter for years to come. At least with the purchase of a finished dog you can see what kind of a hunting partner you will have. There is little reason to worry that the finished dog will not accept your attention, obey you or bond to you and your family. I've raised and trained puppies and I've bought many started and semifinished dogs. Most dogs will, with time and attention, transfer their total allegiance to you as their new master.

Unfortunately, real top-notch, finished dogs are seldom available except in about three or four circumstances:

1. *Field trial washouts.* These are dogs that cannot compete at the field trial level but are very well trained and often exceptional hunting dogs. If you can go this route, ask frankly why the dog is being washed out. Perhaps it will make the dog more appealing to you. For example: He doesn't range out far enough for horseback trialing!

2. *Divorce or family situations.* I've seen a few really great dogs come available through family breakups, families moving, children's allergies, loss of interest or even an injury such as a bad knee, which ends a hunter's ability to pursue his hobby.

3. *A need for cash.* Some rather talented amateur dog enthusiasts are not all that well fixed financially and sometimes they are forced to sell a good dog to generate cash. Somebody will always buy a good dog.

A started dog is an alternative between a puppy and a fully trained dog, usually a yearling that is partially trained. In these cases you can usually see most of the dog's potential, but more training will be needed. Obviously, a started dog's cost is less than that of a fully finished dog. Two of the best dogs I ever owned I bought as started dogs, then finished their training. Both went on to become field champions, then very reliable gun dogs.

PUPPY VS. FINISHED DOG, A COMPARISON

PUPPY

Advantages	Disadvantages
Low initial cost	At least one hunting season is lost as the dog grows up
Joy of raising a puppy	Emotional tie if the dog does not work out
Close bond with the dog	Cost is *hidden* over time
Satisfaction of the training experience	Very time consuming
Able to buy the best	You must do the intense finish training yourself or pay to have it done
Cost is spread over time	Speed, range and retrieving are unknown

FINISHED DOG

Advantages	Disadvantages
Able to see "finished" product	Higher cost?
Ready to hunt now!	Difficult to find
What you see is what you get	Best dogs are seldom for sale

HOW MANY DOGS DOES A HUNTER NEED?

A hunter needs several dogs. Start with one for each type of bird and terrain. Better yet, why not two or three for every bird so a fresh dog is always on the ground? Unrealistic? Of course. Practical limitations of space, cost, time and spousal frustration stops everyone at some more manageable number—one or maybe two at the most.

A hunter will have wonderful and successful days afield with only one well-trained, talented and especially well-conditioned dog. On extended trips you learn that staying power is a valuable attribute in a dog. Some just have natural endurance that allows them to keep going, hour after grueling hour.

Some dogs, regardless of conditioning, are worn out and frazzled after four hours, so if you are a serious, all-day hunter, two dogs to alternate on the ground is ideal. If your maximum number is two, then the selection of the styles and ages of the dogs deserves some careful consideration.

Much can be said for separating the ages of your two dogs by five or six years so that you always have a dog in the prime of its career. In most sporting breeds, the dog's most productive years should be from age three to nine. Generally, in dogs, the larger the breed the shorter the life expectancy and hence the shorter the productive years. I have hunted over old Springers and Brittanies twelve or thirteen years of age that still put out a very productive hour or two on the ground, but I've also seen some large, ten-year-old retrievers that were long past retirement age.

TWO DIFFERENT DOGS

There is a lot to be said for owning two very different styles of dog. But most of us don't. Once we have found a breed we like, we tend to back it up with another of the same breed, style, speed, range and talent. I do that myself and I see it repeatedly in the dog selections of my friends.

What probably makes more sense for the widely traveled hunter is to have two significantly different dogs in his kennel, so the dog can be matched to the task at hand. If he had both a wide-ranging Pointer and a close-working, obedient Brittany in the truck, in the morning he could tackle a five hundred-acre property with ease and let the big Pointer race off searching the edges for coveys. Then in the afternoon he could work out small patches, waterways, thickets and creek bottoms with the Brittany.

Or, with two spaniels, a big-running field trial Springer for wide cover and a close-working Cocker or Springer for ditches and fence rows, you could tackle almost any kind of widely varying areas.

Or, with a Retriever and a Continental dog you could hunt grouse and woodcock in both the broad alder thickets with your German Shorthair and the islands of aspen along the roads with the obedient Labrador.

Owning two dogs of different style makes so much sense that I may even get around to trying it some day.

CHECKLIST

An honest evaluation, using this simple checklist, will help you narrow down your choices to quickly select a dog with the natural attributes of range, style and personality that match your needs. After you have defined your own parameters, finding a dog with those attributes should be a rational process.

HOW DO YOU LIKE TO HUNT?

Is your style physically aggressive or laid-back? Physically active or relaxed?

How well do you shoot on surprise flushes?

Are classic points important to you?

How much property will the dog be expected to hunt?

Is a wide-ranging dog an asset or a liability?

Will the dog's being out of sight while hunting seriously concern you?

Will the prime quarry be pheasant? grouse? woodcock? quail? other?

Will this be your only hunting dog?

Is retrieving every bird key to your enjoyment?

Will you also hunt waterfowl?

Will you want to get involved with hunt tests or pheasant contests?

WHERE ARE YOU GOING TO HUNT?

Very dense thickets?

Woodsy edges and new growth?

Large woody areas in a trekking style?

Small woodsy patches by roads?

Fence rows, sloughs and terraces for pheasants in open country?

Large waterways and acres of dense rough ground near crop fields?

Huge, weedy CRP plots?

Quail plantations?

Tiny rough patches on farms of thirty to fifty acres?

Huge, grassy prairies?

Cactus-covered deserts?

Arid mountain rocks and ridges?

Game preserves?

All of the above?

None of the above?

Your answers to these questions should at least point you in the direction of a dog that will match your needs.

HOW WILL THE DOG LIVE?

Kennel only?

In the house only?

Combination house and kennel?

Will the dog be a pet?

Will the dog be around small children?

Do you have a fenced yard?

How frequently will the dog be exercised? Where and how?

DOG SELECTION BY BIRD SPECIES

ON A SCALE OF 5 TO 0   5 = VERY GOOD   0 = VERY POOR

	Quail	Pheasants	Grouse	Woodcock	Ducks	Geese	Doves
Pointer	5	2	3	2	0	0	0
English Setter	5	2	4	4	0	0	0
Brittany	4	3	4	4	1	0	1
German Short-haired Pointer	3	4	4	3	2	1	2
German Wirehaired Pointer	3	4	4	4	3	2	3
Vizsla	3	3	3	3	1	1	1
Weimaraner	3	3	3	3	2	2	2
Wirehaired Pointing Griffon	3	4	4	3	2	1	1
Gordon Setter	3	3	4	3	0	0	0
English Springer Spaniel	2	5	3	3	4	2	5
English Cocker Spaniel	1	4	3	4	2	0	3
Labrador Retriever	1	3	3	2	5	5	5
Golden Retriever	1	3	3	2	4	4	4
Chesapeake Bay Retriever	1	3	3	2	5	5	5

DOG ATTRIBUTES RATING

SCALES 5–0   5 = VERY GOOD   0 = DOES NOT DO THIS

	Points	Hunts Aggressively	Handles Moving Birds	Easily Trained	Stays in Control	Strong Retrieving	Petability	Water Work
Pointer	5	5	1	2	2	1	1	0
English Setter	5	4	1	2	3	1	1	1
Brittany	4	3	2	3	4	3	3	1
German Shorthaired Pointer	4	3	3	4	4	3	3	2
German Wirehaired Pointer	4	3	3	3	4	4	2	3
Wirehaired Pointing Griffon	3	3	3	3	3	4	2	3
Vizsla	3	3	3	3	3	3	3	2
Weimaraner	3	3	3	3	4	3	4	3
Gordon Setter	4	3	1	3	4	1	3	1
English Springer Spaniel	0	5	5	4	3	5	4	4
English Cocker Spaniel	0	3	3	3	4	4	4	3
Labrador Retriever	0	3	3	4	5	5	5	5
Golden Retriever	0	3	3	3	5	4	5	4
Chesapeake Bay Retriever	0	4	3	3	4	5	3	5

CHAPTER 20
COMBINING A GREAT DOG WITH
A BUSY LIFESTYLE

For the last two years I made a special effort to hunt over many different dogs of many different breeds, as they performed an average day's work for their owners. Some days we had only three or four dogs with us and some days we had as many as a dozen. Over that time, the dogs' performances varied from magnificent to terrible. But one thing was clear, even with some of the worst performing dogs: The hunters with their own dogs enjoyed the hunting far more than those just walking along and shooting. Although I was very tuned into the dog work and careful to observe the dogs' efforts, I'll admit that I didn't enjoy even the very best days of shooting over others' dogs as much as when I'm hunting over my own dogs.

The dog work does not need to be brilliant to bring a hunter great pleasure. Little moments of shining performance can cause great satisfaction: a pup's first wild bird point; a tough retrieve completed easily; a "hunt dead" found; working in range without a heavy whistle; staunchness when out of sight. Any of a number of positive actions can foster great pride in the dog owner. Clearly, the hunter without his own dog misses much of the joy of the sport.

Money is not the main deterrent to owning a great hunting dog. Certainly, high-quality dogs are expensive, but it is lifestyle incompatibilities that frequently prevent the hunter from owning a hunting dog. These incompatibilities include: interaction between family and dog, interference with family and business commitments, space for a high-energy dog and time to keep a dog properly trained. These complex difficulties keep many hunters from owning that one great hunting dog.

Owning and caring for a dog requires a serious personal time commitment. However, I believe a realistic understanding of what is involved and a little creative planning will allow you the pleasure of hunting over your own dog.

A HUNTING DOG FOR THE HARRIED

Unlike hunters in the early 1900s, only a very limited number of bird hunters can maintain extensive breeding and training kennels today. Most of us live in cities, work long hours, have long commutes, travel extensively and have family commitments. For the harried executive or professional, the choices are driven not by hunting needs or cost but more by lifestyle pressures. Almost every family can handle the effort involved in keeping a household pet, but the harried hunter is always concerned about the care of his dog during long work days and frequent business travel.

A few measures can relieve some of these worries. First, a good outdoor run will handle the dog during long days of work. An electronic bark collar will assure you that the dog isn't disturbing the neighbors while you are gone. Next, a carefully nurtured relationship with a nearby boarding kennel can resolve the conflict with business and family travel. If you add in a couple of months of summer camp for the dog with a professional trainer, you can be free for a family vacation. You will not only have summer freedom for family obligations, but your dog will be honed for the fall hunting season.

Some of my most harried friends also carefully cultivate a relationship with a local hunting dog trainer and work *together* to develop the dog. Most dogs will easily serve two masters or even three, just not at the same time. Many of the best trainers have weekend sessions when handlers and dogs show up for school together. Your dog gets trained and you get to shoot some birds. Remember that some of the most important gun dog training is done not in the fields but in your backyard. It is discipline, programmed learning and control that can and should be reinforced in your yard or a local park. I find that five minutes of dog training and play (throwing some retrieves, doing sit, come and stay obedience) after a hard day at the office is both diverting and relaxing. You can even accomplish valuable training after dark if you install a couple of yard lights.

HIRING A PROFESSIONAL

The reasons hunters use professional trainers vary widely. Some owners don't have the skills or facilities; other owners don't have the time. Many have other interests such as golf or boating, or keep a lake cottage during the off-season. No matter what the reason, working with a professional trainer is an accepted part of the sport and anyone contemplating hiring a pro should understand the basics of the process.

Dale Jarvis (left) and Dr. Richard Dorr, of Ann Arbor, Michigan, are about to start off on a Saturday training session. They work together to train Remy, Dr. Dorr's eighteenth-month-old Brittany. This session took place on a spring day while the preserve season was still open. After Remy's first hunting season as a yearling, she is now ready for more complex and comprehensive training, which needs to be completed at this stage of her mental development, regardless of the season.

A good pro really earns his pay and deserves to be paid promptly and fully as agreed. For that pay the trainer should give your dog an appropriate amount of time and effort and tailor his training to the needs of your dog in line with your agreements. Sometimes that training includes birds, shooting and retrieving, but at other times it is just very serious obedience and yard work. Some parts of the training require a significant amount of daily repetition to become ingrained in the dog's psyche. A few steps in the process can involve some risk, and the best pros will discuss this openly.

Dale Jarvis works on Remy's staunchness and pointing firmness as Richard Dorr watches and prepares to shoot. Remy is the Dorr family pet and lives in the house with the family. She is a very small dog, but fully capable of handling rooster ringnecks.

To most of us, our dogs are a bit like our children in that we are a little too emotionally attached to be completely objective. Dog trainers know this, and either by compassion or cowardice, tend to sugarcoat the messages they give us about our dogs. Conversely, a few seem to be almost sadistic in telling us of our dog's latest transgressions. I think those very negative trainers are secretly setting up an easy out: "After all, this dog had a hard mouth when we got him, what can you expect me to do?"

What I expect in a dog trainer is the unvarnished truth. I always say that to the pro when I turn a dog over to him, and because of that, I usually get an honest assessment of the dog's current condition and its long-term potential, along with a realistic estimate of the time and costs to achieve it. I've heard trainers who were described by the phrase, "He can really talk to dogs, but he can't talk to people worth a damn!" For my money, that is a much better set of skills for a dog trainer than the chap who can smooth-talk me but can't seem to explain anything to my dog!

Let me relate a true story about a high-powered field trial pro. I had a young dog of very good breeding being trained by a pro with the hope that it might develop into a field trial dog. The odds of success weren't high, since the original owner of the puppy had left it in a kennel for the first twelve months of its life without even minimal socialization. But the pup had great bloodlines, so I decided to buy it and attempt to have this top trainer resurrect it. Unfortunately it wasn't working out and very soon the pro told me to save my money and quit training this dog for field trials.

I happened to be visiting the pro the following weekend and decided to take the dog out for a basic hunt in the woods. Well, the trainer was exactly right: The dog had no potential as a field trial dog—not enough fire, speed, polish or enthusiasm. But as a hunting dog, especially on grouse and woodcock, his slow, careful, close-working pattern and eager, dependable retrieving qualified the youngster as a very solid hunting part-ner. Within a week I had sold the dog to a hunter from New Jersey who was looking for a dog of exactly this style. As I recall, I got about $1,000 for the dog, which didn't come close to covering my investment. Flight transfer arrangements were needed, but it was during one of those very busy periods of my career, so I asked the buyer to work out the shipping details with the trainer. However, I cautioned the buyer that this trainer "talked to dogs in their own language but couldn't talk to people worth a damn." You can guess what happened. While making flight arrangements the buyer casually asked the trainer his opinion of the dog, and the trainer told him honestly but a little too bluntly, "If that was my dog, I'd shoot the son of a bitch."

Of course, the sale unraveled and was only reconstructed after an hour of my reassurances and with my personal guarantee that if the dog was unsatisfactory I would take it back and fully refund the purchase price. About a week later the new owner called to tell me that not only was the sale final but that this was "undoubtedly the best gun dog" he had shot over in twenty years of hunting, and that he had limited out on woodcock over the dog on all three days he had hunted him, fresh off the plane.

I've related this story to help you understand the mindset of professional trainers. Some focus only on a few outstanding field trial dogs and won't put any effort into an average hunting dog. Others don't have either the knowledge or the guts to tell a client the truth about a dog. Perhaps they enjoy the revenue stream too much, or dislike bearing bad tidings too much, to tell the straight story. Such lack of candor could cost a client another $1,000 during the extra three months it would take to continue to work the dog with minimal results.

At least half the hunting dogs in America are also the family pet. As David Jones says, "There's just something about kids and puppies." This little fellow and the family puppy appear to be having a good time, but who is leading whom?

The best trainers will give you a factual and honest assessment of your dog and the progress that is being made. If you are going to get good results using a professional trainer, be prepared to hear the news you hope to hear, and the news you don't.

Dog trainers usually come in two distinct varieties: those who train dogs for field trials and those who train dogs for hunters. The requirements and expectations for the dogs are very different and the way in which the trainers approach their tasks are also very different. Usually the field trial dog is expected to perform every task perfectly, including some tasks that are fairly insignificant to the hunter. Taking any training shortcuts can potentially result in a flawed field trial performance. But taking shortcuts is the norm when training a hunting dog, and most trainers will use the most efficient method of training even if it results in some minor or irrelevant fault. Most hunters prefer to overlook these minor "faults" in favor of significantly reduced training costs. An example of a minor fault might be dropping the retrieve at the handler's feet rather than delivering it to hand, or perhaps a hesitation in a spaniel's flush, which is a severe fault in field trials but an insignificant problem or maybe even an asset for the hunter. Hence, it is usually better for a hunter to seek out a trainer who is focused on the needs of this particular dog.

The dog training profession covers a broad cross-section of practitioners, from celebrated "wizards" with well-manicured professional kennels of long-standing reputations serving an affluent clientele, to the backyard charlatan with ten stakes, ten barrels, ten chains and ten dollars' worth of business cards. In between there are dozens of reliable, honest, caring, capable trainers. Hiring a dog trainer is an exercise where the buyer should be a bit wary and always makes sure to check references.

You can accomplish a lot of training on your own property, like this snappy retrieve down the driveway by an 8-month-old Springer.

Not every dog and pro will click. I've known more than a few dogs that bombed with one trainer, only to later be rescued and turned into a high-class performer by another. Most importantly, don't be intimidated by a pro. Ask lots of questions, check references, inspect the training grounds and facilities, review the sanitary conditions of the kennels, be specific about what you want and ask the estimated time and cost. Then ask if your expectations are realistic! Once you establish a good, open and trusting relationship with a reliable pro, you are likely to enjoy the benefits of a good hunting dog at all times.

To close this important topic, let's examine some of the myths that have developed over the years about the care of hunting dogs.

Myth: Bird dogs are too big, too crazy, too hyper, too aloof to be proper pets.

Not necessarily. Just carefully pick a breed that fits your home, family and lifestyle. You may have to compromise a little, but it can be done. English Cockers, springers, German Shorthairs, Brittanies, Labs and Goldens are frequently selected as pets. In fact, many prospective buyers visit the parents of the puppy they are considering to evaluate their personalities before purchase. More are owned as pets by nonhunters than by hunters!

Myth: Your travel schedule will confuse the dog, resulting in a neurotic, lonely, sad and confused dog.

Dogs adapt quickly to new surroundings. If the care is proper, your dog will learn to handle change easily. Under the right circumstances, a trip to the trainer is like a vacation for the dog.

Myth: Switching the dog from owner to wife to a pro trainer and back and forth will make training impossible.

Dogs respond to the handler in much the same way children respond differently to parents, teachers or grandparents. Several of my dogs will ignore commands from my wife but obey me. You do need to be sure family interaction doesn't ruin your hunting dog: no tug of war games with the kids, for instance.

Myth: Your family thinks all bird dogs are ugly.

Beauty is in the eye of the beholder. Be sure you see all the breeds and variations from bench and field stock. The real beauty of a dog is its personality, intellect and affection. Appearance is a fleeting criterion and a very superficial reason for selection.

Myth: Classical bird dogs come only from specific, traditional breeds.

The Ruffed Grouse Society's 1990 Minnesota championship was won by a pair of Labrador Retrievers. English Cockers were named for their woodcock ability. English Springers are often used to retrieve ducks and I've seen German Shorthairs retrieving doves. Don't let commonly held misconceptions slant your opinions.

Myth: A dog that lives in the house will not perform well in the field.

Many hunters live in suburban settings where "kennel only" dogs would be difficult, if not illegal. Many of the old theories that the highest dog performance can only be achieved by kennel dogs are simply out of date. Some national champion bird dogs spend their lives as everyday house dogs. A hunting friend, Ham Schirmer, keeps his high-powered English Setter, "Davis," in the house. Davis has even been trained to ignore a cocktail table laden with hors d'oeuvres. This high-powered setter has adjusted to house living while fully retaining his field intensity. Ham is a perfect example of a very busy executive who has learned how to keep a top-notch dog by using local boarding and nearby professional training facilities to share the care responsibility.

Harried people are used to research, planning and juggling a dozen priorities. You can have a high-performance bird dog if (1) Your family will embrace a pet dog; (2) You can select a breed that fits your lifestyle; (3) You have an easy, all-day care facility like an outdoor dog run; (4) You develop a painless boarding plan; (5) You find and plan an effective training system often including some paid professional help; and (6) You learn how to relax and enjoy this great sport wedged in between business and family demands, just like everything else.

ELECTRICITY

One last bit of advice. Busy people often look for shortcuts to cram more productivity into a busy day. An electric training collar has lots of appeal from that standpoint and may be able to overcome some of the training left undone due to a busy lifestyle. But be aware of the pitfalls.

One October, I was grouse hunting with an old pal in the beautiful golden hills of upstate New York. This chap had a bit of a hearing problem so he put a small cowbell on his big, shaggy, old Setter. As she loped along through the woods, anyone with normal hearing could hear her BONG! BONG! BONG! from a mile away. "Lulu" (not her real name) wasn't particularly attuned to her master and the only way he could hunt her productively was with an electric collar. Every hour or so, as she slipped back into her mode of ignoring his yells and whistles, he would pull out the transmitter, yell, "Lulu, damn you, come back here!" then give her a high-voltage jolt. Off in the distance she would let out a yelp and then the sound of the bell would gradually wind its way back to us.

After lunch we took off again, now hunting his other dog, "Mae" (not her name, either). About fifteen minutes into the hunt, Mae, too, was ignoring his whistle, so he decided to give her a little jolt, "just to get her attention." But when he pushed the button, far away in the truck we could hear Lulu wail, "Oooooooo!" My buddy had forgotten to switch the collar to his afternoon dog!

Electric collar stories abound in the dog training world, some funny, some catastrophic. I personally know of at least a dozen dogs that have been wrecked, totally ruined forever, by the improper use of a collar. I know of other dogs that could only be controlled by use of a collar, and when they were bred, their offspring could only be handled using a large dose of electricity. The electric collar is undoubtedly changing the face of the dog world.

I own a collar, two in fact, and I use them on occasion. My wife is a real softy with dogs, but she now believes that judicious and careful use of the collar in training is far more humane than a flushing whip, a fist or a boot. The key is that the dog has to know why it is being shocked.

TWO KINDS OF ELECTRIC COLLARS

Electric training collars come in two varieties: The old kind can be used to shock the dog in response to unwanted behavior, and the new kind can be used in a very sophisticated and somewhat complicated type of training called *avoidance training*. Both have their place.

The old models are widely available from a variety of manufacturers and are rightly known as "shock collars." I have mixed feelings about these. On one hand they are very valuable devices to keep a trained dog under control and obedient. In some cases they can save a dog's life by keeping it under control and out of harm's way. Many of the big-going pointing breeds are consistently hunted with electric collars to maintain control. Some are never let out of a truck without a collar. On the other hand, many handlers (these are not trainers in any sense) shock the dog too soon and too much, before it is fully trained and before it understands what it is expected to do.

The second type of collar is relatively new and expensive and is used for avoidance training. Currently these collars are made only by Tri-tronics. To greatly oversimplify, the collar is turned on and the dog receives an extremely mild and continuous stimulation that is turned off as soon as the dog begins to obey. When you command the dog to "Come!" as soon as the dog starts toward you, the stimulation is turned off. Thus, the dog learns how to "avoid" the stimulation. Once I owned a real nice, young male dog that did everything well. He was just a fine little hunting partner except he had one odd quirk that just drove me crazy. That dog would refuse to go into a travel crate and it didn't matter where the crate was located—back of the truck, sitting in the garage, on the driveway, in the house, didn't matter. He wouldn't go in! To make matters worse, he would run from me whenever he knew I was about to put him in a crate.

Sometimes it's the little things that really bug you and I had just about had it with this dog. I tried every method I could think of with no success and I had finally decided that I had chased him around a motel parking lot for the last time. He was destined for a new owner, when a friend suggested that he was a prime candidate for the new Tri-tronics electric avoidance training method. Well, I read the book three times before I started, then I read it again every day of the procedure. At the end of ten days (and without the collar on the dog) I could say "kennel" and he would run full speed for fifty feet and jump in a crate in the back of the truck. It sure worked in that situation.

This type of electric training is not simple (frankly neither was the old form), so anyone thinking about using avoidance training should attend a Tri-tronics seminar to learn the system. It is most important to properly "train the trainer" *before* the trainer trains the dog. All the experienced dog trainers I know (even veteran professionals) are impressed by the potential of this new device. However, if you are a do-it-yourselfer who hates reading or following instructions, beware! Tri-tronics can be reached at Tri-tronics Inc., 1650 S. Research Loops, PO Box 17660, Tucson, AZ 85731, telephone (800) 456-9494.

In both types of electric collars the danger lies in a quick-tempered trainer who lets go a stream of punishment without serious consideration for its consequences. Some of the very best dog trainers use the collars only sparingly and some of the best trainers I know were even better trainers when they were young and too broke to afford a collar so they couldn't shortcut proper preparation. I have a quick temper, so I have to be very, very careful how and when I use the collar. A collar is a very powerful thing and in the wrong hands will very quickly undo a promising animal. I once saw a very high-potential field trial English Setter that had won numerous puppy and derby titles become so intimidated that it began to blink birds after it was excessively punished by a heavy-fingered trainer. The new avoidance training method offers some real hope for hard-to-train situations and I view it as a real breakthrough for the studious trainer who is really willing to patiently and carefully learn its use.

CHAPTER 21
THE BRITISH CONNECTION: INTERVIEWS WITH KEITH ERLANDSON AND ALAN GYWNNE

Many of our sporting breeds originated in the British Isles: the Pointer, the three setters, English Springer Spaniels, English Cocker Spaniels and almost all of the lesser-known spaniels. Keith Erlandson, who lives in Wales, is known worldwide for his outspoken opinions on everything relating to gun dogs and hunting. I asked him to update us on the current state of the British sporting dog scene.

KEITH ERLANDSON

Dog Trainer, Dog Writer, Dog Broker
Llangollen, Wales, United Kingdom

A man of Scandinavian heritage, Keith Erlandson has lived in the northeast corner of Wales for all of his adult life and has trained and brokered some of the world's best dogs. *Brokered* means he can see a dog's talents and watch the way it works for its owner and from that find a suitable buyer for that dog; sometimes half way around the world. This is a practice very common in art, race horses and real estate, but not one fully understood in shooting dogs. In addition, Keith breeds, raises and trains dogs, judges field trials, authors books and is a prolific writer for British sporting magazines such as *Shooting Times.*

What I find most intriguing about Keith is his worldwide understanding of the gun dog scene, but even more importantly, his willingness to speak the truth (or his interpretation of the truth) regardless of the personal consequences.

Please describe how retrievers and pointing dogs are used in the United Kingdom as compared to American practices. How popular are the various breeds in Britain today?

ERLANDSON—*Retrievers:* The prime function of a retriever in Britain is to sit quietly while its well-heeled master shoots driven pheasants, partridges or grouse over it. At

Keith Erlandson with a German Shorthaired Pointer named "Krupp."

pheasant drives, a retriever's function might be more decorative than practical as many birds will fall dead onto open pasture or winter wheat, wounded birds being picked up by paid help behind the firing line with their retrievers and spaniels. On a grouse moor, the shooter's retriever will be more useful to him, as many grouse will fall into heather where the dead and wounded birds are hidden from view and require a dog's nose to find them. Many roughshooters use Labradors to hunt up and flush game for the gun, but the spaniels rapidly are gaining ground. Many Labradors will reliably stay close to heel while the gamekeeper is distracted by giving orders to his helpers and telling the shooters where to go.

Pointing dogs: One could write a whole book on how the Pointer and the English, Irish and Gordon Setters all developed in the British Isles, then spread to practically every part of the world wherever hunters pursue winged, upland game, yet in Britain have almost declined to the vanishing point as hunter's dogs. In the words of an Irish Setter fan friend, "the nearer to the Church, the further away from God." Just a few bird pointing dogs continue to find employment in the north of Scotland where grouse numbers never reached high proportions and where a good wide-running dog is needed to find limited game. But it is the field trial people who have kept our bird pointing dogs alive. The field trial lobby of bird pointing dog enthusiasts is strange indeed. Very few of them are hunters.

The English Pointer finds a grouse in the heather, but Erlandson explains that English Pointers are no longer common in the land of their origin.

A truly mixed bag from a British roughshoot: hare, rabbits, red grouse and a black grouse.

Most don't own a shotgun and they train for trials. As hunting dogs, the true bird pointing dogs have lost ground to the Continental/versatile breeds.

Both the Pointer and the English Setter have obviously British origins but don't seem to be very popular in the United Kingdom today. Why?

ERLANDSON—*Pointer and English Setter*: On the low ground, farming patterns have changed, which has been disastrous for gray partridge (Huns) survival. The farmlands became more open and partridges would no longer lie for bird dogs. Also, Britain is much smaller than France or North America and in the South where it is intensively farmed, we don't have large areas of rough land where a bird dog could quarter its ground wide and fast and find pheasants.

Some Americans are beginning to use retriever breeds (Labradors, Goldens and Chesapeakes) for roughshooting. These dogs are expected to reach out and quest for game and run a pattern ahead of the hunter in search of game. How do you feel about that?

ERLANDSON—The important function of any hunting dog is that it should perform the desired function to the satisfaction of its master and with the minimum amount of irritation. As the French would say, "Chacun a son gout" (everyone to his own taste). The bottom line in all gun dog work is the bird in the bag. How it gets there is unimportant provided the hunter derives pleasure from putting it there, then enjoys eating it when he gets it home. From my point of view, being a purist in these matters, I don't care to shoot over a questing retriever. For close-range work, I want to see a spaniel hunting in front of me with rapid, dashing style. If any of my friends in the States are happy to use a retriever for upland game hunting and "get after the son of a bitch," who am I to say they have got it all wrong?

Why are Labrador Retrievers so popular with gamekeepers in the UK?

ERLANDSON—In Britain, Labradors generally are complacent animals and not at all hyped-up as rumor suggests many American field trial Labradors are. They fit in well with a gamekeeper's daily work. Always ready to sit down and stay, they make excellent "picking-up" dogs, collecting lost birds and cripples on big-driven game shoots.

The English Cocker Spaniel has recently seen an upturn in interest in the United States and is being imported here in greater and greater numbers. Field trials for Cockers are again in vogue. For what type of a hunter is the Cocker most appropriate?

ERLANDSON—I have exported a limited number of working Cockers to the United States over a twenty-year period. A Cocker can do anything for the upland bird hunter that a Springer can in the game finding and retrieving departments but normally works closer, and so gives a better chance on ruffed grouse or woodcock. They stand a warm climate better than a Springer owing to greater heat loss, but care must be taken when working in water at low temperatures as heat loss can then work against them.

Keith Erlandson, a world-renowned Welsh gun dog trainer, lives high on a mountainside above the Dee Valley. He is shown here with a pair of English Springer Spaniel puppies. The well-burned grouse moors are about the only place in the British Isles where a far-reaching pointing dog can use its range. Burning the moors seems to be an essential management practice to preserve proper grouse habitat.

An English Setter and a Pointer about to be turned loose on a grouse moor.

Are there many Continental pointing breed (Brittany, German Shorthaired Pointer, German Wirehaired Pointer) dogs in Britain at the present time and, if so, how are they used?

ERLANDSON—In 1993, registrations at the Kennel Club for the Continental versatile breeds were as follows: Bracco Italiano 1; Brittany 87; German Shorthaired Pointer 1,016; German Wirehaired Pointer 208; Hungarian Vizsla 323; Italian Spinone 263; Large Musterlander 108; Weimaraner 1,609. These figures, although not large, are deceptive, as a high proportion of those registered are show dogs that never work. We have few handlers who are real specialists with the versatiles and this is borne out by the fact that a championship stake has only been held about eight times for these breeds.

Increasingly, Americans are training dogs using an electric collar. Are electric collars used in Great Britain, and what is your opinion of them?

ERLANDSON—I regard electric collars as an abomination, and even though it is now claimed that the modern devices are less severe, the continued use could mean that strains could develop that required electricity to train them. I'll be damned if I want a transmitter as part of my normal training gear. Regrettably, they are used over here now in increasing numbers and I don't like it. The great dogs of the past made it without them.

This book is mainly about roughshooting—walk-up hunting in heavy cover. How much of that is done in England and for what game species? Is it accomplished in virtually the same manner as in the United States?

ERLANDSON—There is quite a lot of roughshooting done in Britain and Ireland, and the most common quarry species are the pheasant and the rabbit. Woodcock are much esteemed when available as being largely migratory and the same applies to snipe. As one goes further north, hill partridges frequently live on the margins of the grouse moors in rushy pastures. Under such conditions the bag could comprise pheasant, rabbit, brown hare, arctic hare, gray partridge (Hun), red grouse, black grouse, snipe, woodcock and if there are any wet places, mallard and teal. The major difference in the United States is that if you have similar terrain available, the English Setter doubtless would play a major part, whereas here the dogs used would be Spaniels and versatiles.

Most of the field-bred English Springer Spaniels in the United States show a significant number of English dogs in their pedigrees. Because Spaniels are the predominant hunting dogs in England, a significant gene pool of field-type Springers and Cockers exists there. The English Cocker is undergoing a significant resurgence of popularity in the United States and most of the dogs are recent imports from the United Kingdom. Alan Gwynne raises both English Springers and English Cockers in Wales. I asked Alan to answer a few questions about the spaniels he ships to the United States.

ALAN GWYNNE

Spaniel Breeder
Llandeilo, Dyfed, Wales, United Kingdom

To call Alan Gwynne a soft-spoken Welshman is a bit of an understatement. Alan and Jean, his wife of thirty years, live in a charming hundred-year-old shepherd's cottage, tucked into a high green ridge in southern Wales. From here it is only an hour to the sea at Swansea, but the ridges still run hard through the lush green of the Welsh countryside. The winding roads pass through such well-known names as Llandrindod Wells and Powas Castle.

The Gwynnes' home's exterior quaintness belies an immaculate, modern interior and everything in the house and buildings is carefully in its place. If one is lucky enough to have the time for a leisurely visit, Jean may fix her specialty, a home-grown lamb roasted in mint sauce; it's the best I've tasted anywhere in the world.

Many of the very best gun dogs don't come from the big breeding kennels, but rather from very purposeful and focused hobby breeders who only produce one or two litters per year. Such people often focus on trying to match the dog or puppy to the needs and personality of the buyer, and in the long run the results are excellent. The Gwynnes match that profile, a small but conscientious breeding operation.

Alan and Jean Gwynne both tend to busy pharmaceutical drug sales

Alan Gwynne, shown in the sheep pasture on a farm in the south of Wales, is with a well-trained Springer. Alan and his wife, Jean, have exported many quality Springer and Cocker Spaniels to the United States for hunting and field trialing.

jobs by day and play with the dogs in the evening. It is a combination hobby and labor of love that has earned the Gwynnes a strong reputation in the United States for supplying high-quality spaniels, both English Springers and English Cockers.

You have been selling spaniels, both Cockers and Springers, to Americans for quite a while and based on your clients' reactions, you should have a pretty fair assessment of your success at matching their needs. Do most of your clients want a dog for hunting or for field trialing?

GWYNNE—I suppose, over the years, it's been about fifty-fifty, but with the high cost of shipping, etc., the ones to be used for hunting tend to be people with a good background knowledge of the breed who know what they're looking for.

Is there a major difference in the type of dog you would send to an American field trialer versus an American hunter?

GWYNNE—Yes, most definitely. The field trialer wants a high-performance animal, an athletic dog that has what it takes both physically and mentally to compete at the highest levels. To compare it with motor cars, he'd be looking for the Formula One racing model as opposed to the family sedan. He's also very concerned about the pedigree of the dog. The hunting man is more concerned about the temperament of the dog and how he'll fit in with his family. He's looking for a companion as much as an efficient working dog.

What if I told you that I only planned to hunt grouse and especially woodcock; would that make a difference in the dog you selected for my needs?

GWYNNE—Yes, it would make a big difference. I'm lucky that where I live here in Wales we probably have the highest concentration of woodcock of anywhere in the United Kingdom. Consequently, I've learned that the dog best suited for this type of hunting will have plenty of drive in hard cover and is prepared to hunt all day without much evidence of game scent to encourage him. In other words, I'd be looking for a stayer rather than a sprinter.

At what age is a fully trained dog ready to be shipped to the United States?

GWYNNE—I normally like my dogs to be at least eighteen months old before I ship them to the United States. By this time I've had time to assess them properly and give them the sort of training they're going to need.

When I visited you in Wales I was quite surprised at how you were able to limit the working range of your dogs. How do you teach a level of control that limits the dogs to that range?

GWYNNE—Yes, I do like my dogs to hunt close and to win field trials; over here this is what you have to do. I like my pups to have as much freedom as they like until they're about ten months old, to develop their confidence, balance and enthusiasm. However, when their serious training begins, I like to hunt them into the wind in light cover and with voice and whistle encourage them to stay close. When they don't respond, I blow my whistle and move very quickly toward them. This has the effect of making them realize unless they respond instantly, in just seconds I'll be right out there alongside them. They soon get the message that it makes more sense to stay in close than to have a six-foot Welshman bearing down on them!

I know you export both Springers and Cockers to the United States; is there a major difference in how the two breeds perform?

GWYNNE—The biggest difference I find in the two breeds is that a springer (generally) is prepared to hunt for scent, whereas a Cocker performs best *on* scent. What I mean by this is that most suitably bred Springers are prepared to run for the pure joy of it, and only learn to find game at a later stage. The Cocker performs better when his nose tells him there is recent evidence of game being around. I also generally find the Cocker to be a better natural retriever than a Springer. I believe pound for pound the cocker is physically stronger than the Springer, but I often think their mental attitude has a lot to do with it. The Cocker is a tough little dog.

Is there a difference in how the two breeds are trained?

GWYNNE—My training of both breeds is very much the same. However, I find I'm able to free-hunt my Springers before the serious discipline work starts and they're prepared to then accept the change. The Cocker shouldn't generally be allowed much free hunting, otherwise you find he's not prepared to accept the discipline side of the training, which is vital before you can produce a complete dog.

When I visited your kennel in Wales you demonstrated how you used rabbits to help the dogs' hunting ability. Is there any downside to using rabbits to train spaniels for game birds?

GWYNNE—I don't think there is any substitute for rabbits in developing a spaniel's hunting ability. However, everything in moderation! It's vital that he's also given sufficient experience on birds, otherwise things like his marking ability will never develop, and he'll hunt with a low head carriage and will always be hunting for foot scent instead of body scent.

What is the size difference between Springers and Cockers? Are the field strains and the show strains very different in England?

GWYNNE—There is a substantial size difference between Springers and cockers. Ideally I like my Cockers to weigh twenty-five to twenty-eight pounds, and the Springers about 50 percent bigger. Our field and show strains are so different they could be different breeds. The field strains tend to be smaller and much more athletic than the show types.

Is there much American-style "walk-up" roughshooting in Wales?

GWYNNE—Most people in Wales who shoot over spaniels tend to be "walk-up." The type of terrain in Wales lends itself to this type of hunting and I think this is the type of work a spaniel is intended for.

What is your kennel name so we can recognize it in pedigrees?

GWYNNE—Windmillwood. This was the name of the small farm I was born on and where I grew up, and I decided to stick with this, as it reminds me of my "roots."

PART III
GUNS AND SHOOTING

CHAPTER 22
DEFINING A GAME GUN

I once observed an English hunter pick up a long-barreled Browning over-under being shot by an American at a field trial. "My god!" he exclaimed, "This isn't a game gun, it's an artillery piece!"

Game gun is a term used frequently and improperly by Americans without real knowledge of its definition. In traditional parlance, *game gun* is an English term for a gun designed and dimensioned specifically for shooting live, flying game. In England, where guns were carefully designed for this singular usage, traditionally a game gun was a side-by-side of very light weight, usually under 6 1/2 pounds, even in 12 bore. Such a gun was specifically built to handle and shoulder quickly and to point where the shooter's eye sees in order to maximize hand/eye coordination and allow for instinctive shooting.

Some of the most pointed comments concerning the selection of game guns were written by Capt. Paul A. Curtis in the book *Guns and Gunning*, written in 1934 and published by the Penn Publishing Company and *Outdoor Life*. He wrote:

> The most unfortunate thing the American gunner has to contend with is his ingrained preference for heavy guns, which has been encouraged by the gunmakers, as it is easier to make a strong but cheap heavy gun than an equally strong light one. They form the habit of using heavy loads in these ponderous weapons so that when a light weight 12 bore gun falls into their hands they naturally feed it the same fodder, and immediately condemn the light gun because it kicks so viciously. As a result our sportsmen are nineteen times out of twenty over-gunned and carrying around with them about a pound to a pound and a half more metal than is necessary.

Captain Curtis was obviously a man of strong opinion and his book is fun reading.

The game gun's light weight and quick handling traits, which make it ideal for wing shooting, also make it naturally a bit punishing when shooting skeet or trap or when loaded with magnum shells.

The early American doubles (side-by-sides) in many ways followed the lines of English side-by-sides except that American guns tended to be substantial with large pistol grip stocks and splinter fore-ends, a combination that was not always ideal for hand alignment or hand-to-hand relationships. In addition, older American doubles traditionally have long barrels, often thirty inches, conservatively constructed and thick-walled, which tend to make them a bit barrel heavy. A high percentage of these big, older guns, although collectibles, did not fit the definition of a game gun any more than a beautiful old 1939 Packard can be called a sports car.

Game guns of the British variety are a distinct pleasure to shoot and carry. This Cogswell and Harrison 12 bore weighs only six pounds, and is choked cylinder right and modified left. This gun, by a midlevel London maker, is fully engraved and well equipped, including ejectors and a self-opening mechanism.

The hand-to-hand relationship of any gun affects the ease with which you point to where your eye looks. If both hands are on the same plane, it is easier for the hands to work in concert and hence, to point at the target. But if your hands are out of alignment, subconscious muscle memory can continually misalign them. This is why English (straight stocks) or tiny Prince of Wales stocks are generally matched with splinter fore-ends on side-by-side guns. Deep frame design over-unders, like the Belgium Brownings or auto loaders with large hand-filling fore-ends, almost always have a substantial pistol grip to align the hand-to-hand relationship.

When a gun is barrel heavy, as many older American guns are, it results in a slow pointing and less agile gun. Heavy-barreled guns are often harder to accelerate or slow down, to keep them on an undulating target like wild birds dipping and swirling and weaving through the trees. The very attribute that makes long-barreled trap and skeet guns so effective—their momentum and consistent movement once the barrel is swinging—makes them much less responsive for tracking the movement of wild birds in flight.

The opposite of a slow-moving, barrel-heavy gun is a tiny little light-barreled or ultrashort-barreled gun that moves so easily that the hands and muscles overpower it. A gun that responds to any minute input of force is said to be "whippy"; excessively responsive to the handler's efforts. It takes a very accomplished and calm shooter to properly handle a whippy gun without overpowering it.

In general, game guns handle best when the gun is properly balanced, that is, when the weight is centered between the hands: a gun that is neither barrel-heavy nor butt-heavy. The extra three to five inches of length in the receiver of a pump or automatic gun and the heavy production line barrels of such guns move the barrel weight just that much further forward, making most of them a bit barrel-heavy or at least making the goal of "between the hands" balance harder to achieve. It is not easy to define one measure that determines if a gun is properly balanced. However, gun-makers have known for years that such a balance is most easily achieved in a double gun with medium length barrels (usually twenty-eight inches).

Finally, you are going to walk many miles in a day of roughshooting, at all times trying to be ready to instantly snap the gun into place for a quick shot. To make this as comfortable as possible, a gun needs to be easily carried. Rarely is this mentioned, but it is an important factor in the pleasure one derives from a day of shooting and the success one achieves in the process. A gun that fits the body, the hand, the crook of the arm, the shoulder and feels good all day is part of the definition of a "game gun" and a significant part of the pleasure of roughshooting.

In the end, only a lightweight, well-balanced and properly dimensioned gun meets all the criteria to truly be called a game gun.

GUN FIT

Most Americans never in their life hold, shoulder or shoot a gun that fits them *perfectly* and matches their physique in weight, balance and length of barrels. The average shooter either doesn't know that a gun can be adjusted, cut or bent to fit him, or he has an absolute paranoia about having a gun modified for fear of diminishing its value. Gun fit is much more important in hunting than it is in the clay bird games of trap and skeet, where the gun is shouldered and fixed before the "pull" of the clay bird. In sporting clays and real hunting you snap the gun to your shoulder and fire, so it must fit naturally and be on target when it comes up. Knowledgeable shooting instructors such as Rex Gage will explain that in a snap shooting situation, when the gun is instantly and reflexively snapped to the shoulder, pointed and fired, gun fit is essential.

Fit is obviously affected by your overall physical measurements. While some people can wear a suit right off the rack, most people can't. If you are average in every way, you will probably shoot a gun of average dimensions fairly well. But if you are tall or short, lean or heavy, or have a unique shooting style, gun fit may be very important to your hitting ability.

I wouldn't worry much about diminishing your gun's value. It is true that a radical or oddball stock alteration of an irreparable nature will hurt the value of the gun. An example would be cutting the stock length to less than fourteen inches. Somehow fourteen inches seems to be a magic number, but it is quite rare for an average-size American to need a stock much shorter than this. However, even a stock cut to less than fourteen inches, say 13 1/2 inches or even thirteen inches, would probably reduce the gun's value by a maximum of 25 percent. You need to put gun value into perspective. You will fly to a hunting area of your choice, rent a car, wear $500 worth of clothes and boots, stay in a good motel, eat quality food—all of which will add up to about $1,000

Here Pat Leiske analyzes the fit of George Wilson's new Beretta Sporting Clays over-under. He uses the same method as most gun fitters to view where the gun comes up instinctively. NEVER DO THIS WITHOUT CHECKING TO SEE THAT THE GUN IS UNLOADED. Only well-trained specialists are able to properly fit a gun; unfortunately that skill is woefully rare in the United States.

per week, but you won't get your gun altered to fit you because it would reduce the value of a $1,000 shotgun by $250? Think about it! If you ever shoot a gun that fits you like a glove, you will never want to go back to a rack gun.

Another very realistic alternative is to scour the gun shops and gun ads for a gun that has already been modified to your dimensions. If those dimensions are really unusual, when you do find a gun that fits, you may be able to buy it at a bargain price. I once was able to purchase a neat little 16-bore English side-by-side that had had the stock shortened for a woman. I paid substantially less than its unaltered market value, then had a good gunsmith extend the stock with a spacer. Then he bent it to my prescribed drop and castoff and I now use it as my favorite grouse gun. It fits me superbly, so I am shooting a high-quality game gun at a bargain price. Due to the short stock and its already well-used state, it will never qualify as a collector's item, but I've collected many memories with the gun. That counts for a lot.

Getting a gun properly fitted and altered in the United States takes some effort. It's not something you trust to the gunsmith down at the local discount store, especially if it is a high-grade double gun. You need to meet with the fitter personally, perhaps at a shooting range. Bring your gun and allow enough time to let him determine your correct dimensions. Every fitter uses a slightly different method. I was first fitted by Rex Gage, a crusty old Englishman who worked many years in England as a shooting instructor for Holland and Holland. Rex then spent the years before his retirement touring the United States, conducting shooting schools at some of our best gun and hunting clubs. Rex fitted me on a sporting clays course in Michigan. He stood about ten feet from me and had me snap the gun into place, pointed directly at his nose (the gun was unloaded, of course). Then he measured my gun, watched me do some shooting and then repeated the "point it at my nose" routine. From this he could tell how the gun I was shooting fitted me and what alterations were needed to point at his nose instinctively. He scribbled my prescription on the back of his card and I took it to a properly certified gunsmith to have it filled. My dimensions have since been confirmed by some other gun fitters and haven't changed much over the last fifteen years. I find it is much easier to shoot a variety of guns if they all have the same basic dimensions.

SAFETIES

I'm sort of a nut about gun safeties. They serve a very basic need and most of us would absolutely refuse to go afield with a gun if we knew it had no safety or a defective safety.

Actually, at one time some extremely high-grade guns were produced without safeties, for live pigeon shoots. In these cases the shooter did not

Here the breech of the Darne is open to accept shells. The Darne is a lightweight, great handling game gun but the unusual safety makes its usage very difficult for surprise shots.

want to risk the chance that a mispositioned safety could spoil a critical shot; hence, *no* safety. When the gun was closed it was ready to fire.

While most of us are quite familiar with the safety of our own gun, few people have seen all the many configurations of safeties available on various brands of guns. If you've hunted far and wide and with many partners you will recall at least a few times when a shot was missed and the shooter admitted to fumbling with the safety. Perhaps this was because the safety was balky, or because the safety was in an unfamiliar location. Perhaps the shooter's finger simply didn't move to it naturally, as a reflex, or perhaps the button was too small and the finger slipped past it.

One gun that I love is a French-made Darne side-by-side of a unique sliding breech design. I love the fit and feel of the little Darne, but the safety is not only in an inconvenient location, but it is so tiny that my clumsy fingers won't work it. For that reason even though I have a Darne in the closet, I almost never hunt with the gun; what a shame.

By far the most common safety is the trigger guard type found on most semiautomatics and pump guns. Some are in front of the trigger while others are in the rear of the trigger guard, as is this one on a Remington 1100.

I grew up shooting a gun with the safety on the top tang. That location is so natural to me and so easy for me to reach, that I release it instinctively. One time in my midlife I tried hunting with an automatic with the safety down on the trigger guard. In the excitement of the flush, the millisecond of delay while I fumbled with the safety usually meant a missed shot. For instinctive snap shooting you want to minimize every needless obstacle.

Safeties are usually either on the top tang (side-by-sides and over-unders) or on the trigger guard (pumps and auto loaders). Either works well, but mixing the two usually leads to lots of fumbling, delays and missed birds. The gun you select must have a safety you can operate easily. Some guns have top tang safeties that also function as the barrel selector. By sliding the button left or right the barrel is selected, then by sliding the safety button forward the safety is removed. The safety can hang up if moved incorrectly, potentially causing a hesitation. The solution is simple: pick a type of safety and then buy only guns in that format.

W.W. Greener, the legendary gunmaker, got patent number 1,623 and 1,877 for the side safety. Many of the older Greener guns are equipped with this safety and it works very well once the shooter learns to use it instinctively. Both the gun and the hand in this picture belong to Barry Noland of Ontario, Canada, and he shoots the gun very well indeed.

The top tang safety, common on most side-by-sides and over-unders, is familiar and can be operated by reflex even when changing guns.

AN ALL-DAY GUN

Obviously you will be lugging that six, seven or even eight pounds of gun all the hunting day long, and because of that, many books and articles discuss gun weight as a key factor in hunting fatigue. In response, many shooters opt for small-gauge guns. Most assume that the smaller the gauge the lower the weight. But do your homework. Recently I read a lengthy article about the wonderful attributes of a new European-made 28-gauge over-under. The article filled several pages with data and statistics, but subtly buried in the text was the fact that the 28 gauge weighs more than the same model 20 gauge by the same maker! In fact, the 28-gauge weighs 6 1/4 pounds! What is the reasoning? Weight is important in a game gun, and a 28 gauge that weighs more than most 16-gauge guns and as much as some 12's doesn't make much sense.

Just as surprisingly, aside from weight, I have rarely seen much reference to how comfortable the gun is to carry, hold or cradle all day long. Maybe it is not mentioned because it is such a subjective discussion, for seemingly there is no way to measure or put numbers on the "*comfortable to carry*" factor. What is most comfortable to one shooter may be unbearable to another. I reiterate that we are not talking about shooting attributes here. This discussion is about how a gun fits your hands, the curve of your elbow, lays back against your shoulder or balances in one hand as you walk along all day.

Some of my best shooting guns, guns that come up naturally and point well, just don't carry well. I currently own two side-by-sides of mid-1960s vintage that are both sweet-shooting, easy-pointing, hard-hitting guns, but for some reason neither carries well. By 10 A.M. I am always fidgeting for a more comfortable hand hold. By nightfall I can't wait to put the gun in the case. Although both guns weigh only 6 1/2 pounds and are well balanced for shooting, I find their bulky, hand-filling pistol grips and loaf-of-bread, beavertail fore-ends carry poorly, for me. Others of my guns must be better suited to my hand size and stature because I can carry them all day with minimal carrying fatigue. In my case a very slim oval hand grip on the butt stock and a slim splinter fore-end seem to go a long way toward carrying comfort. You may find that a different combination of stock and fore-end is the most pleasant to you. But carrying comfort is a personal thing.

I have never, ever heard of a gun purchaser who asked the dealer to "Let me walk around carrying this gun for an hour or so to see if it is comfortable," but that makes a lot of sense for a roughshooter. Gun carrying comfort is a far more important attribute than is generally acknowledged.

HOW MANY GUNS?

How many guns does a roughshooter really need? The question, although a legitimate one, is better stated as, How many *game guns* does one hunter really need for American roughshooting? The answer is simple: *one*!

There is an old English saying, most likely coined in the 1800s, to "Beware the man who shoots only one gun." Shooting only one gun has distinct advantages, and these advantages are enhanced if the gun is perfectly suited and fitted to the shooter and reasonably matched in gauge, weight and chokes to the task at hand. In many cases the *one gun* would be a compromise, a little too short-barreled and too lightweight to be a great pheasant gun and a little too long-barreled and heavy to be a great quail or woodcock gun. However, it is possible to have one all-around gun of surprising adaptability to different game situations. There is much to be said for the value of familiarity in fit, balance, safety position and muscle memory, so using one very familiar gun that is slightly mismatched to the task is probably more effective than several guns each perfectly matched to the task but each a bit unfamiliar in the hands of the shooter.

Within the last decade a major gun innovation has been perfected completely: the screw-in choke. For years these lightweight little tubes were available only in factory installations, but now they are widely installed by some of the more competent gunsmith services in older guns. The use of choke tubes instantly tailors the gun to the task so that today more than ever, one gun can be used for a wide variety of shooting situations.

Unfortunately, using one gun would mean giving up the thrill of buying another beautiful or interesting gun and I could no longer justify owning a collection of good guns, which is one of the greatest pleasures of shooting.

I don't heed the one-gun advice. Personally, I shoot several different game guns in roughshooting, sometimes two or three in the same day. To me that's part of the fun of the sport and although I acknowledge that I'd probably shoot better if I picked just one and stuck with it every day, I'd miss playing with my toys.

So the question has two answers. For shooting? A roughshooter needs only one well-fitted and reasonably adaptable game gun. But for interest and the satisfaction of collecting a trove of treasures, one lonely gun may not fulfill the psychic needs of many hunters.

KNOWING WHY A GUN WORKS

Some gun lovers feel they need to know every detail of how and why their guns function. They do research into the most minute background facts and to a great extent they become collectors and statisticians as well as hunters or shooters. While that can be great fun, some of the best hunters and shooters I know simply find a gun that fits properly and that they can point on target instantly by reflex. All they know about a gun is how to load it, point it and pull the trigger. You need not know all the ins, outs, complexities, statistics, design subtleties and nuances to be a great shooter—just as one need not be an automotive engineer to be a good driver. At least half of the success you will have with any gun is your own confidence. If you love the heft and balance of a certain gun and if in your hands it feels perfect, if it gives you confidence and if you think you could shoot a perfect round with this fowling piece—you very well might! Confidence is a powerful ally.

CHAPTER 23
SELECTING A GAME GUN

LESSONS FROM THE OLD LEFEVER

I was one of those leading-edge baby boomers who was handed off Grandpa's old double-barrel when Dad, home from the big war, bought a new Remington, Browning or Winchester pump or automatic. In 1950 new pumps and autoloaders were in vogue, as the high-style "way to go." Pheasants were plentiful in the Midwest, so a third or fourth or fifth shot was highly valued. Few of those World War II veterans, freshly back from years of sleeping with an M-1 and hungry for new-fangled technology, would have believed then that the basic design of grandpa's old side-by-side would ever again be acceptable. I have heard stories from the 1950s when old Parkers and Smiths were piled in the corners of gun shops, unsold even at $5 or $10. But all those old side-by-sides, even while sitting in a dusty closet, contained the germ of gun design genius that still makes them the finest live bird hunting guns ever made.

When my father was ready to teach me to hunt rabbits, squirrels and quail at age ten, Grandpa's old 20-gauge Lefever side-by-side was relegated to me while Dad sallied forth sporting a shiny new Mosberg. My mother frankly considered even the bargain basement Mosberg to be a needless extravagance, considering that my dad already had one gun in the closet, albeit Grandpa's. I, of course, lusted after that Mosberg. Although I was glad to be taken along—glad to be learning to hunt, glad to be trusted with a gun—I always wanted to shoot the best gun: the Mosberg. It was years later before I realized that I had indeed learned to hunt with our "best gun"; not just the best gun but the safest and most reliable gun in our closet, too!

When Grandpa died several years ago, his old Lefever, which had already been in my closet for thirty years, officially became my permanent property, and I still shoot it on occasion. Surprisingly, I seem to hit with it as well as any gun I own, so perhaps muscle memory really does win out in the end.

The only reliable method for checking the constriction in a barrel is with a choke gauge. It is fast and easy and most good gun shops routinely stock such gauges. Cylinder bore is "0.0" constriction, while a full choke is about .030 in a 12-gauge gun.

I learned a lot from that old Lefever, like an understanding that most hunters overchoke their guns. After I had used the gun for fifteen years or so and shot it at everything that flew, including big Iowa pheasants and even a few ducks, I got a surprise. One night while cleaning the gun I carefully examined the ends of the barrels and noticed a few signs that indicated that they had been cut off. Somehow I had overlooked this for all these years while thinking that it had factory chokes; maybe improved cylinder/modified or even modified/full. I immediately called Grandpa to ask if the gun had ever been modified. "Oh, sure," he said. "I bought that gun back during the Depression to hunt quail on Wednesday afternoons with my card playing buddies," he explained. "First trip out I missed every bird. I was real embarrassed, so I came home, took it down to my shop and hacksawed two inches off the barrels. Near as I could tell I sawed off all of the chokes." He fairly beamed through the phone, "But I didn't miss many quail after that."

That was an eye-opener. For years I'd heard these complex arguments about chokes and watched people worry about having the wrong gun for the job; or feverishly screwing and unscrewing their Cutts chokes. All the time I had been shooting grouse, woodcock, quail, pheasants and even ducks with a gun with cylinder bore barrels and a 20 gauge at that! That experience convinced me that most Americans are far too concerned about chokes and tend to err on the side of *too much* choking in their field guns.

The next lesson I learned from the old Lefever had to do with gun fit. That gun fit me to a tee. When it touched my shoulder it was on target! The gun, by luck or by heredity, fit me. "Gun fit" is a subject that the average American gunner has never worried much about. Later, when I knew enough to measure the stock, I learned that it was fairly short (about

13 7/8 inches) and had a lot of drop at the heel. By chance, this was a fair match to my five-foot, nine-inch stature, stocky build and full face. My current stature is not all that much different from that of my grandfather when he picked the gun off a hardware store rack back in the 1930s. It fit him then and it still fits me fairly well. However, if I stood six feet, six inches, was thin, long-armed and lean-faced, this gun would be a disaster for me to shoot. Most Americans try guns off the rack and then "accept" the dimensions of the one that feels good.

Today, I have a carefully defined set of stock dimensions that I try to match in my game guns. Although my ideal gun dimensions may change slightly as I age, I expect to reach old age with guns that still fit fairly well.

Another lesson I learned from my grandfather's old Lefever was to withhold judgment on barrel length. For years while shooting only the Lefever, I was convinced that barrels longer than twenty-six inches (the Lefever's altered state) were detrimental to good shooting, needlessly clumsy and out-of-date. I have now grown to understand the value of longer (or shorter) barrels for different purposes. The key, of course, is balance, swinging style and in the end, handling characteristics. The proper length of barrels is a function of hunters' build and size and the quarry being pursued. The appropriate gun for a fellow who stands six feet three inches and weighs 230 pounds is different than for a five-foot, eight-inch, 150-pound shooter.

A significant lesson from the Lefever had to do with the gun itself, its level of finish and its inherent value. The Lefever started life as a basic, assembly-line field grade gun. It wasn't worth much even when new and the hacksawed barrels further reduced its market value to almost nothing. The years of hunting, traveling and storage have left their marks, including thin bluing, no case colors, worn checkering, numerous scratches and a few dents. The old Lefever helped me come to understand that the visual condition of the gun does not effect the gun's basic and inherent handling and shooting characteristics. The Lefever Nitro Special was never a masterpiece, but it is fairly well balanced. Its lack of artistry and its plain, outward appearance do not affect its shooting characteristics one whit. Thus, I am always a bit surprised when a shooter chooses to use a gun that fits poorly and is ill suited to the purpose, but is selected for its beautiful wood or intricate engraving. For the same price a hunter could have a gun of more durable design: well balanced, sleek, well fitted, but with less artistic embellishment or a worn level of finish. Such a thought process is tantamount to a symphony musician selecting his instrument based on its beauty rather than its tonal qualities or playability.

The final lesson from the Lefever was how to shoot and enjoy the feel of a side-by-side shotgun. All the muscle memories of my youth and my view of a rising bird naturally include the feel of a side-by-side game gun. Side-by-sides are not for everyone, but for those that love them they are the only gun.

In summary, what did I learn from the old Lefever?

1. CHOKES ARE LESS IMPORTANT THAN BEING ON TARGET, and most Americans shoot guns with too much choke.

2. GUN FIT IS A VERY PERSONAL MATTER. Few Americans ever consider gun fit as a part of the shooting equation but it is the essence of maximum gun enjoyment.

3. BARREL LENGTH MUST BE CORRELATED TO THE OVERALL BALANCE OF THE FIREARM. Too short, too long and just right all depend on the ultimate usage, the total package, the balance of the gun and the build of the shooter.

4. BEAUTY IS ONLY SKIN DEEP; it is the inherent balance, handling and quality of a gun that really counts. Bluing, case coloring and varnish are nice but not essential.

5. JUST BECAUSE IT IS NEW DOESN'T MAKE IT BETTER. My father's once-new Mosberg is now lost somewhere in the attic, but Grandpa's old Lefever is still in my gun case ready to be used.

ONE-BARREL GUNS

Every year millions of game birds are shot in the United States using one-barrel guns, or at least it seems that this should be the case. Certainly more one-barrel guns have been sold over the years than all the side-by-sides and over-unders combined. One-barrel guns have several advantages, but their main attractiveness is their low initial cost and relatively durable construction. Such field guns are rarely collectors' items, so they can be hunted without worry about scratches or dings lowering their value. Under heavy usage they are tough, reliable and can generally be inexpensively repaired

Pump guns generally cost less and are a bit more reliable than automatics, but require a complex set of reflexes to bang out a series of rapid shots. Some shooting instructors think a pump can actually result in more accurate shooting since the shooter is forced to pump then *re-aim* before pulling the trigger a second time. The esteemed Winchester model 12 and the earlier model 97 are two of the most revered old pump guns, and many old-time quail hunters and duck hunters used them religiously. These were followed by the lightweight Ithaca 37 and very common Remington 870 Wingmaster. Those four models comprise most of the pump guns one encounters being used in the field for roughshooting. There can be something magical about a shiny old pump gun, a smooth shucking gun that can bang out shot after shot in the hands of an expert.

The advantage of an autoloader is its very rapid three- or five-shot power package. Some hunters just do not feel comfortable without a magazine full of shells at the ready. Of course, when hunting woodcock, a migratory bird, the magazine must be plugged to hold only three shells. But many hunters place high value on the five-shot magazine when hunting slow-rising coveys or when shooting at fast-crossing pheasants. Several automatics are common in the United States, with the Remington 1100 and the old Browning A-5 (Humpback) being the most common of the older guns. Today one sees Remington 11-87s, Berettas, Benellis and Browning A-80s as well. The newer automatics tend to cycle more reliably than their 1960s counterparts and generally, if kept clean, will eject and reload shell after shell without a hang-up.

The most common bird guns in America are one-barrel models like this Remington 1100 semiautomatic held by Erik Warren.

The receiver of a one-barrel gun adds about three to five inches of overall length to a gun, most of it in the ejection area.

Screw-in chokes are now available in most one-barrel guns directly from the factory or by purchasing a replacement barrel. Generally these durable guns are built to take the wallop of American magnum loads and keep on shooting. The cushioning effect of the autoloader mechanism helps soften the guns recoil, an important asset to sensitive shooters.

The biggest drawback to one-barrel guns is their weight, length and handling characteristics. They tend to weigh more than double guns of the same gauge and the guns are always three to five inches greater in overall length than a double gun with the same length barrel. This added length is due to the receiver mechanism that fits between the stock and the barrel, making the guns less agile and some even tend to be a bit barrel heavy. This extra length is especially noticeable in dense cover situations like the grouse woods where gun agility is necessary for snap shooting. To minimize these characteristics, several manufacturers have offered scaled down sporting guns of various configurations. The Remington 1100 Special was an example, an autoloader with an English stock and a twenty-one inch barrel to reduce length and weight and make the gun handle quickly. At just over five pounds in 20-gauge this is a quick-handling little fowling piece. I've hunted with a few guys that handled and scored as well with one of these little guns as any double gun.

THE OVER-UNDER SHOTGUN

The side-by-side has tradition going for it, and the one-barrel guns, automatics and pumps, are far and away the most common in the field. However, if a survey of all roughshooters were taken to determine the most desirable gun, I have little doubt that the modern over-unders would emerge as the victors. The over-under has a level of cachet and desirability today that a gun of no other configuration seems able to challenge. Most of this preference is due to its easy pointing style and single sighting plane. Indeed, consistently winning trap and skeet scores would suggest that the over-under guns do have some significant shooting advantages in clay bird games. A plethora of specialized new sporting clay over-unders are now on the market so it looks like the tide in sporting clay guns is headed toward the over-under as well.

However, even though most bird hunters and roughshooters aspire to an over-under, lightweight, quick-handling stack barrel guns are not so easy to find or afford. Most of the older over-unders for sale in the United States are rather substantial guns, long barreled and heavy, not particularly well categorized as game guns. The over-under shotgun, inherently more difficult to build than a side-by-side, accounts for much of the delay in its commercial development until the 1920s. The difficulty came about in the complexity of developing a lightweight and streamlined locking system that would properly secure the barrels to the breech and keep the gun tight and safe without adding a pound of bulk. Volumes

Among over-unders, there are few that can outdo this beautiful Beretta SO2 game gun owned by Don Alexander of Michigan. This is a very unusual over-under: a side lock, two-trigger, straight-gripped gun.

have been written about this painful gestation period, the labor pains and the technical aspects of the delivery, but in the end the baby has been highly accepted and widely revered.

By the time the venerable Browning Superposed models were introduced in the United States, they found an eager market panting in anticipation for a reasonably priced over-under. Built in Belgium by Fabrique Nationale, the Browning Superposed was designed by John Browning, an American, for an American audience that was often moving up from a pump or an automatic. These early guns were substantial, long-barreled, pistol gripped, with large, full fore-ends and built tough to handle the magnum loads sure to be used by American gunners. Almost all the old Brownings weigh in at nearly eight pounds, which is pretty heavy for a true game gun. In Don Zutz's classic book *The Double Shotgun*, the author candidly discusses the various over-unders for sale in the United States both in the past and today. His observations explain in great detail the difficulties involved in building over-unders in a true game gun configuration, and he gives his unvarnished assessments of all the various brands and models.

Ohioan Dick Siciliano uses a Belgium Browning superposed model with the fairly unusual straight stock.

Today, a whole range of reasonably priced over-unders is available, but virtually all are imports from Belgium, Japan, Italy, Spain or Germany.

OVER-UNDER GAME GUNS

The challenge the over-under shooter will face is to find a reasonably priced over-under in true game gun configuration. Although hundreds of thousands of over-unders are available in the United States, both new and used, a high percentage are target guns and as such are quite long barreled and heavy. If it is reasonable to say that a game gun should weigh no more than 7 1/2 pounds in a two-barreled configuration, then no more than half of the 12-gauge over-unders match the description. Many hunters have attempted to solve this dilemma by dropping down to a 20-gauge gun, but the weight of many 20-gauge over-unders still approaches seven pounds because most of the newer 20-gauge guns are chambered to shoot three-inch shells.

The American shooter's love for small-gauge, lightweight guns is too often negated by our equal love for magnum loads. The three-inch, 20-gauge gun is built to handle almost as large a shot charge as a 12 gauge and thus it is bulked up to the necessary strength to handle the chamber pressure. Truly lightweight game guns are often not built to handle the hottest magnum loads, so ironically, a 12 bore built to handle light loads often actually weighs less than a 20-gauge magnum gun of similar design.

Some of the over-unders of lightest weight are the less available models including: Merkel, Beretta, Franchi, Citori Sporter, Perazzi's MX12 light game gun, Sauers and some other hard-to-find guns like the rare 16-gauge Brownings. A roughshooter seriously looking for a lightweight over-under would be well advised to put the gun on a scale. Beautiful over-under game guns do exist. Don Alexander, a good friend of mine from northern Michigan, had a Beretta Sidelock SO-2 over-under made to his specifications years ago. His gun has a straight English stock, slim fore-end, twenty-eight-inch barrels, two triggers and ejectors, weighs just 6 3/4 pounds and is set up as a true game gun. Another hunting pal, Dominick Santarelli from New Jersey, shoots a Browning Citori Upland Model with twenty-four-inch barrels that weighs just seven pounds, and Dom seldom misses a grouse or a woodcock.

THE SIDE-BY-SIDE

Many avid shotgunners, including some who are also accomplished roughshooters, have little appreciation for the side-by-side shotgun. To them the side-by-side, commonly referred to as a double barrel, is antiquated, clunky and restrictive when compared to the multitude of over-unders or single barrel multiple shot pumps and automatics available today. Most serious clay target shooters (trap, skeet and sporting clays) opt for a single-sighting plane, single trigger gun in the legitimate belief that each of these features will account for a clay bird or two during the competition. Statistically, there are very few side-by-sides ever seen on the clay bird ranges. The side-by-side, with its broad sweep of barrels and wide sighting plane, is uncomfortable to some shooters, who feel the wide set of barrels subconsciously distracts them from quickly pointing the gun. This seems to be mainly a personal idiosyncrasy that the shooter either can or cannot overcome. I cannot refute this fact, but the side-by-side still rates high in the hunting field where wild bird shooting scores seem the same.

The side-by-side lover discounts all those arguments when he reaches for the gun that he feels is a true work of art. The shooters that can handle a double well, recognize it as the ultimate game gun. For the contemporary American shotgunner, the side-by-side is an acquired taste, but like single malt scotch, caviar and the symphony, it qualifies as one of the finer things in life.

The side-by-side, like all shotguns, comes in many configurations, gauges, sizes, weights and qualities. But a significant number of side-by-sides will meet the criteria in weight, handling and balance to truly be considered game guns. Certainly the side-by-side buyer must be very careful, for the guns have been built for more than a hundred years in this same configuration, and older guns must be carefully scrutinized for safety. Older steels and Damascus barrels may not be safe when shooting modern ammunition. However, some magnificent older guns are still in shootable condition and after the inspection and approval by a competent gunsmith, many older guns are able to withstand the force of hunting loads for woodcock, quail and grouse. However, they may not be up to the stiff loads needed for pheasants in open country.

Out of favor for some time, the side-by-side, the most traditional and nostalgic of all upland game guns, recently sparked renewed interest among knowledgeable shooters. I have been pleasantly surprised to see several ardent hunters uncase neat and trim side-by-sides before we started off through the cover. Several of my hunting friends have switched from over-unders to side-by-sides in the last ten years with no change in their shooting scores. They all switched for different reasons, including tradition, a desire for lighter guns and value for the money.

THE AMERICAN SIDE-BY-SIDE

By the late 1880s the British had pretty much perfected the design of the side-by-side shotgun. As a result, almost all the high-quality side-by-sides made in the world over the last century in Belgium, Germany, Italy, Spain and Japan, are direct copies of the legendary British designs. For the most part the old English guns were expensively hand-crafted tools of genius.

Using that genius of design, numerous American firms sprang up to build basic variations of the side-by-side. However, the American manufacturing processes incorporated a greater and, in some cases, extensive use of machine-made parts and assembly line methods. This varied radically from the hand-made, hand-fitted, piece-by-piece one-off guns of England. Naturally, many of the low-cost American guns failed to achieve any level of success in design or workmanship. However, during the first half of the twentieth century there were a few American makers who were capable of producing high-quality, well-designed and carefully finished side-by-sides. Most roughshooters have at least heard of Parker Bros., L. C. Smith,

When I first started hunting with George Wilson, he was a confirmed over-under man with a nice set of guns, like this 20-gauge Browning Superposed.

Later (without any urging from me), George began to shoot side-by-sides and now hunts mainly with this 12-gauge Parker Reproduction.

Lefever, Ithaca and Fox. These were the premier names in American manufactured side-by-sides and the huge number of guns bearing these names that still survive today testifies to their longevity.

Additionally, half a dozen other high-quality American side-by-sides were produced in much smaller numbers. These include Baker, Iver Johnson, Tobin, Winchester (Model 21) and a smattering of Colts and Remingtons. Some were low volume or a quality step just below the five major brands. The Model 21 Winchester, however, was an exceptional gun of low-volume and extremely high quality. Unfortunately, the side-by-side, regardless of its inherent balance and sophistication was, by the 1940s, seriously out of favor in the United States and by World War II all but three of the companies were out of the side-by-side business.

The side-by-sides sold in America today have undergone a significant style change from the side-by-sides built and sold in the United States in the early part of this century. The early guns—Parkers, Lefevers, L. C. Smiths and Foxes—tended to be rather large and substantial weapons with barrel lengths of twenty-eight or thirty inches and even a few with thirty-two-inch barrels. Generally they were 12-gauge guns with a relatively bulky pistol grip and a splinter fore-end. Double triggers and extractors were common, mainly as a cost-saving practice.

Most new, quality side-by-sides sold in the United States today are of Italian or high-grade Spanish manufacture and they tend to be lightweight guns with shorter barrels, straight English stocks and almost always splinter fore-ends. A high percentage are small gauges (20 gauge or smaller) with a single trigger and ejectors. This is in contrast to the more traditional English side-by-side configuration of straight English stock, splinter fore-end, double (two) triggers and ejectors.

My own taste in side-by-side guns falls somewhere in between. If I were designing my own ideal gun, it would be a six-pound, six-ounce, 12-gauge (for pheasants) with twenty-eight-inch barrels, two triggers, extractors, English stock and splinter fore-end. Actually, I shoot a slim line Prince of Wales (semipistol) grip as well as a straight English grip. I see no need for ejectors in an American game gun. Environmentally and practically, if you are not shooting driven game where you need very, very fast reloading, ejectors are a pain, shooting out empty cartridges on the ground. For grouse and woodcock I'd drop down to a 16 gauge of similar dimensions but the gun would weigh about eight ounces less.

Many older American side-by-sides were configured like this 16-gauge L. C. Smith, a beautiful lightweight game gun. A surprising number of nice guns by the classic manufacturers are still on the market.

Some great shooters are capable of shooting wild birds with a 20 gauge but dropping down to a 28 gauge or a 410 is an exercise in ego that generally results in far too many wounded birds that are destined to be lost, only to die within a few days of being hit.

The differences in configuration between side-by-sides and over-unders are usually significant. I estimate that more than 90 percent of all the over-under shotguns ever sold in America have a substantial pistol grip stock, a large handful of fore-end, a single trigger of some form, automatic shell ejectors and a safety that doubles as the barrel selector. Since the late 1980s most of the over-unders sold in the United States have some form of factory installed screw-in chokes.

When we hunt pheasants in the prairie states, Erik Warren usually shoots this Winchester model 21, a rugged, well-built gun that is able to stand up to heavy game loads. Erik has made some great shots with this gun.

Conversely, a higher percentage of side-by-sides have a straight (English) grip or a very small bump called a Prince of Wales grip (most older American side-by-sides have the small pistol grip) combined with a splinter fore-end, two triggers, extractors and a single-purpose top tang safety. It is still rare to see a side-by-side with screw-in chokes. Over-unders tend to weigh more than 7 1/2 pounds, with many approaching eight pounds, while the side-by-sides, even the older guns, generally weigh seven pounds or less.

ONE TRIGGER OR TWO?

A controversial decision that always accompanies the purchase of a good break-open gun is the choice of one trigger or two. The inventors of side-by-side guns almost always used two triggers, a system that is simple, inexpensive, instantly selectable and reflexively fast. Anyone who has learned to shoot a two trigger gun successfully can switch from trigger to trigger instinctively. Double triggers are common on British guns and are often seen on European guns as well. Due to their low cost and simple reliability, they were very common on older American-made side-by-sides and most old Parkers, Smiths, Foxes and Lefevers have two triggers in the lower grades.

If you can find a copy of Steven Dodd Hughes' article on triggers in the September/October 1994 issue of *Shooting Sportsman* magazine, you'll have a much better idea of why side-by-side purists generally shoot two-trigger guns. Once you've had the frustrating experience of shipping a gun back and forth to a gunsmith to have a single trigger adjusted while he questions your shooting technique and you question his gunsmithing knowledge, you'll begin to understand. Most over-unders are equipped with very reliable, modern, single trigger systems, but as Hughes explains, most old side-by-sides were not really all that adaptable to single triggers and the numerous patents for single trigger devices testifies to the difficulty of the undertaking.

Many Americans, especially those who grew up shooting one-barreled pumps and automatics, find two triggers to be clumsy, unsightly and out of date. Therefore, most over-unders sold in America include a selective, single trigger that can alter which barrel is fired first. The single triggers in modern over-under guns are extremely reliable and seldom need repair. Buying an over-under with two triggers today is virtually impossible, as the one trigger buyers rule this part of the gun world.

Which is right for the roughshooter? Either. Two triggers are simpler, less expensive, instantly selective and generally almost 100 percent reliable. The drawbacks are appearance (to some eyes) and the dexterity necessary to operate the shots quickly. Single triggers are easier to operate, more expensive, more complex and a few need occasional repair or adjustment. I have mostly two-trigger guns but I also have a few one-trigger guns. I find I am able to switch back and forth without a thought. It is as simple as owning two cars, one with a stick shift, the other with an automatic. Within a few seconds the mind adjusts!

EJECTORS VERSUS EXTRACTORS

Much is made of the complex mechanisms that eject spent shells from the chambers of both side-by sides and over-unders. Virtually any significant gun book will devote page after page to diagrams and cutaway drawings of this aspect of fine guns. In England, where driven game shooting is still practiced, ejectors add significant value to used classic guns and an ejector gun may fetch up to 50 percent more than an extractor gun. But this is not so true in the United States. What is the real value of the ejectors and what do they add to the roughshooters usage of the gun? Over and over in a field situation I have watched hunters put their hands over the breech of an ejector gun to catch the shells as the gun is opened. Many hunters reload at least some percentage of their shells, and few knowledgeable sportsmen simply blow out the shells, to lie on the ground and litter the habitat. As for the cost differential of extractors versus ejectors, were I choosing between a well-made, high-quality, sleek and well-balanced gun with extractors versus a solid, reliable, slightly heavier, lower-quality gun with ejectors, I'd select the extractor gun every time.

WHAT IS A TWO-AND-A-HALF-INCH GUN?

Once in a while you'll see an ad for a gun (especially English or European made) that says "2 1/2 inch chamber." This means that the gun was originally built to shoot only 2 1/2 cartridges. This is still a common shell length in England and Europe. Many years ago some short-chambered guns were also made in the United States, but by the late 1930s almost all guns made in the United States were chambered for the standard 2 3/4-inch American shells. The standard shotgun shell sold in the United States today is 2 3/4 inches long (before crimping). *So beware!* If you fire 2 3/4-inch shells in a 2 1/2-inch gun, the shell will extend too far into the chamber, causing extremely high barrel pressures. Many of the very lightweight, imported older game guns for sale in the United States still have the old 2 1/2-inch chambers. Most are proofed only for light loads. They are ideally suited to roughshooting, but not with 2 3/4-inch shells! Today

2 1/2-inch shells can be purchased in the United States through a few sophisticated gun dealers who handle such guns.

MY GAME GUNS

I came to my own game guns by a long and serpentine path. Starting with some battered, old low-grade American side-by-sides, I worked my way up through a couple of Ithaca Flues models, an SKB model 150 12 gauge, a Parker VH, a Fox Sterlingworth, a Lefever DS sidelock 12 gauge, a Darne

16 bore, a beautiful, old 5E L. C. Smith and an Iver Johnson Skeeter. Along the way I had a non side-by-side period when I experimented with a Remington 1100 automatic (I couldn't work the safety), a pump, a Winchester Model 12 (I kept forgetting to pump it) and a Franchi over-under (it just didn't feel right), but in the end I came back to my first love, the side-by-side.

The first English gun I bought was a Birmingham-type boxlock by Fred K. Williams, an obscure maker. The midlevel gun was in good, tight shooting condition, with good bores but a bit worn with little blue and no case colors. I had never experienced such a mar-

This is my J and W Tolley side-by-side, an old long-barreled English gun that is very special to me.

velously agile-handling gun before and once I found the English guns I stayed with them. I've swapped and traded up some and now my most used guns are a J and W Tolley sidelock, a London gun weighing six pounds, six ounces with thirty-inch barrels, two triggers, extractors, straight grip and a splinter fore-end. This is a 2 1/2-inch gun, but I use it for pheasant hunting and for mixed bags of pheasant and quail. Although its chokes, cylinder and full are a bit unusual, the combination is very effective for the way I use the gun. My wife bought the gun for me as a gift while we were in Scotland on a wonderful and memorable vacation, and it has been a constant pleasure, one of the best gifts I've ever received. The second gun that I use frequently is a 16-gauge George Gibbs boxlock. Gibbs is best known as a rifle maker from Bristol, England, but he also made a few shotguns, and this five-pound, fourteen-ounce gun with twenty-six-inch barrels, two triggers and extractors is a lively and quick-pointing gun for woodland birds. It has a tiny Prince of Wales bump of a pistol grip and a splinter fore-end. Both the Tolley and the Gibbs were bent to my specifications and although they are very different guns they both and come up on target instinctively.

These two guns give me great pleasure and add immensely to my joy of roughshooting. The fact that both are souvenirs of memorable trips to the United Kingdom also adds to their essence. I've watched men develop great affection for a battered old game gun based on the wonderful memories collected in the gun's presence. The Tolley and the Gibbs hold such a position with me.

All the discussion of guns comes down to what happens when you instinctively snap the gun in place, point and fire.

My personal beliefs and opinions on guns, chokes and loads have gradually jelled into a moderately coherent structure. But for most of my shooting and hunting life I've been just a bit out of step. For example, I like side-by-sides; most people don't. I like larger gauges (like 12 or 16); most people lust after 20s and 28s. I like light guns but most Americans shoot heavy guns. I opt for open chokes while most people shoot at least modified, and I hunt with really light loads while most Americans load up with magnums. I pay attention to gun fit and don't shoot clay birds from a fixed stance or a shouldered gun. Most Americans do neither. It's not that these ideas haven't been around a long time; it's just that few people (in the United States) believe or practice them. But suddenly I find I'm not alone! Recently several articles espousing these concepts have shown up in the most prestigious places, like *Greys Sporting Journal* and *Shooting Sportsman*. I don't feel quite as out of step anymore.

C H A P T E R   2 4

ON FINE GAME GUNS: CONVERSATIONS WITH MARK CRUDGINGTON AND HERSCHEL CHADICK

MARK CRUDGINGTON

Gun Maker
I. M. Crudgington and Sons
Bath, England

Mark Crudgington is a precocious young Briton, not at all shy, nor the stuffy proper stereotype of *Upstairs/Downstairs* image. Except for his strong west of England accent, his exuberant and straight-forward approach might make you think he was a "Yank." I first met Mark when I popped into his father's shop in Bath, England, while on a family tour to Stonehenge. If you ever go to London, you'll probably opt for a quick day trip to see Stonehenge; from there a tour of the beautiful architecture of Bath is just another hour west.

The small shop on Broad Street houses I. M. Crudgington and Sons Gun Makers. Crudgington acquired the rights to the George Gibbs gun maker name and now builds guns under both names: Gibbs or Crudgington. The shop is owned by Mark's father, Ian, co-author of the beautiful book *The*

194

History of Shotguns, Volumes 1 and 2. When I was in the shop, Ian and Mark took me on a tour of the family gun collection, a treasure trove of unique and exotic shotguns of the last two hundred years.

Like most English gun shops, the facilities of I. M. Crudgington of Bath are not all that large, nor modern, nor impressive, but Mark Crudgington and his father run an interesting business out of this provincial location and seem most accommodating compared to some big-city shops. Crudgington has the rights to the George Gibbs name and continues to deal in guns and other sporting gear so popular in England.

I took an immediate liking to Mark, a straight-talking, no-nonsense, thirtyish chap of obviously broad knowledge and strong views, similar to my own. He apprenticed in London before joining his father in the trade. Bath is not the "nose-in-the-air" London gun trade. Here you can ask an uninformed question and get a straightforward, common sense answer. The shelves usually hold thirty to fifty used English guns of varying price levels but relatively few Purdeys or Bosses or matched pairs.

I was specifically looking for a woodcock gun, light and quick with open chokes. I found a George Gibbs 16 bore, a 2 1/2-inch gun proofed only for one ounce of shot, so I'd have to buy imported shells or load my own. We negotiated a price, then Mark measured me, agreed to alter the stock to my dimensions and open the chokes to .004 in both barrels. I paid for the gun, bought a pair of rubber Wellies, collected the family and we all headed back to London. All the way home I worried. I had purchased a gun in less than an hour, from a dealer I didn't know, paid for extensive modifications and departed. Back in the States, I immediately called Mark to inquire about his progress. Perhaps he could read the tone in my voice, because in his typically direct way he stated bluntly, "Mr. Roggenkamp, we are gun makers, not gun butchers! If you are not completely satisfied when the gun arrives in the States, just send it back for a full refund!" Needless to say, I love that little Gibbs; it is such a neat, perfectly fitted little fowling piece and although it is far from a collector's item, it is a very special gun to me. It feels just right.

You spend a large percentage of your time working with side-by-side guns; what type of side-by-side would you recommend for an American shooter for woods birds: grouse and woodcock?

CRUDGINGTON—I would recommend a gun that is not too heavy for the owner/user; that is, if you are six feet, six inches tall and weigh two

Mark Crudgington at his bench working, as usual, to custom fit a typical English gun for a client.

hundred pounds, a 7- or 7 1/2-pound gun may be fine. If, like me, you are closer to five feet, eight inches and 150 pounds, a 5 3/4-pound or 6-pound gun may be better. If you carry a gun that is too heavy or too long, your shooting may deteriorate, as your reaction times are slowed by the strain on certain muscles. Barrel length should suit the stature, twenty-six to twenty-eight inches for my type of build; twenty-eight to thirty-two inches for someone over six feet tall; the dimensions of the gun must be in proportion to those of the owner.

Would your recommendation change much for which gun to use for walk-up pheasant shooting over a flushing dog or quail shooting over pointing dogs?

CRUDGINGTON—No, one gun should be capable of all tasks; familiarity with a gun helps instinctive shooting.

You've said that most Americans shoot too-heavy loads: too much powder, too much shot. Can you elaborate?

CRUDGINGTON—The temptation is to think the more lead in the air the more chance you have of bringing down game. This is true to a point, but overlengthening the column of shot in the cartridge (heavier the load, larger the column) causes problems in creating long, uneven patterns; it is much better to have a load balanced to the bore diameter, e.g., 1 1/4 ounces for 10 bore; one ounce for 12 bore; 3/4 ounce for 20 bore and 1/2 ounce for 28 bore. With modern plastic wads, superb even patterns can be created with such loads that will do nearly any task required of them within the limitations of any shotgun.

How heavy must a 12-bore gun be to handle 1 1/8-ounce loads?

CRUDGINGTON—For 1 1/8-ounce loads, a gun of around 7 pounds to 7 1/4 pounds seems ideal, but this only really applies if a lot of shots are to be fired in a relatively short space of time. For upland hunting you could go down to a gun that weighs between 6 1/4 pounds to 6 1/2 pounds.

How much effect do plastic shot cups have on patterns?

CRUDGINGTON—They appear to have a great stabilizing effect giving good regularity of pattern in a quality loaded product.

Do low shot weight target loads (but with relatively fast burning powders) fully take advantage of the smaller shot weights, or do the fast powders blow patterns?

CRUDGINGTON—High velocities do appear to blow patterns in fiber wadded cartridges, but plastic shot cups (as most are) appear to help stabilize the pattern.

Does the choke have any bearing on the ideal size of the shot load?

CRUDGINGTON—Really, patterns should be regulated via the choke to suit the conditions of use, therefore, you should have your gun's patterns professionally checked for the type of shooting you require.

What chokes would you recommend for grouse and woodcock? pheasants? quail? doves? Ducks over decoys?

CRUDGINGTON—In all cases, if a plastic wadded cartridge were to be used, an ideal would be improved cylinder in the first barrel and quarter choke in the second, so long as the patterns were checked on a plate before use (.005 inch and .010 inch constriction).

Do most people tend to overchoke or underchoke?

CRUDGINGTON—Most people believe what they are told. We once had a customer who was the finest shot in the country; bets seemed to be taken on the occasion of a missed shot. He was convinced, having been told by a so-called expert, that his guns had full choke in both barrels. He pulled off many, many legendary, long-range shots with these guns on quarry as diverse as snipe and geese. Upon his death we were given the guns to sell and discovered that both guns had *true* cylinder barrels! No chokes whatsoever!

Do you recommend short or long barrels when you build a gun?

CRUDGINGTON—Refer to my response to your first question. I also listen to the customer's needs. If he is five feet, two inches and really insists on thirty-four-inch barrels, I'll build them for him, but I'll be ready to make a pair of twenty-five-inch barrels in a couple of years when he has made up his own mind rather than listen to the glossy magazine experts!

Some Americans don't like the wide sighting plane of side-by-sides. Does any type of rib lessen the perceived width of the barrels?

CRUDGINGTON—Sighting planes are only applicable, in my view, to rifles. If you shoot a shotgun like a rifle, using the barrel/rib as a reference point, then use an over-under. If you shoot instinctively with a properly fitted gun then use either an over-under or a side-by-side.

Most older American guns have a pistol grip; most older English guns have a straight English grip. Do you believe there is much difference in the way the guns handle?

CRUDGINGTON—The left hand (in a right-handed person) controls the gun, so what the trigger hand does is of little consequence in terms of handling. There are so many different types and shapes of grips that it is nearly impossible to answer this question accurately. All I can say is pick a gun you like the feel of.

What is your opinion of beavertail fore-ends?

CRUDGINGTON—I like them so long as they are long enough and light enough not to make the gun feel clumsy and are shaped to suit the user's hand.

Americans seldom have a gun closely fitted to their dimensions. On the other hand, English shooters almost always have their guns fitted. How much difference will it make in the hunter's shooting accuracy?

CRUDGINGTON—I always tell my driven game shooting customers that all the money they spend on fitting will only help them with 2 to 4 percent of the shots they take. However, these are usually the shots that stand most prominent in the memory. Most people can hit 50 to 70 percent of skeet-type birds with an unfitted gun; they eventually fit themselves to the gun.

How risky is the stock bending process (especially in older guns)?

CRUDGINGTON—I have bent nearly eight hundred guns' stocks in sixteen years. I've only had one break and that had already been broken and very cleverly repaired.

What is your opinion of the tiny gauges, 28 gauge and 410s, as hunting guns?

CRUDGINGTON—I use a 28 bore for most of my shooting now, using a 2½-inch, 9/16-ounce load. We have regulated the barrels to deliver the whole charge in a thirty-inch circle at thirty yards!

For the average hunter, does a sidelock have any real advantages over a boxlock?

CRUDGINGTON—No.

What would you look for if you were purchasing a used English side-by-side in America for hunting only?

CRUDGINGTON—I would go to an English-trained gunsmith/maker preferably with fitting experience. I would find a gun I could (a) easily afford including stock and barrel alterations, (b) a gun that felt light enough for me to carry all day and (c) a gun that appealed to me aesthetically. After that I would have it altered to my requirements.

Can the average layman see or feel much difference between a good quality English gun (say a quality Birmingham) versus a London Best?

CRUDGINGTON—Yes, the same argument carries through to all quality hand-crafted goods. You only get out what you put in and seven hundred hours feels less "polished" than fifteen hundred hours.

What single gun dimension will have the most impact on the shooter?

CRUDGINGTON—Length of the stock has a dramatic effect. If the stock is too long people tend to be slow and shoot low; too short a stock can end in bruising to the shooter's face and the gun will shoot slightly higher.

Do you install screw-in chokes and what is your opinion of them? Do they effect gun balance in any way?

CRUDGINGTON—No, I don't install them. I have personally found no need for them. Some chokes, such as the "Teague" choke made here in England, have no effect on balance. In my opinion screw-in chokes are for people who like to fiddle with things.

HERSCHEL CHADICK

Gun Dealer
Chadick's Fine Guns
Terrell, Texas

The Chadick gun store in Terrell, Texas, is beauti-fully decorated and well stocked with sporting gun inventory and antiques related to outdoor activities. However, it is a bit off the beaten path and most of the trading is carried on by telephone and mail order.

It is a part of assessing every true game gun to deter-mine its accurate weight.

About twenty minutes east of Dallas, you'll find the dusty little Texas town of Terrell, population 12,490. Terrell is an unlikely place to find a store like Chadick's, where an inventory of the world's finest vintage shotguns and rifles await the loving approval of buyers from all over America. About noon on a typical day the phone begins to ring persistently as gun buyers and gun sellers from around the nation begin the daily ritual of gun trading.

Herschel Chadick has been dealing in high quality "game guns" for about twenty years and Chadick's Fine Guns has a nationwide reputation as a place to find some of the best. I still think of Herschel as a Parker expert even though the inventory now includes fine guns from around the world. At some point almost every dedicated roughshooter decides to splurge, to buy one truly special gun. When you do, there are a limited number of gun dealers that can fill your order. Just like the antique shops that specialize in rare types of furniture or paintings, the gun shops that truly cater to the whims of the double gun fanciers are rare. If you call Herschel on the phone, he'll patiently describe the gun in a deep Texas drawl as he carefully examines it. Few people who purchase a gun here ever visit the pristine refurbished shop full of antiques and gun artifacts, but if you are typical, when the package arrives with the Chadick label your fingers will tremble and your pulse will race.

Do you specialize in hunting-type guns?

CHADICK—Yes, absolutely. We sell mainly hunting guns and we don't see many trap shooters or clay pigeon shooters. Most of our customers want to hunt with the guns they buy.

What percentage of your sales would be to shooters versus collectors?

CHADICK—I would say 90 percent of the guns go to shooters and maybe 10 percent to collectors. It's a funny thing about shotguns. If the gun doesn't fit a person, he doesn't want it. It just has to fit the hunter. He must be able to envision shooting a quail or a grouse with it and if he can't, he won't really want to own the gun no matter how rare or collectable it is. So to me that means such people are really shooters!

What percentage of your business is side-by-side versus over-under?

CHADICK—The ratio is about 90 percent side-by-sides simply because we sell guns to shooters. A very high percentage of over-unders are not in real hunting gun types of configurations. We always have six or eight here and we would like to sell more over-unders if we could find them in the right configurations.

Do you see many over-unders in real game gun configurations?

CHADICK—Unfortunately not. Predominately the game over-unders are bigger, heavier guns made for live bird shooting or trap and they tend to be pretty bulky.

So your business is really focused on live bird hunters?

CHADICK—Yes. We sell a few guns to people that are going to put screw-in chokes and maybe shoot the gun for sporting clays but mostly they want to hunt with it.

The guns I see here are high-grade guns. Can someone buy a high-grade gun and take it hunting without hurting its value?

CHADICK—Definitely. Especially if you don't abuse it. We have a gunsmith on staff here named Tom Chapman who is one of the best wood men in the world. I hired him away from Browning eighteen years ago. He can make any blemish or scratch go away. So if you have a good gun, you ought to shoot it and use it and enjoy it. That is what it was made for and if you put a few scratches in it, Tom or five or six other really good people in the United States can remove those dings or scratches or barbed wire messes without hurting the gun's value at all.

What about a new gun?

CHADICK—That's another story. With a new gun, once you take it out of the box and shoot it and scratch it and use it, you can't claim it to be new and unfired any more so you are going to lose some value. But, just think of the lucky guy who back in 1935 bought a new Parker and took it out and used it and enjoyed it and it's worth a lot more now than it was in 1935. Guns are to enjoy, to use, new or not.

Do you sell any new guns?

CHADICK—Very few. I don't get a chance to buy new guns that I can buy and resell at a reasonable price. I mainly deal in good used guns that I can buy and sell reasonably.

Can a buyer take one of these guns and have it fitted to himself in the United States?

CHADICK—Yes, but we don't do fitting ourselves. There are some people in America that have try-guns and they can actually fit you to the sixteenth of an inch in every dimension. But you are probably never going to find a gun to fit those measurements exactly anyway, so my recommendation is to get measured so you know basically what you need. Then when you order a gun from a legitimate dealer, he can tell you the dimensions and the weight and everything so you will know about how closely the gun already matches what you want.

Can a shooter go out and find a reasonably priced, good quality gun in a game gun configuration that is lightweight and fast handling?

CHADICK—Yes. You can find them for $2,000 and up depending on what you want to spend. It won't be a Parker 28 gauge, but you can get some really nice guns for between $2,000 and $10,000 in almost any configuration you want.

Do you specialize in small-gauge guns?

CHADICK—No, not really. I appreciate them, and the 28 gauge is one of my favorite gauges and 16 is a very nice gauge for lots of reasons. But my personal favorite gauge is still a traditional 12 gauge, thirty-inch barrel, full and modified choke. It lends itself to just about anything you want to hunt except for close-in quail or woodcock. I think small bores have their place and they're fun to shoot, but by and large 16s or 12s are still my favorites.

What about two triggers and how does that effect value?

CHADICK—Some people will pay more for a single trigger, and sometimes they will pay an inordinately high price for a single trigger and ejectors, but double triggers are preferred by probably 75 percent of today's shooters.

How about ejectors versus extractors?

CHADICK—I like extractors. I like to be able to pull those old paper hulls out that I have saved for years and shoot them because they smell so good. Something about the old paper shells smells a lot better than the new plastic shells. If you have ejectors you have to cup your hand over the barrels to catch the shells or bend over and pick them up and I am lazy and I don't want to do that. Extractors are reliable; they don't break, they don't cause you any trouble and you get to pull out the shells and catch that sweet smell before you put them away.

Does stock configuration, whether a straight stock, a pistol grip or a Prince of Wales have much effect on value?

CHADICK—Generally no, but sometimes yes. A straight grip will sometimes command a little higher price because fewer were made. Back then fewer people wanted them. Back in the heydays of the American double most Americans wanted pistol grips, and that's the reason there were more made that way. Back then people could order what they wanted. They could get pistol grip, or straight grip or round knobs, or full grips, but most Americans ordered pistol grips. Right now there is kind of an English trend and some people will pay a little more for a straight grip. I am always excited when I get in an older American-made short-barreled straight grip gun with a butt plate because that's what some buyers want these days. Still, all in all, I believe that most Americans still want a pistol grip.

Do you use the term game gun *much?*

CHADICK—Absolutely. Most of the guns we sell here are really "game guns." Guns that you can take out and shoot. They tend to be lightweight and quick handling, very aggressive game guns.

C H A P T E R 2 5
TOWARD BETTER SHOOTING

You can't learn to shoot or play golf or tennis from a book, but you can better understand the principles that affect athletic movement. You can also better understand the mechanics of the equipment and how that affects your actions. During my hunting years I've probably read twenty books on shotgunning. To my frustration, most got quickly and deeply into the complex, technical aspects of gun design, shot strings, point of impact and on and on. Frankly, only a few people have the patience to wade through this and even fewer can fully use the information to improve their shooting. When deep into these treatises it is easy to lose track of the fact that the purpose of a hunting gun is to shoot birds!

Shooting birds involves only two aspects: (1) placing the gun pattern over the moving target and (2) selecting a load that throws a pattern that puts enough shot into the bird to bring it down. The first involves shooter skills, gun fit and gun balance. The second involves gauge, chokes and loads, all of which determine the number of shot that reach each area of the pattern. If, for now, you can separate the two (being on target versus pattern) in your mind, I think it makes the whole equation easier to understand and it makes it easier to change the things that truly affect your shooting success.

Better shooting is everyone's goal. But let's face it, we all miss sometimes. All it takes is the rear view of three or four Dakota roosters flying unscathed into the sunset while you stand there with barrels smoking to convince you that a little better shooting would be appropriate. Anyone's roughshooting can almost always be improved with some personal effort in five areas:

1. Get some good shooting advice or instruction. Even the best shooters occasionally need a little tune-up. A good instructor may see tiny errors in your movement that when corrected can greatly improve your scoring.

2. Practice, practice, practice—both shooting and quick gun mounting. Target shooting and gun mounting in a "roughshooting format" is a year-round need.

3. Be sure your gun fits. A gun that really fits always shoots better, which means you can relax and mount the gun instinctively. A fitted gun matches you, rather than you adjusting to the gun.

4. Pattern the gun so you are able to properly select chokes, shells and shot size to match the game bird you are after. What works on quail at twenty yards may not work on pheasants at forty.

5. Get in shape physically. No one shoots fast or well when dead tired and out of breath.

SNAP SHOOTING PHEASANT AND GROUSE

When hunting pheasants or grouse, even over the finest quality pointing dogs, there will be times when due to some unseen condition, presumably weather or wind, the birds will not hold for points. During these days the only shooting will be snap shooting over surprising flushes at surprising times. This seems to be especially true on windy days or when hunting wily birds that have been hunted extensively. Cover that gives the birds many easy escape routes also allows the birds to move away from the pointing dogs and flush at some distance. Pheasants have always been notorious runners but grouse of late seem to be adding the pheasant's propensity to run more with each passing year.

Recently I charted the actual flushes of each bird for ten days of pheasant and grouse hunting and found that the vast majority of the pheasant flushes came without a point and at least half of the grouse flushes were wild flushes without a point. That is not to say that the dogs had not in some way indicated that birds were in the area by a false point or a flash point, but at the actual time of the flush the gunner was caught by surprise. Even over pointing dogs, the individual who is able to shoulder the gun quickly, instinctively and on target has a far better chance of success.

SHOOTING IS A LEARNABLE SKILL

Shooting is a physical activity, but real roughshooting is a *reflexive* physical activity. Most really great roughshooters mount, point and fire instinctively without even a conscious realization of the action. How well one shoots live birds in a roughshooting situation is always a result of how well a whole group of physical actions in the firing sequence work together to put the pattern of shot over the target.

A shooting coach should be able to give helpful insights specifically designed for the type of shooting at hand, to any shooter. If a tournament golf pro on the PGA Tour occasionally takes a lesson (and they do), or if a tennis player at Wimbledon has a traveling coach (and they do), why should anyone be embarrassed to take a shooting lesson? I asked Pat Lieske, a shooting instructor from Davison, Michigan, to give me his viewpoints on how the average roughshooter could become a better overall roughshooter, and Pat's insights are included in chapter 26.

TRAP, SKEET AND WING SHOOTING

Several of my hunting acquaintances are also avid skeet or trap shooters. These are fellows that can regularly troop out to the range and powder twenty-five in a row. There is no way that I could ever achieve such high scores and I frankly don't care to make the effort to do so. However, I generally feel able to shoot wild flying birds, over dogs, in the company of these gentlemen without too much fear of embarrassment. The shooting is so different that the highly skilled trap or skeet shooter cannot always take advantage of those skills in the woods or on the prairie. I would stop far short of saying that formal trap and skeet shooting won't make you a better wing-shooter; however, there are differences that keep the formal shooting skills from being directly transferable to the hunting field.

Shooting a few rounds of skeet or trap may help your hunting marksmanship a little, but you can really make a difference in your shooting if you use that bird throwing machinery in a training format. In both games some of the stations are much more valuable than others. So to save time, shoot only the stations that simulate flushed bird situations. Secondly, when hunting you rarely have a situation where you can plant your feet and shoulder the gun, so why practice shooting that way? I like to practice by using the five center stations on a skeet field. First, stand with the gun in a field carrying position then tell the thrower to surprise you by throwing random birds from the high or low house at his decision. This is challenging shooting, kind of a poor man's sporting clays and very representative of roughshooting. If you have a thrower with a bit of imagination and a bit of time you can greatly improve the speed of your reactions and build more hitting power into your reflexes.

On the trap field use the same technique, setting up the toughest challenges with little or no warning. Distance is not as important as surprise, so you can almost stand on the trap house so long as you get no warning of the release. Again, hold the gun low and don't plant your feet.

AN APPROPRIATE PATTERN

The density of the pattern is a function of three factors: gauge, chokes and loads. Why gauge? Because gauge determines the amount of shot that can realistically be stuffed down the barrel of the gun. Most 12-gauge game guns can easily shoot 1 1/4 ounces of shot, a load of about 431 number 7 1/2 pellets. On the other hand, a 28 gauge loaded to the maximum of seven-eighths ounces of shot holds only 302 number 7 1/2. Obviously the 12 gauge has the potential to put 40 percent more pellets on the target than the 28 gauge. That does not automatically mean that the pattern density and spread of pellets from the 12 gauge will be better than from the 28 gauge or that it improves your chances by 40 percent, but it should help!

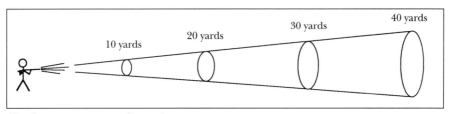

How the pattern opens up as distance increases

Now, having selected the gauge of our choice, the next effort must be focused on selecting chokes and loads that produce an ideal pattern for the birds we are pursuing. Let's use, for example, the woodcock. We generally hunt woodcock in dense, spiny, briar-infested coverts often holding foliage in one hand and the gun in the other. Woodcock flush almost underfoot, so the shots are short, no more than twenty yards and require very quick reflexes. Many woodcock are dropped at ten or fifteen yards. Beyond that distance the birds are often out of sight in the foliage. The swirling flight style of this bird makes it hard to keep the pattern centered on the bird. Hence, it helps if the gun throws a rather large pattern at short distances such as a thirty-inch pattern at twenty yards. That usually means using a very open choke. But because the woodcock is fairly small, a dense pattern with a minimum number of openings is needed. Because woodcock are fairly easy to knock down with small shot, even a small load of number eight or nine shot, with a high number of pellets, will fill most patterns thoroughly. One ounce of number nine shot holds 585 pellets.

If the number of shot in the load was the only factor to consider, all hunters would carry a 10 gauge (the largest legal gauge), but the weight, bulk and clunkiness of the 10 bore make most of us opt for a smaller compromise. The larger a gun's gauge the larger the shot load it can accommodate easily and hence, the more shot you can put into the pattern. Unfortunately, with larger gauges always come more weight and bulk thus affecting the desirability as a game gun. We choose to carry a smaller gauge gun not only to save weight, but to also improve fit and feel, knowing full well that we are trading off the amount of shot we can place on target for the lighter gun.

This exotic shotgun patterning kit sells for about $15 if you can't find a surplus sheet of four-by-four plywood lying around the garage. Just find a safe place to shoot, then nail the plywood to a tree or post with the top slightly above eye level. Next use thumbtacks to attach the paper. Then "X" the center of the paper, record your gun, barrel, choke, distance and shell and fire away.

Putting ego aside, an ethical shooter should always shoot the largest gauge he can comfortably carry in order to minimize the number of wounded and crippled birds left in the field to die. For most people that is a 12, 16 or 20 gauge. The 20-gauge gun can be chambered for three-inch shells, but in doing so the gun must be strengthened to the point that it often weighs as much as a lightweight 12 gauge. Unfortunately, ego often gets in the way here. I've seen average shooters go afield with tiny guns, 28 gauge or 410 guns, that throw such small patterns that even the very best (or luckiest) wing shots could not have consistently killed birds with the gun. These beautiful little guns could not reliably provide a proper pattern for wild bird hunting in the hands of an average shooter and the result was many wounded birds left to fly off and die later. A realistic assessment of a gun's ability to put a sufficient number of pellets into an appropriate pattern at real bird shooting distances is needed.

PATTERNING A SHOTGUN IS EASY

Patterning a gun is a simple matter that can be completed in a couple of hours during the off-season, and doing so will give you a much better understanding of how your gun shoots.

I still remember the first time my father took me into a cow pasture to pattern my old Lefever double barrel. He didn't need to see the pattern for he had seen it many times, but I needed to understand how and why and what the pattern meant. We just tacked the Sunday newspaper on a big old locust tree and fired at it from thirty yards or so. The mosaic of little holes in newspaper is not very easy to see or evaluate, but we didn't have any plain white art paper or brown wrapping paper or factory-prepared patterning targets back then. Today I just use white art paper to get a good idea of the gun's performance. The pattern will become quickly obvious.

My complete patterning kit consists of thumbtacks, a roll of thirty-six-inch art paper, a felt-tipped pen and a four-by-four-foot sheet of plywood nailed on a tree. The actual patterning is easy to do. First, I write all the statistics (gun, distance, choke, shell type, shot size, etc.) on the sheet before I shoot and I always shoot at realistic distances that match the game species and the true length of shots when hunting. Most importantly, I try out the exact shells I'll be shooting in the field. You'll learn plenty from this, especially that it is hard to aim a shotgun directly at the exact center of a pattern board from forty yards.

Shotguns, by their nature, throw slightly different patterns in each shot, so you will need to shoot each "set-up" (example IC choke barrel,

Shoot at realistic hunting distances to match the quarry. The gun's pattern at forty yards is unimportant if you are shooting at a woodcock at fifteen yards.

twenty yards, federal target eights) three or four times to get a true view of the gun's consistent performance with that combination of choke, distance and load. But when you are done you will have a much better idea of how your gun performs a specific task.

I once bought a Remington 1100 autoloader for goose shooting and thought I'd gotten it for a terrific price because it had a big unsightly adjustable choke collar on the end of the barrel. I took it out to the trap range and hit only three of twenty-five targets. Although I'll admit that I'm not a great trap shooter, I can usually do better than 12 percent! Later that day at the pattern board I learned why the gun had been such a bargain. When I examined the paper, there was not a single shot hole in the right half of the pattern. The adjustable choke had been installed out of alignment with the barrel so the gun did not shoot where it was aimed. Ninety dollars later the gun had a new screw-in choke system and now at least it shoots where it is pointed, even if it is no longer a bargain. It took a pattern board to understand what was wrong with the gun.

BALANCING SHOT SIZE WITH PATTERN DENSITY

When selecting a shot size to use for a particular game bird the hunter is always balancing two factors: shot size versus pattern density. Shot size is important because the larger shot carries more energy, penetrates deeper and the larger shot sizes will carry their range of killing power much further. It is a fact that larger shot hits harder than small shot; a simple matter of physics. The disadvantage of using large shot is that there are far fewer shot in the load and therefore there will be holes in the pattern, with some holes large enough for a bird to fly through. These holes are random in every individual discharge so the bird may not be hit even when the overall pattern covers the bird.

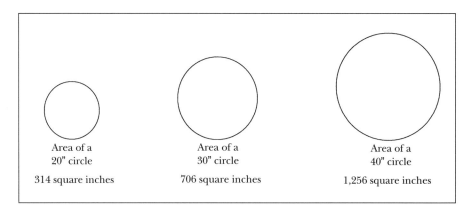

Area of a 20" circle	Area of a 30" circle	Area of a 40" circle
314 square inches	706 square inches	1,256 square inches

For purposes of illustration let's use the two extremes: number two shot versus number nine shot. Suppose that we shoot two identical shells in the same gun, except one is loaded with an ounce of number two shot (88 pellets) and the other is loaded with an ounce of number nine shot (585 pellets). Assume for now that we have patterned the gun and it throws 100 percent of the shot into a forty-inch circle at forty yards. Thus, the forty-inch circle at forty yards will contain all 88 number two shot or all 585 number nine shot. Now divide the area of the forty-inch circle by the number of shot to see the size of the holes in the pattern. In this case, the forty-inch

Now examine the pattern. Some people analyze each shot very carefully, while others just want a general idea of how the gun is shooting. This pattern is for the thirty-inch full-choke barrel of my brother Kelly's Mosberg pump, a three-inch, twleve-gauge duck gun. At fifteen yards it throws a pattern the size of a dinner plate, not much good for woodcock.

circle has an area of about 1,256 square inches, when divided by the 88 pellets, yields one number two pellet for each fourteen square inches, while the 585 number nine shot yields one pellet for every two square inches.

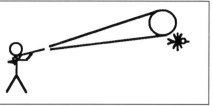

#2. Pattern not on target

Assuming that the body of a pheasant when flying away represents an area of roughly six square inches, it would be very easy for the pheasant to fly through the pattern thrown by an ounce of number twos. On the other hand, it is very likely that the number nines would strike the pheasant several times. The question is whether the number nines would have enough retained energy at forty yards to drop the bird. Therein lies the question of balance between shot size and pattern density. The largest shot sizes, number two and number four, retain

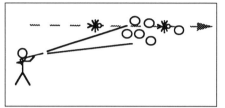

#2. Pattern on target but insufficient to drop bird

#3. Pattern on target and sufficient to drop bird

tremendous power at long ranges, and one or two pellets in a vital area often have the power to bring down the bird. On the other hand, the limited number of pellets will leave many holes for the bird to fly through.

Generally, the smaller the bird, the smaller the amount of energy it takes to knock the bird down. Very small shot will bring down a woodcock but hardly sting a pheasant, and the smaller birds are also generally shot at shorter ranges. Many woodcock are shot at fifteen yards, where even number nine shot still retains a significant portion of its energy. Prairie pheasants are often shot at forty yards, meaning that the smaller shot has dissipated much of its energy. Pheasants (and plains grouse) also tend to be shot flying straight away from the dog and gunner. Straight-away birds are always harder to bring down, since the shot must drive through the rear tail feathers into the body cavity to reach the vitals. Any bird flying across the path of the gunner or toward the gunner is easier to drop because the shot is likely to strike in the head, neck or front part of the body.

On a recent South Dakota hunting trip we hunted on a day with a forty-mile-per-hour wind. The pheasants were very spooky and were generally flushing out in the distance. Even the few that held a bit, still jumped up at twenty yards and the wind rifled them away on a few hard wing beats. We all wrestled with the choice of shot. Some chose number fours, others opted for number sixes. I found a compromise box of number fives. In the end we made some great shots, missed many others and could draw no conclusions as to which shot size was the most effective compromise.

MAGNUM SHELLS

Over the years I have hunted with a plethora of unique individuals, some very sophisticated, some very down-to-earth people from all walks of life.

What seemed almost universal among this wide-ranging group of hunters was the *bigger is better* mindset of shot shell selection. Generally speaking, it was their attitude that if one and one-eighth ounces of shot is good then one and a quarter ounces must be better and one and three-eighths ounces must be downright wonderful. If three and a quarter drams of powder is good, then four or more must be great. I look back a bit chagrined that on one occasion when a friend missed a bird, I suggested that perhaps he should drive to Des Moines to buy a box of three-inch magnum loads for his 20-gauge Winchester 101. I remember well the days when I would not have considered a trip to Iowa without a couple of boxes of 12-gauge magnum loads of one and three-eighths ounces copper-coated buffered shot pushed by four drams of powder. If something hotter had been for sale I'd have bought it!

All the time I was shooting a 12-gauge Ithaca SKB side-by-side that only weighed about six pounds, eight ounces. Even in a hunting situation with the adrenaline flowing I would feel the full-force wallop of those loads. Since all my friends and hunting cronies kept espousing hot magnum loads I was absolutely sure that was the right thing to do. I was operating on "the bigger is better" American theory for just about everything.

Then several of my friends went to England to shoot driven game. They came home raving about the hitting power of those tiny little 2 1/2-inch light load English shells. These guys boasted of fifty-yard kills. How could that be? The loads were standard three-dram, 1 1/16-ounce British loads. These light loads have always been the norm in England and really reflect a very different philosophy of gunning: Develop a very efficient pattern from the gun using the minimum amount of shot and powder rather than trying to overcome poor patterns with large amounts of shot and powder, magnum shells. I have since come to believe that careful use of a light but balanced load in a well-patterning gun may actually result in more uniform hitting power at the target than the blown and swirling patterns so common with magnum shells. Some of the experts cited in this book seem to agree.

Consider this: Many American hunters think they must have magnum 12-gauge loads in order to hunt properly, while many others think they are such great shots that a 20 gauge or even a 28 gauge is enough gun for wild birds! Both positions seem a bit extreme to me.

CHAPTER 26
A CONVERSATION WITH PAT LIESKE

PAT LIESKE

Shooting Instructor
Davison, Michigan

Pat Lieske is one of those unique people who can both do and teach. In the 1994 USA Sporting Clays Championship, Pat tied for third in a field of nine hundred competitors, but he spends every weekend when he is not competing, teaching shooting at a prestigious shooting club in Michigan.

Pat, a tall, muscular young man, is a financial analyst by trade. He has also been heavily involved in competitive shooting sporting clays at the national level for several years. Many of Pat's teaching methods are grounded in the quick, reflexive, instinctive shooting techniques necessary for sporting clays, using a low gun to shoot widely varying targets; the clay bird game most similar to roughshooting.

The use of a shooting instructor to help improve skills was relatively rare in the United States until recently. However, many hunters have come to realize that keeping their skills constantly honed and ready for the hunting season pays off.

Pat focuses on taking control of the many variables of shooting to develop instinctive shooting skills. With his height and long arms, he finds off-the-rack guns do not fit him well. He shoots a custom-stocked Beretta Automatic on the competitive circuit.

Some people delve deeply into the technical aspects of guns and shooting. Do you need to know these aspects to be a good shooter?

LIESKE—Not at all! It's like any other sport or activity. Some people get as much enjoyment from reading and learning about the technical aspects as they do from getting out and actually doing the real thing. I find a lot of people in sporting clays and shotgunning, in general, have just as much fun thinking about what choke is good at this distance and planning different reloads as they do shooting. In the end you can have the best gun, the best shells and know everything there is to know about shooting and guns.

But if you can't put that shot in the right spot to hit what you are shooting at, you are going to have trouble. Knowledge alone won't necessarily make you a better shot.

Pat Lieske (instructor) explains to George Wilson some small detail of the gun shouldering movement that may be reducing his ability to come up on target instinctively.

What method can the average shooter use to help his shooting and can you give us a brief description of the various shooting methods that are taught?

Now he watches to see if the action change was positive. Note that Pat and George are not shooting from the standard positions on the trap or skeet field.

LIESKE—There are about three so-called standardized shooting methods. One is called *pass-through* shooting or what most people in the United States call the Churchill method. Churchill came up with this idea and it worked well with the type of guns that Churchill made: short-barreled, lively guns. If you are shooting a real fast gun it works great, as you come from behind the target and virtually see no lead. Shoot right at the target and, of course, the lead is developed as the gun keeps moving between the time you see the target, pull the trigger and when the shot gets to the target. Obviously, the barrel has moved in front of the target because there is no way you could hit a moving target without shooting in front of it.

A second method is called *maintained lead* or you may hear people call it *sustained lead.* You start in front of the target at a predetermined length and maintain that distance of lead. With this method you have the ability to kill the target at any point because you always have a lead. As a general rule, that may be fairly hard to do on wild birds in heavy cover or if they fly erratically. The third method is called the *pull-away* method. The Clay Pigeon Shooting Association of England has adopted this as its preferred method of teaching sporting clays shooting and for teaching generalized shooting. In the pull-away method you start by inserting the gun on the target then pull away from the target to generate your lead. As you perceive the lead opening up, you then pull the trigger and deliver the shot. I think, for most hunting situations, the pull-away method is probably the best.

The difference between pull-away versus sustained lead and pass-through shooting is that in pull-away you are always tracking along at the speed of the target and you are always starting on the target. If a bird flies up in front of you, you're moving the gun with the target; you're always with the bird and moving at speed. You are always pointing in the general vicinity of the bird, no matter what. Then all you have to do is get the proper lead. You naturally adjust, depending on what the bird is doing, so with experience your mind will automatically calculate how far in front you are going to pull away before you pull the trigger to deliver the shot. You are just going to instinctively do it and that's really the key to any shooting style. Realistically, there is no such thing as an instinctive shooting method, but you begin to shoot instinctively when you commit your method or style of shooting into your subconscious and it automatically happens. That is what instinctive shooting is all about.

How would you define snap shooting?

LIESKE—Snap shooting, in the truest sense, would be what we call spot shooting. You see the target, you pick a spot and you shoot that spot and hope that the bird is there when the shot gets there. For most people it is a form of pass-through shooting. Even though it is a very quick, short movement, they are still coming from behind and shooting the target.

Do you teach only one style or do you take the shooter's natural style and work on that?

LIESKE—There is definitely no one shooting style that is best for everybody, nor is there one shooting style that is best for every target that you might encounter. To be a good shooter you need to be able to adapt to whatever happens.

Is pass shooting geese from a blind totally different than shooting grouse in the woods?

LIESKE—Yes. Almost every situation requires a slightly different technique, so if you are going to be a good all-around shooter you need to be able to do more than one shooting method, because there is no way that one method is going to work for every situation.

How do I learn to get the gun up and mounted in place quickly and correctly almost by instinct?

LIESKE—The key is mounting the gun with your left hand. If you mount your gun with your left hand, the whole gun moves out away from you as you mount it and the gun goes right to your cheek. However, about 95 percent of all hunters try to mount the gun with their right hand, but the left hand is more important than the right hand! It's the left hand that mounts the gun and points it as well.

In roughshooting, flushed birds always come up fast and many are surprise flushes. Can you give us some key pointers that help get the gun up fast and on the target quickly?

LIESKE—The key is in making shotgunning a natural extension of your body. Try to make the gun a natural part of you, just like anything you might use in everyday life, something you do every day. When you point at something with your left index finger with both eyes open (if you are right-handed) you will be pointing directly at whatever you are looking at. You don't have to think about that. You don't have to look at your index finger (or at your barrel) to see if you are on target; it's just going to be there. The more you can make shooting a shotgun similar to something that you do every single day, the better. Every day you wake up and go through your day with both eyes open. You point simply by extending your finger to indicate something and that is the way you should shoot a shotgun. Both eyes open, then reach out and point. It's just natural.

But how much do I have to shoot? If I shoot fifty clay targets a month from a low gun position, will that keep me reasonably tuned up?

LIESKE—More would be better, but fifty is a lot better than none. But there is something else that you can do that doesn't take much time, energy or money. About two or three times a week break your gun out of the gun safe, make sure it is unloaded, then, in a safe place go ahead and pretend to shoot a flying object. It costs nothing and it works great. It's a proven fact that your muscles have memory and any time that you mount the gun and visualize shooting you are building muscle memory and training your mind. You are visualizing, making muscle memories and committing those factors to your subconscious.

When I go out to the skeet or trap club to shoot by myself I may shoot a whole round on just two or three stations. I may shoot eight or ten targets from the one station that best simulates a flushed grouse, but I never see anybody else doing that. Why?

LIESKE—Because there are very few hunters at most clubs. Very few hunters put in the practice time it takes to become a good shot. They wait all year for the hunting season to come, and long for opening day, and then they are not prepared. They have their gun ready, their outfit ready, their dog ready, but they're not ready to shoot.

So a hunter should not feel embarrassed to ask at a trap range to throw birds from any station while he practices?

After the lesson, Pat is off to the Sporting Clays Range to work on his own skills for the next big tournament.

LIESKE—It's not a problem if the range isn't too busy. In my experience, the best way to do that is in the afternoons. I wouldn't try to go out on a Saturday or Sunday morning and ask for something special, but if you go out on Saturday afternoon when the football game is on, they will work with you. They want your business and if they can get an extra fifty hunters to come out and use their operation every month, it's worth it to them, and you.

So you think playing clay games really does make a difference in your shooting?

LIESKE—Yes, without a doubt.

Pat goes after a fast left to right double.

Then how come when I hunt with guys that can shoot a hundred trap targets straight they don't hit wild birds any better than I do?

LIESKE—That's because as the games of trap and skeet became more competitive, their shooting has nothing to do with shooting live birds. They're shooting a repetitive game that is based on concentration, a very regimented game. But if you go hunting with guys that shoot a lot of sporting clays, you will notice that they are also very good wild bird shots.

Do chokes really make a major difference in a hunting situation?

LIESKE—Probably for about 75 percent of all the shooting that you will ever do, you can shoot an improved cylinder choke. That gets rid of one of the variables in the process. I have seen people break targets at fifty or sixty yards with improved cylinders and they were broken hard enough that if it had been a bird it would have been killed at that distance. As good as commercial ammunition is today, unless you are shooting real large, tough birds at long distances the choke is not that important.

PART IV
ROUGHSHOOTER'S MISCELLANY

C H A P T E R 2 7

GOOD GEAR MAKES AN IMPORTANT DIFFERENCE

Well-fitting and appropriate gear enhances your enjoyment of any physically taxing sport. Roughshooting is no exception. Your gear need not be expensive or fancy, so long as it is well constructed and durable. A basic $30 hunting vest, well fitted and rugged, will be far more comfortable for hunting than a stylish but restrictive $250 hunting coat. The goal of proper gear is not to impress your friends, but simply to allow you to enjoy the hunt with minimal interference.

If you spend many days afield, you can expect to encounter a wide variety of weather conditions, and nothing ruins a hunt faster than being cold, wet or in pain. Most hunters I know are on a lifelong search for new and fascinating equipment for the hunt. I have a large closet devoted to my numerous experiments in outdoor clothing. My wife swears that if I wore nothing but the hunting clothes I already own, all day, everyday, for the rest of my life, I could never wear them all out. Because hunting is such a rigorous physical activity, your clothing should be nonbinding for easy walking and quick-shooting agility. They should provide protection from briars and brush and incorporate methods for easy temperature control. It is easy to find gear that accomplishes one of these objectives, but it is combining all of them that is complex.

First, to really enjoy hunting you need to dress for temperature control. Think about the extremes you face in a morning of hunting. When you leave your vehicle at 8 A.M. it is cold, perhaps 27 degrees, frost is still on the grass, a bit of a breeze is blowing, and the sun is low in the east. You

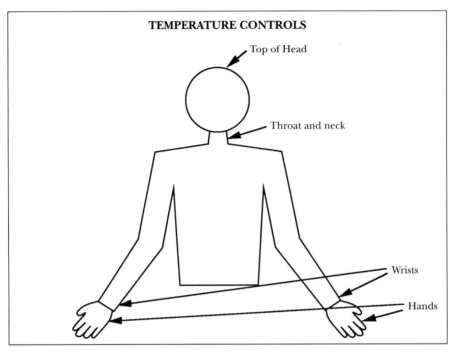

TEMPERATURE CONTROLS

Top of Head

Throat and neck

Wrists

Hands

Controlling your body temperature during a day of arduous hunting can be accomplished by covering and uncovering the six spots on the upper body where blood flows closest to the skin. These are the top of the head, throat and neck, wrists and hands.

are warm and cozy from a long ride in the truck and your stomach is still working on the last of the pancakes you ate an hour ago. A warm jacket, a snug hat and gloves make you toasty as you turn the dogs loose and start into the woods. But by 11 A.M. the sun is bright, it is fifty-eight degrees and after slipping and sliding across a half-mile-wide milo field of ankle-deep Kansas mud you are roasting. The sweat trickles down your back, your gloves are off, your jacket is tied around your waist and your hat is stuffed in your pocket. You must still reclimb three big hills before you get back to the truck for lunch. You now understand the hunter's adage, "Always start out cold." As the day warms and your exertion level intensifies, you will still be comfortable.

NATURE'S WAY OF KEEPING WARM

I'm never afraid to appropriate someone else's good ideas, so I've adopted temperature-control ideas from hikers and cross-country skiers. Years ago I purchased a very well-designed mountain parka and with it I received a small booklet that explained body temperature control in varying conditions. The booklet outlined the six major heat control spots on your upper body: the top of the head, the throat, neck and upper chest, both hands and both wrists.

These six "hot spots" are where blood circulates near the skin surface. When you cover them, you shield your body from heat loss. You can uncover these areas and the blood circulation will transfer body heat through the skin to the atmosphere. This is how I use my gear in each of the six spots to remain comfortable regardless of temperature or physical exertion.

Bill Vander Mass starts a hunt warm and covered; hat on, collar up, gloves on, sleeves buttoned—smart shooter.

HEAT CONTROL ZONES

Your head is one of the highest heat-loss areas. Wear a snug, warm but lightweight cap when it is cold, then stow it as the day heats up. Carry a visor or a mesh-top cap with a wide bill to wear during the heat of the day and to shield your eyes for shooting. Flat caps that can be easily stowed and carried work best.

Wear shirts that can be opened and closed. When you're cold, button the shirt and raise the collar to cover the back of your neck. As you warm up, unbutton your shirt and roll down your collar. Open the top of the vest and undershirt. *Never* wear a turtleneck, unless it has a front zipper that can be opened. Wear a small scarf around your neck. It can be removed and stowed as needed.

Wear shooting gloves: gloves on when cold, gloves off when warm.

The blood flow through your wrists is very near the skin. Wear shirts with button cuffs that can be unbuttoned and rolled up and a long underwear shirt with sleeves that can be pushed up. *Avoid* jackets with sleeves that cannot be adjusted.

String mesh undershirts (sold by L. L. Bean) trap warmth when your overshirt is closed but allows air to reach your skin when the top buttons of the outer shirt are opened. A Henley collar undershirt also helps regulate warmth by allowing you to button or unbutton it at the throat area.

Long underwear bottoms are totally inflexible to control body heat. The only way to cool off is to take them off, boots and all.

Hunting vests provide both flexibility and heat control. My friend Frank Sylvester, a long-time hunter, swears that fifty years ago hunting vests were virtually unavailable and his uncles had their wives remove the sleeves of their hunting coats to make the equivalent of today's shooting vests. A hunting vest provides the maximum level of utility, carrying capacity, shooting flexibility and comfort. The price of a vest has little to do with its comfort, fit, utility or carrying capacity. Your vest will keep your torso warm, but give you great mobility for shooting.

Three hours later, the hat is stowed, the collar is open, the gloves are in his vest pocket and the sleeves are rolled up to the elbow. Such a simple system, wearing a vest and stowable gear, is a painless method of body temperature control.

LAYERING

Often *layering* clothes is proposed as the ultimate solution to warmth and flexibility in strenuous outdoor activities. To a point I agree. Three light layers—a Henley-necked duofold undershirt, a thick canvas hunting shirt and a sturdy canvas shooting vest—should provide adequate warmth in most autumn roughshooting situations. But sometimes an additional layer is needed. The problem with the practice of adding and removing layers to control your body heat is, what do you do with the removed layer when you are three miles from the truck? The answer is you carry it, or drag it or stuff it in your vest. None would seem very appealing. That is why I embraced the "six-spot" temperature-control system. It helps me avoid the "extra" layer consequences.

PROTECTIVE CLOTHING

The most expensive protective clothing is made of rugged, briar-resistant fabrics that are guaranteed to turn aside even the most vicious thorns, but unfortunately those same fabrics tend to be stiff as a board. Clothing made from these fabrics make long, arduous walks and quick, reflexive shooting impossible. I don't have an easy solution, but I never wear protective fabric above the waist. A rugged canvas shirt seems to protect my upper body effectively even in the most brutal woodcock cover. Below the waist I wear lightweight briar pants. In really brutal cover I sometimes wear a protective pair of lightweight leggings over my briar pants. Two layers of lightweight protective fabric provide more comfort and flexibility than one pair of superheavy briar pants *and* seem to effectively turn briars away.

FLEXIBILITY AND AGILITY IN CLOTHING

We are lucky to have so many new, warm, lightweight and flexible fabrics available. In my father's era only brittle canvas and stiff heavy wool would provide the same level of comfort and warmth we get from Polypropylene, polar fleece and Thermomax. These fabrics are designed to wick moisture away from the body during high exertion periods, keeping the wearer warmer and more comfortable.

Having the right gear neatly organized can be fairly simple. This truck holds two dog crates, plus (left to right) shooting box for shells and tools, shell belt, vest, side-by-side shotgun, Wellingtons (boots) for rain, Russell leather boots for dry weather, dog bowl and water jug.

BOOTS

No single item of gear (except your gun) contributes as much to the comfort of a day of roughshooting as a proper pair of boots. An ill-fitting gun is a nuisance, but ill-fitting boots will spoil the day. The proper boot helps you tackle widely varying terrain and many different levels of moisture and traction without strain, stress or aches. At the risk of oversimplifying the proposition, a boot must satisfy five criteria:

First, the boot must fit properly. Without proper fit, comfort is impossible and soon pinches, blisters, slips or flaps will be diverting your attention from the hunt to your feet. If you are hard to fit like I am, a pair of custom-made boots is well worth the cost. A couple of hundred dollars for great-fitting boots can save the day.

Second, the boot must provide support to your foot, ankle, arch and lower calf. As you grow older and heavier (as most people do), this will become increasingly important to your comfort and your safety as well.

Third, the boot must keep you dry in wet weather. Unfortunately, the same materials that keep you warm and dry in cold, wet weather tend to make you wet and sticky in warm, dry weather. So, although rubber boots are the best and most foolproof solution to really wet conditions, they also tend to be hot and sticky on warm days and provide minimal support. Some leather boots are guaranteed waterproof. I've never found that to be completely true.

Fourth, the boot must match the temperatures encountered. Today's space-age materials (like Thinsulate) can provide warmth and comfort in a very thin envelope. However, if you plan any hot weather hiking or hunting, the Thinsulate will cook you in its cocoon of warmth. Often the best all-around temperature range is found in a plain leather boot teamed with varying types of socks.

Fifth, every step expends energy and therefore the greater the weight of the boot, the greater the energy expended. Obviously you want the lightest weight boot possible *but* one that will provide the support and protection necessary to walk all day over rough terrain. The bigger and clunkier the boot, the harder to push through heavy grass and weeds, making it harder to walk briskly. Occasionally I see someone trying to bird hunt in the big, clunky pack boots that deer hunters favor. The result is usually just what you would expect: a substantial loss of agility and mobility for the roughshooter who wears them.

In addition to those five key characteristics, the boot should also protect your feet and shins. If you are a really aggressive hunter, you tackle rough cover that provides the perfect recipe for thorn pricks and bruised shins.

The big question is how to combine all these needs into one boot? In my opinion it can't be done, and any boot that tries is at best a compromise. I have been accused of suffering from a boot fetish, but I think it is just my own realistic understanding of the strengths and weaknesses of each type of boot, and my willingness to buy several pairs of boots to meet *each* of my hunting needs.

HOW MANY BOOTS DOES ONE REALLY NEED?

At the minimum it is tough to get by without two pairs: a pair of dry weather boots (usually leather) and a pair of wet weather boots (usually rubber), or at least a rubber bottom like an L. L. Bean bird boot. A third, often needed in the north country, is a knee-high all-rubber boot for those really wet days in the marshy country.

I always take at least three pairs of boots with me, even though I seldom use more than one or two pairs per trip. I never know which ones will be needed until the morning we head out to hunt, and even then the weather might change by noon. Boots don't take up much space, but having a spare pair along has saved many a hunting trip. Boot dryers are also a great invention that when plugged in at dinner can usually provide you with dry boots by morning.

These are the various types of boots and the pros and cons of each.

TRADITIONAL LEATHER BOOTS

This is still the most popular and most critical boot in your hunting wardrobe. You need a long mileage, heavy effort, power carrying boot. Some people like the molded toe models that purport to be waterproof. Timberline and Danner sell these by the millions. They must be great boots because friends of mine swear by them. But because of my foot shape I get a much better fit in the moccasin toe boots (stitching around the toe seam) like those made by Russell or Gokey, a better-quality boot that provides better support and lasts longer. This is the high-mileage prairie boot for pheasant and quail hunting. You won't want much of a lug on the sole unless you enjoy hauling Iowa mud along on every step. Comfort, support, fit, relatively cool (or warm if insulated) and medium in weight—this boot should be your first choice, for use about 50 percent of the time.

RUBBER BOOTS

The knee-high, all-rubber molded boot is the driest boot of all. These are made both in the United States and overseas and are extremely popular in England where the climate is so inclement. The English call them "Wellies," short for Wellingtons. Manufactured in a variety of weights and insulation levels, these molded boots are totally inflexible in the way they fit or conform to your foot. You may need to try several different manufacturers and models before you find a comfortable pair that fits you properly. These are the boots for pouring rain days and standing puddles. However, they offer minimal support, are hot and sticky in warm weather and can be difficult to fit.

L. L. BEAN-TYPE RUBBER BOTTOMS

These are an American classic now available from a wide variety of manufacturers. Some are very cheap, imported imitations guaranteed to kill your feet. Bean's are still the premier in quality and durability. They will do a fine job of keeping you dry on wet days, but won't handle standing water more than a couple of inches deep. These boots were originally designed for grouse and woodcock hunting where a few inches of ground water, shallow creeklets and marshy ground are so common.

They are reasonably priced, waterproof in damp conditions and have a comfortable lace-up top to improve fit. However, they offer minimal foot support and foot fit can be hard to match exactly. They need to be fitted with a support insole to cushion the impact of normal hunting activity.

HIKING BOOTS

In early season or warm-weather conditions, a top-quality hiking boot like a Hi-Tech, a Merrill or a Vasque can make outstanding hunting footwear. They are light, comfortable and provide terrific support. What they don't provide is protection and durability. Their lightweight materials are easily punctured by thorns or torn by rough cover. Only a few provide any warmth, insulation or waterproofing. The low-cut style can allow your legs to suffer most of the abrasions of hunting.

SUPPORT INSOLES

The space-age insoles we have loved in running shoes are available at most shoe repair shops and can turn many otherwise comfortable boots into a great pair of well-fitting supportive boots. Even the best quality rubber boots with a steel shank embedded in the arch perform best when properly fitted with a high-tech arch support. Running shoe-type insoles work very well.

Top-quality *custom fitted,* moccasin toe, leather boots are made by both the Russell Moccasin Company of Berlin, Wisconsin, and the Gokey Boot Company of Tipton, Missouri. I wear an odd-size shoe and I need a boot with lots of support. Russell has made several pairs of custom boots for me and I really love them. The neat thing about Russell is that they will add or subtract any feature to their custom boots, such as speed lacing or heel counters or kangaroo leather or any one of *twenty-four* different soles, and you can have the boots made exactly to the size and shape of your foot.

RAIN GEAR

Everyone has a little different idea on how to stay dry and keep hunting on rainy days. Fortunately, over the last twenty years the quality of rain gear has

When it gets really cold and the snow hangs on the ground, it may take a shooting coat to stop the chill.

In the British Isles it frequently rains, so Alan Gwynne wears the appropriate rain gear for a field trial, including "Wellies" and full rain pants.

improved significantly. Both technology and newly imported clothing have contributed to this improvement. Barbour Brand Clothing is the best example of gear that is now widely available in the United States that was unknown here just a decade or so ago. The Barbour line, a British style, is made of Egyptian cotton, a natural fiber, then treated and retreated with a waxing process to impart moisture turning properties. The fabric breathes, it flexes and it ages softly over time. However, it is heavy, it smells bad and it stains the seats of your vehicle unmercifully. I love my Barbour gear for outdoor wear, especially field trials on rainy days. Unfortunately I can't shoot worth a damn in my coat. It's just too heavy and too restrictive. A dozen Barbour look-alikes are now on the market including a Filson waxed jacket that has all the flexibility of a taco chip. I've been able to find some lightweight Gore-tex shooting coats that turn rain water reasonably well and still give me shooting flexibility. They don't seem to handle abrasion very well in the woods so they must be replaced every few years, but that's a small price to pay for staying dry.

Barbour does make full rain pants, which I consider indispensable for rainy-day hunting. These are not chaps but full pants with a drawstring waist, and they seem to prevent the dreaded soggy underwear problem. Rain chaps can allow the water from your hunting coat to drip onto the unprotected seat of your pants above the chaps.

Also bothersome is the rain that flows off your cap and down your neck. A wide-brimmed waterproof hat drains the water out onto the shoulders of your coat. These are now available from numerous manufacturers.

SHOOTING BOXES

Neatness and organization of personal effects has never been one of my long suits. My basement shelves are a jumble of odd tools, parts, electrical switches, bolts, nuts, screws, nails, bits of wire, paint rollers and the like. It is often easier to go to the store and buy more rather than look for the odd part I need on those shelves. During a busy shooting season, my garage and gun bench also get very cluttered. However, I keep my dog gear and my gun gear organized in a series of cases that I can easily toss in the truck at a moment's notice.

Years ago every hunter had a hand-made wooden box to hold his gear, extra shells, gloves or any other essentials. I've seen a few of these ancient, battered chests for sale from time to time in antique shops and flea markets. I always lusted after one of these old pieces of history, but the prices were usually as high as the condition of the box was low. Then a friend pointed out that a twenty-five-pound box loaded with another twenty-five pounds of gear becomes a very cumbersome load in the back of your vehicle. The hand-crafted shooting box of old has now been replaced by a neat plastic tool case; inexpensive, easily washed out at the end of the season, strong, durable, very lightweight and available at any hardware store.

Alas, another time-honored tradition succumbs to technology.

BODY SUPPORT

It is a fact of life that physical efforts result in more aches and pains as we age. Some people claim not to experience this rite of passage, as they reach their era. But most of us do. Previous generations often restricted their physical activities as they got older. However, today the "use it or lose it" and "if you rest, you rust" generation keeps pounding out the miles year after year. That is not to say that we don't awaken each morning with that familiar dull ache in our muscles from exercise. None of us wants to overtax our muscles and one of the best ways to avoid muscle strain or injury is with the use of good gear.

Most hunters' aches and pains come from the feet, knees and lower back. Fortunately, today's technology has produced some assistance devices for all three: back braces, knee braces and support insoles. The simplest by far is the new high-tech back brace. It is easy to wear, comfortable, light-weight and inexpensive. You can protect yourself and greatly reduce the wear of a day-long hunt for under $40. These marvels of nylon, elastic, spandex and Velcro are a miracle for the lower back pain sufferer. A second wonderful invention is the spaghetti strap knee brace. It, too, is lightweight, comfortable, supportive and inexpensive. Constructed of plastic, neoprene and Velcro, it can go a long way toward keeping a sensitive knee from ruining your hunt. Finally, the great new space-age foot support products slip into a pair of standard boots and instantly transform the old foot gear into versatile boots as agile as a running shoe. I find the back brace, knee brace and support insole indispensable to my hunting comfort.

As you pursue roughshooting for yourself, doubtless you will adopt many of the foregoing suggestions and plenty that come from your own particular needs based on your own preferences and experiences. And, after all, customizing to suit your own needs is a large part of the fun in the planning of and satisfaction in your success.

CHAPTER 28
GUN SAFETY

"Nor all the Pheasants that err been bred are worth the price of one man dead."

—Old English saying

Many years ago the retired president of General Motors, Harlow (Red) Curtice, was duck hunting with some fellow GM executives on Lake St. Clair when a horrible accident occurred. Curtice shot and killed a retired GM vice president and hunting companion. The hunting partner stood up directly in the line of fire as Curtice raised his gun to fire at an overhead flight of ducks. His long-time friend was killed instantly. Gentleman that he was, Curtice took it upon himself to go to the man's home and break the news to his companion's wife that he (Curtice) had that morning accidentally shot and killed her husband. The story made national news and I remember it well. I've often wondered if I could be so brave as Mr. Curtice, and prayed that I would never be in such a position.

More recently I was flipping through the television channels when I came upon one of those celebrity hunting shows that have become *de rigeur* for January Saturday morning television. Why pheasant hunting with a country-western singer is more interesting than pheasant hunting with a banker, factory manager or postman is beyond me, but anyway, that seems to be the current format of choice. In this case an army of far too many people were pheasant hunting in South Dakota as a group. Some were walking through standing corn while the celebrity and the host narrator blocked the end of the field and chitchatted while they waited for the birds to fly out overhead. Even knowing that no serious mishap had taken place (if it had I wouldn't have been watching this video months later in the comfort of my home), I cringed as I watched supposedly experienced guides and hunters shoot toward each other. Of course, depth perception is fuzzy at best in a video, but nonetheless, the potential for serious damage occurs anytime a firearm is discharged in the direction of another hunter, especially when shooting large shot sizes—fours, fives or sixes—at Dakota rooster pheasants.

Only a few other sports have the potential of hunting or sport shooting for instant death or serious injury. Sure, you can wreck a race car or sink a boat or drop a bowling ball on a buddy's foot, but none of these has ever presented the potential for instant death of a loaded 12 gauge at close range. Unfortunately, the more one handles a gun, the more distant this possibility seems. Over time, many otherwise safe hunters begin to relax just enough to let an unsafe habit creep into the equation. Four careless situations account for *most* of the unsafe actions:

1. Shooting in the direction of another hunter, usually due to overexcitement, or losing track of the other hunter's location.

2. Waving a loaded gun past, over or at a person, either while hunting or alongside your vehicle.

3. Forgetting to unload or disable a firearm when no longer hunting.

4. Failing to have the safety on at all times.

It was evident in the previously mentioned video that the hunters using break-open guns, side-by-sides or over-unders effectively unloaded their guns (by opening the gun) when talking to the camera or moving from one field to another. Even on video, I could quickly see that the gun was opened and over the arm of the hunter; however, the one-barrel guns made me nervous. Although those hunters may have unloaded them just as conscientiously, I could not tell that by looking. Because I can't readily tell if a one-barrel gun is unloaded, whenever I hunt with anyone carrying a one-barrel pump or auto loader I am very careful to avoid his muzzle. Their guns seem to make me more nervous than they make them.

Another unsafe situation results when a hunter wants to enjoy a beer with lunch then head back to the fields. That is an absolute no-no in my book. There is no place for a drink during the day's shooting. After hunting is finished and the guns are cased for the night I almost always have a drink or two, but the shooting field is no place for a noon nip.

Unfortunately, most hunting books don't say much about safety and there seems to be an almost unspoken rule about broaching the subject to an unsafe shooter. I've watched otherwise boldly outspoken people hold their tongue when someone makes an unconscious but stupid safety mistake. I've felt the same discomfort myself and on many occasions with-held comment. Frankly, I've reached the point where I will no longer hunt with anyone who makes me feel even remotely unsafe, regardless of how good the shooting. We all owe it to ourselves to dig out or reorder the booklet used to teach a hunter safety class and read it every few years.

BLAZE ORANGE

Blaze orange is a fairly recent invention that only came into its own after World War II. Orange clothing sales took off when it became mandatory for deer hunting in many states. Amazingly, some states still don't require blaze orange for upland hunting.

A few of the most gentlemanly hunters find blaze orange repugnant and feel that it links them to the armies of fence busters and beer guzzlers that add little to our hunting reputation. I, too, wish to distance myself from that element of hunting, but not so much that I refuse to wear blaze orange. In 1960, when the wearing of blaze orange was first made law in the state of Massachusetts, accidental shootings while deer hunting fell by 67 percent. In the grouse woods or the deep pheasant CRP fields, only a splash of blaze orange marks your spot.

Dr. Dennis Scherer savoring the results of a day of his favorite recreation. What more could a hunter ask for than a sunny day in North Dakota, a favorite dog and three roosters in the bag. Dr. Scherer wears a blaze orange hat and vest in the hunting field.

Last fall, a hunting party that I was in was following up a covey flush by hunting quail singles in a Kansas CRP field of chest-high weeds. As a bird erupted and skimmed away just at weed-top level, one of the hunters fired off two quick shots, then exploded into a stream of expletives. The reason was soon obvious. One of our fellow hunters had walked in from the other side, a very dangerous practice, and his blaze orange hat was so old and faded that it was invisible against the fall colors. The shooter had fired directly at the other hunter at fairly close range. We dug out new hats for our partners as soon as we got back to the trucks.

SAFETY GLASSES

I wear glasses at all times and have for many years, so I don't even think about it, but no one should ever go afield to hunt without protective eyewear. The proper pair of glasses can protect your eyes in so many ways, from errant pellets, sticks and weeds, to harmful ultraviolet sun rays. There really is no excuse for hunting without proper eye protection.

I've been on a few hunting trips that were ruined when the whole crew had to pack up and rush to a local hospital to let the doctors check out a minor eye abrasion. Most of us expect to spend our days in the woods, not waiting in an emergency room. Many different types of shooting glasses are available, but be sure to buy the type with tough lenses, the kind that is most likely to stop a pellet.

MEDICAL ASPECTS OF HUNTING

Somehow when one mentions hunting, many people envision a dangerous sport where dozens or perhaps even hundreds of people are killed or wounded annually. Fortunately, the reality is that hunting is far down the list of sports in terms of injury and fatality rates. Although the potential for catastrophic injury is always present when loaded firearms are involved, the facts place hunting injuries far below snow skiing, football, baseball, tennis or even golf. The statistics relate that the lowest injury rate sports are *hunting*, with nine injuries per hundred thousand participants, and swimming, with ninety-three injuries per hundred thousand. The highest injury rate sports are football, with 2,171 injuries per 100,000 players, and baseball, with 2,089 injuries per 100,000.

However, one should not trivialize the inherent potential for injury or death during a hunt, not just from gunshots but from falls, eye injuries, muscle sprains or heart attacks. Put in perspective: Every day people die from heart attacks or injuries in the most surprising places. Three of my friends have died on the golf course; one acquaintance fell over dead at age fifty-three at, of all places, a cocktail party at an engineering society conference; another hunting buddy in apparently great health fell over dead while shooting at a bird dog field trial. In that case, I had the unpleasant responsibility of calling his wife, who was at home four hundred miles away, and breaking the news of his death. She didn't lose control but told me very calmly, "He died doing what he loved so much. If he had to go at least he was happy at the time!"

A CONVERSATION WITH DENNIS F. SCHERER, M.D.

Dr. Denny Scherer is a medical doctor who practices in Grand Rapids, Minnesota. He is a great guy, fun to be with, a pretty fair shot and he has a high-quality dog or two in his kennel. "Dr. Denny" has for many years been the resident acting medical advisor for the National Grouse and Woodcock hunt sponsored by the Grand Rapids Chapter of the Ruffed Grouse Society. Every year for four days about a hundred hunters and fifty guides are in the woods under Dr. Scherer's watchful eye. My math says that is about six hundred person-days of hunting, so Dr. Scherer has good insights into the types of potential injuries involved in such a large group. Although no major accident has ever occurred, he gives us some advice on what to do in case of a bad accident or a serious health emergency.

What are the most common minor medical situations on hunting trips and how does one treat them?

SCHERER—First, to prevent injuries it is important to know your own physical abilities and limitations. Prevention and treatment of sprains and strains begin long before the hunting season with preseason conditioning, including walking through heavy grass and cover with heavy hunting clothes and boots. Actually, strains and sprains sometimes develop slowly, resulting from the fatigue of repetitive activity. Treatment includes rest, use of ice packs and anti-inflammatory medication. And then, be sure to start with adequate warm-up and stretching exercises the next day before resuming activities.

Other injuries often happen quite suddenly when the hunter steps in unseen holes or trips over a dead fall. Often these result in sprains, bruises or muscle tears. Again, these are best treated with rest, elevation, ice packs and anti-inflammatory medicine such as aspirin, Ibuprofen (Advil, Motrin or Nuprin) or Naproxyn (Aleve).

Many well-planned hunting trips have been ruined by twigs, weeds and other sharp objects poking people in the eye. Almost all these injuries can be prevented simply by wearing protective eyewear. Polycarbonate is probably the best lens material for protecting the eyes and it is fairly effective against shotgun pellets.

If the hunter gets a penetrating wound from a knife (while cleaning birds) or a sharp object, irrigate the wound as much as possible with clean water and soap such as Betadine, Hibiclens or PhisoHex, then control bleeding with direct pressure. Wounds requiring sutures should be seen within six hours to reduce the risk of infection. Older wounds sometimes have to be left open to heal slowly because of the increased risk of infection when such wounds are sutured shut.

Hypothermia is more of a concern in duck or deer hunting, but can be prevented by the use of proper clothing, appropriate food and liquids and a reasonable exercise level. Rain gear is essential to keep dry in wet weather to prevent evaporative heat loss. Chills and shivering indicate significant temperature drop and indicate the need to seek additional warmth. Risk of hypothermia is reduced if adequate liquids are taken throughout the day in quantities large enough to maintain regular urine output.

Another condition that often ruins hunting trips is diarrhea. Avoid drinking water from lakes and streams. Wash your hands well if possible before meals and properly refrigerate any prepared foods you plan to use. Diarrhea should be treated with large amounts of clear liquids, replacement fluids such as Gatorade and medications such as Pepto-Bismol or Immodium AD. If the diarrhea is associated with severe abdominal pain, fever or blood in the stool, medical attention should be sought immediately.

Believe it or not, a significant number of hunters suffer dog bites when they break up a dog fight or attempt to kennel or handle their hunting partner's dog.

What critical things must one do in case of a serious illness or injury?

SCHERER—In case of a potentially serious illness or medical injury, *first* the situation must be assessed. The problem may be fairly simple and straightforward, such as an ankle injury where it would be important to see if there is any obvious deformity and if the injured party can bear weight, or in the case of a penetrating injury, the extent of injury and bleeding must be assessed. *Second,* act quickly. If there is no breathing or heartbeat, cardiopulmonary resuscitation should be attempted. If someone is choking, the Heimlich maneuver may be necessary or if there is serious bleeding, direct pressure may be adequate to control this.

The *third* step is accessing the emergency medical system by dialing 911 and arranging for transportation. If hunting in a group, this should be started immediately. It may require bringing a vehicle to the scene of the accident or driving to the nearest phone. If you have a cellular phone with you, this step can be greatly expedited. This is why you should know where you are at all times, in order to direct emergency assistance.

When hunting in a new area, it is always worth taking a moment to learn the locations of the nearest emergency services and closest telephones.

With most sprains, lacerations or fractures, the victim can be assisted to a vehicle or the vehicle can be brought to the victim. A cardiac event is often characterized by chest, neck, shoulder, arm, back or upper abdominal pain, and is usually associated with shortness of breath and profuse sweating (and usually aggravated by exertion). The victim should be made to sit or lie quietly until transportation is brought to the scene or he can be carried out.

What things should be done in case of an accidental gunshot wound?

SCHERER—First, assess the extent of injury and the source of bleeding. If the injury involves the head, neck or chest, it is important to clear the victim's airway and be sure he is breathing.

The second, and probably the most important, action is to control the bleeding. Usually this is best done by applying pressure directly to the source of bleeding.

The third, and often most important, thing of all is to access the emergency medical system (911) as soon as possible. Exactly what is done, and in what order depends on the location of the wound.

In serious injuries to the head, neck, chest and abdomen, quick transport to a medical facility within an hour may be mandatory to save a life. The victim's airway should be maintained by positioning to allow blood to drain from the mouth and throat. If you are alone with a victim of a serious head, neck, chest or abdominal wound and no help is expected, you may have little choice but to go immediately for help or evacuate the victim yourself immediately.

In penetrating injuries to the eyeball it is best to avoid direct pressure to the eyeball, which might result in extraction of the intraocular contents.

With gunshot wounds to the extremities, the initial emphasis is placed on control of the bleeding. In such a situation, control of bleeding should not be compromised for speed of transportation. Too many people have bled to death while sitting in the front seat of a pickup truck speeding to a hospital when the time would have been better spent maintaining control of the bleeding. Sometimes stopping at the first source of assistance or telephone is preferred to racing on to the hospital when bleeding is not adequately controlled. Avoid giving the victim food or water, since this may obstruct the airway or (extravasate) force blood from surrounding tissue into the abdomen if there is a bowel injury.

In the case of all true emergencies, you will need to stay calm, access medical assistance quickly and address any life-threatening situations, such as excessive bleeding, choking or air passage obstructions immediately.

CHAPTER 29
HUNTING ETHICS

Humans have been hunters and gatherers since the dawn of time. It was only after they adopted an agrarian way of life that the practice of hunting was considered anything other than a way to collect enough food to survive. But as societies bloomed, city living and subsistence by trades became a way of life and the need for daily hunting waned. Even in ancient times the value of hunting was questioned, and the Greek historian Xenophon argued that hunting was an asset to society, that the recreation promoted the well-being and health of the hunter.

Excessive hunting was always a possibility and there is no doubt that at times humans overhunted areas, sometimes decimating the game populations. To counter this, the first game laws were instituted in the thirteenth century when Kublai Khan forbade his subjects to hunt during the animal breeding seasons. By the Middle Ages sport hunting as we know it was reserved for the nobles, and the feudal lords of Europe imposed hunting restrictions on their subjects, thereby limiting hunting only to the ruling classes.

In America, the native game populations provided sustenance for generations of European settlers until their agricultural base of survival was established. In the nineteenth century, Americans took a plentiful supply of wildlife for granted, but a long list of thoughtless or unethical shooting practices—including market hunting of waterfowl, the decimation of the bison and the total extinction of the passenger pigeon—are well-documented facts.

When America was an intensely rural nation, wildlife populations often suffered. When people tried to survive and feed a family on 80 acres of ground, all manner of moving creatures were subject to overharvesting, and the white-tailed deer and wild turkey are examples of native species that became nonexistent over wide stretches of the Midwest. Both had to be reintroduced to their native landscape in the early 1900s. Today's hunter, more than ever, must be attuned to the delicate balance between wildlife and humans, and the complex habitat needs for the continued propagation of each species. Each sportsman should carefully obey the laws designed to protect our wildlife.

As Dave Richey of the *Detroit News* wrote:

> There is much that is right and good about hunting, and a few things that are wrong, and breaking game laws and winking at violations have become common faults among some sportsmen. Ethics are important if hunting is to survive and prosper. It behooves everyone to understand that without rules and regulations, we would have no game. (January 15, 1995)

The more you hunt, the more likely you are to see serious breaches of even the most rudimentary code of sportsmanship, fair play and safety. For example, once we had just completed a field trial using pen-raised hen pheasants. As we stood in the parking lot a middle-aged man and his pre-teen son pulled to a stop. They immediately pulled out and loaded up a couple of old pump guns right in the parking lot. That in itself was enough to disperse the crowd. But it was state land and they had a right to be there. Some small game seasons were open, but not pheasants and certainly not hen pheasants, on which there is never an open season in Michigan. As the man and son walked past, one of the trialers cautioned them, hoping to keep them out of trouble. "The season's not open on hen pheasants." "Hell, we ain't huntin' pheasants, we're huntin' rabbits," growled the father, but within a hundred yards they walked up to a hen, shot it twice, put it in the game bag and hunted on. I've often wondered if the son now has the same ethics as the father.

A Minnesota farmer friend told me about an incident during a snowstorm when a road hunter rolled down the car window and shot a pheasant huddled under a pine tree in the farmer's front yard. In this case the shooter's teenaged son ran out on the lawn to retrieve the dead rooster.

I suppose people who lack ethics have always been around, but with so much antihunting sentiment in the air, we must stand united against such behavior. Certainly we must educate our sons and daughters in proper ethics and we must face up to our best friends and hunting buddies when they transgress.

Once I was hunting in northern Michigan with a fellow I really didn't know very well. We had met through a mutual acquaintance and he invited me to join him for a day of grouse hunting. As we walked down a dirt two-track on our way to the first spot, he suddenly snapped the gun to his shoulder and blasted a ruffed grouse out of a tree. I was stunned, he was thrilled. But I was his guest, and I didn't say anything. I just never hunted with him again.

Another time in Iowa with three in the party we separated so each of us could hunt our own separate ways for the morning. When we met back at the Suburban at noon, I had two roosters and another hunter had two roosters, but the third hunter (again, I didn't know him very well) had five birds, two over the three-bird limit. This time I lost my temper because he was hunting out of my truck. "The limit is three, why did you shoot five?" I asked heatedly. "Well," he replied, "the dog was really working well and I had good shots, and I got excited, and I didn't figure you guys would both get your limits so I got carried away." Not only did this jerk break the law, he was a greedy bum who thought he had the right to shoot my birds as well as his own! Had I and the other member of our party also limited out at three, the party would have been overlimit and it was my vehicle that would have been in jeopardy, if checked.

A very well thought-out and articulate article by Charlie Waterman in the November 1993 issue of *Gray's Sporting Journal* carefully examines the differences in peoples' perception of what constitutes hunting ethics and a proper code of conduct. Ethics go far beyond merely living within the law. Waterman's sage observations made me realize that my code of ethics was not universal, even among honorable upland hunters. Although Waterman has a low tolerance for what he considers to be unsportsmanlike conduct, he points out that these are unwritten rules of conduct that each of us carry along on a day of shooting. This code can vary widely from hunter to hunter and our own code may not be considered appropriate or even reasonable by other ethical hunters.

Ethical conduct, obeying the laws, playing by the rules, respect for the land and fair pursuit of the quarry are all a part of our sport, but other than the laws of the state, you must write your own code. Whenever a hunter uncases a gun and sets loose a dog, he is almost sure to experience a situation that will check his code of conduct. The laws are clear, but for many hunting decisions you must rely only on your own ethical compass.

This is my simple code:

1. OBEY THE LAW. Do not shoot more than the legally specified daily limit and never break a game law.

2. EARN EACH BIRD. I must sweat and puff to earn every shot. Do not ground-swat or tree-shoot any bird. Do NOT engage in road hunting. The quarry must be walked up and in the air when shot.

3. HONOR THE LAND. Destroy nothing—not fences, not crops, not seedlings. Do not litter. Pick up every shell casing and every lunch wrapper. Leave only footprints.

4. GET PERMISSION. No trespassing. Hunt only where you will be welcome. Thank the land owner profusely, for he has shared a precious gift. Send a thank-you note.

5. RETRIEVE EVERY BIRD. If I knock it down, I must retrieve it. It is a limited natural resource and it is my obligation to find it! Use a dog that will retrieve aggressively.

6. DO NOT WOUND BIRDS OUT OF EGO. Never use a gun of such small gauge that it won't kill cleanly; that is, a gun that leaves wounded birds destined to die later.

7. SUPPORT HABITAT ORGANIZATIONS. Make a habitat effort by joining Ducks Unlimited or the Ruffed Grouse Society or Quail Unlimited or Pheasants Forever. Get involved, contribute hours or dollars to make the world better for the next generation of hunters and wildlife.

8. ENCOURGE OUR GOVERNMENT TO HELP. Support laws, government programs and tax regulations that support wildlife habitat, conservation, protect the environment and sustain our wilderness.

9. THE NESTING SEASON IS SACRED. NEVER disturb game birds during the nesting season.

10. LITTLE CONSIDERATIONS MEAN A LOT. Examples include: Don't shoot pheasant hens, even when legal (except pen-raised birds). Don't shoot out a grouse woods. Don't hunt quail late in the evening on very cold days. Never shoot a covey numbering below a dozen birds. And the list goes on with many other additions you can surely supply.

11. NEVER HUNT THE COVERTS OF A FRIEND. Those are his, and they are personal. It is my task to go out and find my own spots.

12. SAFETY, FIRST, LAST AND ALWAYS.

If you are going to be a hunter, you have to take a position. You either obey the law or you don't. You operate by a code of ethics or you don't. You give time and money to ensure the future of the sport and the groups that protect it or you don't. It is easy to take a free ride, to walk the fence, to enjoy the sport without ever going back, but true sportsmen see that as freeloading.

C H A P T E R   3 0

FARAWAY PLACES WITH STRANGE-SOUNDING NAMES

If you are going to chase wild birds you must get used to spending your leisure nights in exotic places with names like Orr, Dyke, Sheds, Farson, Speed, Thistle, Tolstoy, Iron Bridge, Fine, Blind River, Damascus, Ollie, Cologne and Lively. By and large these are places that time has passed by, and although a few hardy holdouts still call them home, these are mostly places from a bygone era. Were they not, instead of being a home to bird shooting these spots would surely be covered by tract houses and shopping malls.

In many ways the charm of such places is their lack of pretense. The accommodations are basic and the cuisine bona fide American. Generally you can dine on a wide variety of entrées, as long as they are all fried and you plan to finish eating by 8 P.M. when the local diner closes for the night. However, in Canada I recently stumbled onto a menu that included one bottle of Dom Perignon and six buffalo wings for $127.95. "It was a slow seller," the waitress explained. Small wonder!

Staying in rural motels is a lesson in minimalization and here you often have to invoke the "basic three" rules of motel approval, which are:

1. Clean as a whistle

2. A firm bed

3. An abundant supply of hot water

And don't be afraid to ask for an inspection before you check in. Many are surprisingly comfortable. Be sure to advise them up front that you plan to let six dogs out in the yard to relieve themselves. Luxurious accommodations rarely exist in the rural areas, but the "basic three" can usually be found.

Billy Welk, a grandnephew of the bandleader Lawrence Welk and a native South Dakota rancher and consummate sportsman, has now diversified his holdings into motel franchises and real estate. Billy has a simple theory about operating motels. "If you are in the motel business, the rooms better be clean every day 'cause nobody ever comes back two weeks later just to see if you have cleaned up the place since their last visit."

I keep a little diary of places that pass muster in remote locations. Every serious roughshooter should.

MIDWEST ROADS

When the hood of your vehicle crosses the Ohio border heading west, leaving the winding mountain regions of Pennsylvania behind, you enter a new world of square-mile navigation. In any direction—north, south, east or west—at one-mile spacing, an intersecting network of farm roads grid the land. This vast web, consisting of thousands of miles of mostly gravel county roads, divides the fertile Midwest corn belt into 640-acre blocks called sections, each one square mile, each block one mile to a side.

This pattern holds true through most of the flat or rolling glacial Midwest, including the northern tiers of Ohio, Indiana, Illinois, most of Iowa and the southern tiers of Michigan, Wisconsin and Minnesota. The pattern continues into Nebraska and the Dakotas, as well as parts of Missouri and most of Kansas. In the Dakotas and Kansas, and some of the more sparsely populated areas, some of the section roads have now fallen into disrepair and today many are no more than unmaintained, muddy tracks.

A through-the-windshield view of the rolling prairie is a large part of the experience and the veteran hunter can read the terrain and the cover to interpret the likelihood of birds in the area.

In the more hilly regions, like Missouri or southern Indiana, the roads meander a bit around high hills and wildly roaming creek beds. Both hills and rivers play havoc with the Teutonic order of our forefathers and must have driven the early surveyors of the region to despair. When the settlers first turned the sod or cleared the land those 640-acre sections generally held at least four and often eight families, each eking out a rustic living on only eighty or 160 acres. Today, any farmer with less than a full 640-acre section will struggle to reach the economies of scale necessary to survive economically.

Travel and direction here are easy compared to the northern grouse woods where twisting roads and vast stretches of rough and trackless terrain make getting lost so easy. Understanding the layout of the road network in the Midwest makes navigation simple and precise. There are places where you can cruise a gravel road forty or fifty miles straight without much interruption, even as you pass from county to county or from state to state. This is not the land of wide vistas or soaring mountains; just the rolling prairie, now mostly covered by corn or milo or "beans" (the natives' nickname for the soybean crop). Wheat is grown in western Kansas, but it is a rarity in the Midwest and other crops like oats, rye and barley are so rare as to be almost extinct in this part of the world.

Covered bridges still exist in places throughout the Midwest.

There are a few landmarks here, but not many. The covered "Bridges of Madison County" really do exist. They are not the fictional figment of some novelist's imagination and there is a plaque on the side of a little-used highway in southwestern Iowa beside a worn, rusty railroad track. The plaque commemorates the spot where Jesse and Frank James's gang robbed a train back in the 1800s. Or you could visit Herbert Hoover's birthplace or the Amana Colonies or the site where Grant Wood painted his famous *American Gothic.* But mostly it is just miles and miles of gravel roads, one mile apart where each section holds the secret of many lives and many hours of toil settling and farming this vast land. Today, most sections hold at least a few acres of prime pheasant cover.

IOWA

Hunting in Iowa is neither romantic nor scenic. Iowa is farmland; no vistas, no mountains, just some of the world's best farmland. It varies somewhat in character from north to south and east to west, but it is all agricultural. The north central part of the state is the flattest and best for real top yield row crops of corn and soybeans. At the peak of the agland boom some whole thousand-acre farms changed hands at $5,000 an acre. But then the "bust" came and prices for "best ground" dropped like a stone to around $2,000 an acre—ruining lives, banks and mostly the dreams of those that hadn't sold for big bucks. Even at today's $2,000 prices the farmer can't waste any land, so in much of Iowa, especially north of Interstate 80, the fences are gone, the livestock is gone and the deep black earth is turned over in the fall just as soon as the corn or beans are trucked off to the elevator. Fall plowing means the ground is prepped and ready for a quickly planted crop in the spring. But with no winter cover, no fence rows, no weeds and no ditches there are fewer pheasants. It's that simple. Nothing is absolute and there are spots of rough land and swales that hold a few birds, but the best farmland is generally not the best hunting. For pheasants you'd best look for rougher property: east, west or south.

Hunting in Iowa is neither a wilderness experience nor a solitary experience. During the fall, somewhere within earshot, a combine is always whining. You'll never, never be more than a half mile from a gravel section road, for in Iowa it seems that God intended for all His land to be divided into neat 640-acre squares. Always square, never curved.

Accommodations are at small local motels or economy chains that cater to truckers and construction workers and the food is basic. Practically speaking, real gourmet food does not exist in rural Iowa and with few exceptions, bar and bottle of wine restaurants with tablecloths survive only in the four or five significant cities of the state. But these are minor inconveniences that can, depending on how you see things, be overcome, ignored or even enjoyed.

As for terrain and scenery, the rolling prairie and tree-lined river bottoms of the less "prime" land have an innate character just like the hard lines in the faces of these wind-blown prairie farmers. The deep soil and ample rain grows brutal brush and roosting cover in the sloughs that makes even moderate terrain a challenge. The nearness to roads lends a sense of comfort to people that can't seem to settle easily into the vastness of a grouse woods without looking at their compass every ten steps. You can often catch sight of a farmer hurrying a giant green John Deere towing a grain train of hopper wagons to the storage areas. You are in the midst of the farmer's most critical production phase and even if you are welcomed as an old friend you are expected not to intrude. The farmers are working at a fevered pace, often far into the night, to put the crop in the bank.

Over the years I have learned to enjoy the taciturn hospitality of the prairies, where the sparse motel rooms, three-channel TVs and basic stick-to-your-ribs "down home cookin'" are the norm. As for libation: You'd best bring your favorite with you. I have cultivated the habit of saving some rare liquid treat such as a special bottle of single malt scotch and a unique bottle of red wine for my annual Iowa hunt. A nip while the stories of the day are retold, each dog's work critiqued and the loads, ranges and shots are thoroughly assessed, soothes the sweet muscle aches of a day already on its way to becoming a golden memory.

Hunting in Iowa begs for a good and true friend for a hunting partner. Someone you know, respect and whose company and intellect you enjoy and appreciate.

But a word of caution here. Two is fine, three is a crowd and four is persona non gratta. One or two tagalong friends may be welcomed graciously by an Iowa farmer, but if you show up with an army, the reception will be cool and dry. Most Iowans see hunting permission as a favor, a gift that they bestow on good friends, and they will not be pleased if you bring along a gang to trash, trample and decimate the place.

And don't expect to shoot your three-bird limit without skill or effort. Opening day will harbor a few naive and foolish birds, but by mid-November, two weeks into the season, you are pursuing a wild and wily quarry. Pheasants need to be flushed and peppered only once before they get to be very cagey. There are often days when even experienced, hard pushing, capable hunters fail to shoot a three-bird limit. Knowing how and where to hunt, having good dogs that are up to a challenge and then having the endurance and shooting skills to cash in, are the keys to Iowa success.

DAKOTA PRAIRIES

The long, flat horizon of the eastern Dakotas was treeless for centuries, and man's effort to plant a few rows of trees as windbreaks and house shade has been largely unsuccessful. This is a broad, flat land with a dryness bordering on arid and a cold winter wind that chills the soul. One doesn't talk to a Dakotan long without some reference to the bone-chilling winters. But that is later, much later it is hoped, for now, in November, it is pheasant hunting season and the wind is cold but snow is still days or weeks away.

Pheasant hunting here is far different than in Iowa or Michigan, for this is horizon to horizon hunting on big land in huge fields of waving CRP weeds or corn stubble. The deep sloughs of Iowa are several hundred miles east and here in the Dakotas the land is humbling in its vastness.

There doesn't seem to be a textbook definition of when a farm grows into a ranch, but more than two thousand acres seems to be a reasonable cut-off point. By that definition, there are many ranches in the Dakotas.

Finding birds here means miles of walking through dozens of likely covers and each one must be searched out to find the spot where the birds lurk today, for it is guaranteed that they won't hole up and hunker down in the same places where they were yesterday. In an average day of determined drive hunting you are likely to walk anywhere from six to fifteen miles.

Pheasants are fast becoming a Dakota cash crop as more and more ranchers charge for hunting and cater to out-of-state shooters. I hate to see the time-honored tradition of hunting on old friends' land simply for the asking falling by the wayside.

In the end a big, well-orchestrated pheasant drive is great fun if you are with a congenial group of safety-minded, hard-working hunters. Big luncheon spreads are often laid out in the barn of the host farmer and posthunt cocktails and dinner is a chance to swap stories and exaggerations. So who you hunt with is often as important to the enjoyment of the hunt as the shooting success itself.

A large group of hunters is part of the Dakota pheasant drive experience.

A trip to the Dakotas is a welcome respite from the clogged freeways of urban America and a fanciful trip back to the era of sod houses and Indian raids. A few days on the open prairie quickly reminds one of the vast openness of the great plains of our nation and the isolation one can still find in America.

MINNESOTA

The far reaches of northeastern Minnesota, west of Duluth, reflect an earlier time of iron ore, taller timber and Scandinavian immigrant farmers struggling to grow a living on poor soil in a harsh climate. The transition of the local economy from iron ore and timber to pulp wood for paper has accelerated in recent years. But, the demise of the marginal farmer happened far enough into the past to allow most of the farmsteads to collapse from neglect. Today, in many cases the old buildings have collapsed and are now disguised as clumps of greenery smothered in honeysuckle and berry briars. Beware of old cisterns and collapsed root cellars when you hunt in this part of the world.

This is the beginning of the American plains and the population thins out quickly from here west. Towns of significance become further and further apart and often it is fifty or seventy miles between oases large enough to support a decent motel. A hundred miles north is the Canadian boundary waters, and two hundred miles west, Minnesota rolls into the ever-widening spaces of the Dakotas.

To drive here means putting on miles by the thousands, before you are back home in your own bed. But the drive into this wilderness can be one of interesting contrasts. You can get there via the rolling prairie route through Iowa and the farms of southern Minnesota, by the "dairy route," a long and winding trip through several hundred miles of crisply manicured Germanic Wisconsin dairy farms, or you can tackle the far north route through the tired old towns and Indian reservations that border the Great Lakes in northern Michigan and Wisconsin. Either way, don't miss the surprisingly neat and well-cared-for little twin cities of Duluth, Minnesota, and Superior, Wisconsin, on the edge of the cold, deep Lake Superior. I personally like the Duluth area a lot whether I am staying at the Barker's Island Inn or eating at the Pickwick Restaurant on Duluth's beautiful brick-covered Superior Street. You can feast on the wonderful Chinese food at the China Inn on Belknap Street in Superior, Wisconsin, which features an extensive selection of fiery Szechwan delicacies.

Duluth's frigid reputation belies its charm, for it is only 100 miles to the boundary waters, or 167 miles to International Falls, always one of the coldest spots in the lower forty-eight states.

By any route, northern Minnesota is a wild and isolated place that piques the yearning for space and freedom hiding in the heart of most urban-dwelling Americans. The grouse woods from Minnesota to Maine pretty much all look the same. When you are deep in the grouse woods your locale becomes disguised. Across the grouse range, the birds (both grouse and woodcock) are found in the same kind of regenerating woodlands, mirror images of the places where new growth follows, cutting or fire or wind or farming.

THE ARCTIC WATERSHED: CANADA

It is said that 90 percent of the Canadian population lives within fifty miles of the U.S. border. That leaves only two or three million Canadians to stand

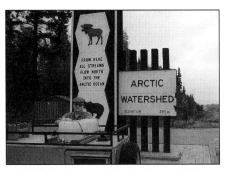

This is "bush" country. In the Arctic watershed you can feel the remoteness in your bones.

guard over the other zillion acres of "bush," lakes and wilderness outside this popular fringe. No wonder that two hours north into Canada the signs of urbanization fall away and the woods encroach upon the smooth ribbons of pavement. At one point, eight or ten hours into the North Woods, I topped a ridge and a sign on the left informed me that I was "now entering the Arctic Watershed." The fine print explained that from this point on, each drop of rain that falls drains into the Arctic Ocean. *Here you are alone.*

As the intersecting network of side roads dwindles, the sense of being truly alone stirs in your mind, the isolation grows and you realize it is both a blessing and a curse. The blessing is the vast bounty of accessible crown land and perfect habitat for grouse and woodcock. The curse is the vastness and the realization that if you become disoriented, lost or disabled you are truly on your own.

This sparks, in most rational hunters, a keener sense of caution, use of the compass, attention to the lay of the land and notice of landmarks. Careful attention to finding one's way back is of utmost importance. Here the careless hunter flirts with disaster.

But the freedom of the North Woods draws one to this mecca, and leads the genuinely enthusiastic hunter to reach outside his comfort level for a new and greater hunting experience.

ROUGHSHOOTING IN NEW JERSEY

My experience is that some fast and furious woodcock shooting on migrating birds exists in New Jersey. The problem is both access to the land and knowing when the flight birds are passing through. Most of the Garden State's migration passes down the Delaware River valley and a large population holes up near Cape May waiting for a favorable north wind to help blow them across the Delaware Bay. But throughout all of rural New Jersey the birds are found in tiny and isolated pockets of cover, or sometimes on state land most of which is now tending to be far too mature to attract birds.

It is no great secret that the woodcock numbers in the eastern flyway are declining. Many theories for this decline have been put forward, but the most knowledgeable experts lay it all at the foot of dwindling habitat. The habitat loss is the result of two key societal changes. One is urban sprawl, brought on by the American trend to move out of the city and into the tract house. With that movement has come more roads and more stores and more schools, all of which pave over the habitat. Just as critical are the changes in the way land is cared for in the northeast corridor. The Northeast was never a farming mecca, but at some point in the past much of the land was cultivated in at least a rudimentary way. However, after World War II a huge amount of farmland was abandoned in the Northeast, and as that abandoned (or untilled) land reverted back to woodlands, the saplings and woody growth was perfect for grouse and woodcock. Unfortunately today, several decades later, these saplings, now mature forests, are unsuitable habitat for either grouse or woodcock. With reduced forest regeneration in progress in the Northeast, woodcock habitat will continue to be sparse and populations will continue to fall.

If you can gain access to the property, there is some decent woodcock hunting even in the high-population Northeast corridor. Further north, in Vermont and New Hampshire, the terrain is rugged but the shooting can be spectacular.

NEW YORK: WHERE TIME STANDS STILL

Unless you have watched it over a long period of years and then compared it to other places of high growth such as the sunbelt or the far West, you might miss the fact that for the last twenty-five years time has stood still in upstate New York. I haven't lived there in almost twenty years, but when I return, very little has changed in the towns, small cities or countryside. The lack of population growth (unlike Vermont and New Hampshire) has not pushed urban sprawl or vacation home boom towns throughout the eroded old mountainsides of the Empire State, nor has its old farm community raced to keep up with the latest technology. Indeed, much of that farm effort was always focused on dairy farming, which has of late fallen on hard times. The timber industry, long ago focused mainly on pulp production for the paper mills, continually rejuvenates the forest with new growth, the perfect habitat required for the ruffed grouse.

The land in the state is a mixture of small patches, medium-sized farms and vast tracts of state or commercially owned property. Getting permission to hunt is usually no more difficult than a knock at the door. But be sure to ask if you can hunt "partridge," because thereabouts no one has ever heard of a ruffed grouse.

It was very late October, almost to Halloween, when we were hunting. I always remember Halloween because it is such a big holiday for small children and I always tried to be home for the holiday to see my own kids in their latest exotic costumes.

The southern tier of counties in New York State butts up against Pennsylvania and some excellent grouse hunting. It is mostly grown over farmland and third- or fourth-growth pulp forest. The terrain is ragged, rolling hills with a few high bumps in the topography that someone might mistake for a mountain.

Once you are deep into the cover, the feel of the grouse environment is almost always the same. The basic tree population is tag alders, birch, maple, hawthorn, swamp beech and popple (aspen). This pattern is nearly the same from Maine to Minnesota and far into the Ontario watersheds. The terrain varies a bit but the feel of a grouse woods is consistent even in Montana or Oregon or Alaska and you feel you could jump in at any spot and give it a go using your favorite dog and your reserve of grouse hunting knowledge.

The mountain regions of New York state are still a summer and a winter playground of lakes and ski resorts, but the woodcock flights pass through during the off-season. After the leaves have fallen and the fall color tour buses are gone, it is very quiet and you can enjoy the echoing ambiance of years past. Generally, New York is an area of fading opulence and grandeur, and in some towns so tiny that you can hardly find an open filling station after 7 P.M. you can find a quality restaurant with white linen table cloths and a menu to match. A town of this size in North Dakota might have a diner where you could get a chicken fried steak. But in New York you just might find a restaurant boasting quite a sophisticated menu. Parts of upstate New York still cling to a remnant of the glorious days when the Empire State dominated America's image of itself and when the Northeast set the tone for American style. But mostly it is a place where time seems to stand still and the history of the hills still echoes in the woods.

DEEP IN THE HEART OF TEXAS

As native quail populations have crashed in the Deep South, the populations in other areas have held steady. The reasons are simple. The farm and ecology changes that have reduced habitat in the Southeast are not practiced in Texas.

Once you leave the hustling, booming, crowded chrome and neon of Houston it is a long, flat, fast drive toward the Gulf of Mexico. The first hour is through good cropland, so flat that it is planted to irrigated rice crops. But further south it begins to roll and get rough and the vegetation turns to scrub and pasture.

If you get down to south Texas on a quail hunt don't miss a chance to stop at Hinze's Barbecue on Route 59 in Wharton, about sixty miles south of Houston. The barbecue of every variety is superb, and everyone in Texas seems to be stopped there for lunch. Just as special as the barbecue are the ten or so different kinds of "salad." Now anyplace south of the Mason-Dixon line, people use the term *salad* loosely. I once recall being served a

In some spots, the fields where pheasants lurk abut the woodcock woods—the best of two worlds of shooting.

Roadside parks are perfect for luncheon picnics.

"salad" in Kentucky that was equal parts Jell-O, marshmallows and Cool Whip. But at Hinze's the salads really are made from vegetables; they taste great and the tartness of the salads is a perfect contrast to the smoky richness of the barbecue.

This is Texas in its native form and the little towns survive on ranching and products from the land. This is the land of pick-up trucks and country music, gun racks, wide belts, silver buckles and pointy-toed boots. Without these accouterments you *will* be noticed.

Big southern quail hunting "off-trucks" (that means riding along in a truck) as the big-goin' Pointers run for the horizon isn't really roughshooting, but it is great fun.

These are the places of big, wide, wonderful America: constant contrasts, bustling cities, sleepy hamlets, deep woods, open prairies, fine folks and precious memories for any dedicated roughshooter to cherish.

C H A P T E R   3 1
AMBIANCE AND THE ROUGHSHOOTER

*The cold-weather cuisine of Provence is peasant food. It is made to stick
to your ribs, keep you warm, give you strength and send you off to bed
with a full belly. It is not pretty, in the way that tiny and artistically
garnished portions served in fashionable restaurants are pretty, but on a
freezing night with the mistral coming at you like a razor there is nothing
to beat it.*

—PETER MAYLE
A YEAR IN PROVENCE, 1989

American roughshooting by its nature usually takes place in remote and
isolated territory. In a bygone era, many wealthy individuals enjoyed all the
luxuries of home by establishing elaborate hunting clubs with lodges in far-
off places. Today some hunters simulate that by hunting with outfitters who
provide some of the luxuries of old. But most active roughshooters hunt
without an outfitter or a guide. With the exception of the hotels and restaurants in some of the classy little resort towns in New England or the quail
plantations of the Deep South, roughshooters are often forced to stay in
some rather basic accommodations.

Since I spend most of my fall weekends bird hunting or field trialing, I
have rarely attended any of the football tailgate parties that are such a part
of contemporary Americana. But there is no reason why the tailgate tradition cannot be transferred to the grouse woods. I got hooked on camp
ambiance some years ago when I fell in with a group of hunters who
believed that the only restriction on food and wine was the capacity of the

These gentlemen share the memories of a successful hunt on the deck at Harry Henriques's "Wild Wings" Lodge.

truck or the cooler. The whole thing sometimes got a little out of hand and on occasion turned into a "can you top this" sort of thing. We used to visit Bob Burger's deer camp in northern Michigan for an annual weekend of grouse shooting, and it was there that I best learned that some planning, a bit of creativity and careful packing can transfer all the gourmet pleasures of the city to even the most remote and rustic places. We all expected to do the cooking at Burger's grouse rendezvous and the place was laid out as a world-class deer camp with beamed castings, rustic fireplace, bunkhouse-type kitchen and all the amenities. Breakfast was Bob's specialty and he would be up before dawn cooking stacks of pancakes, crisp bacon and well-done eggs. In the evening cocktails and dinner reflected sort of a contest as everyone brought or cooked their own specialties—several different chilis, pastas and sauces, venison and wild game steaks and sausage, and batter-fried bass filets.

HUNTING CAMPS

For many years Fred Gray or Bob Michels and I rented a vacation cottage on a little bass lake in southern Iowa as our base camp. We'd hunt all day then wind our way thirty miles or so back to camp where we'd clean birds and feed dogs and have a cold beer. More often than not, when it was time to eat we were too tired to make the twenty-mile trip to the nearest decent restaurant. We finally accepted the cooking chores and began to take easily prepared meals that hit the spot. It wasn't fancy but it was great fun.

Some of the more interesting spreads have included smoked and barbecued Texas wild boar on whole wheat buns served by Chad Betts at his hunting camp in central Kansas. Our friend Tony Hopp once brought wild turkey, venison and pheasant sausages to Burger's place. Once, someone even brought a whole slab of elk roasts.

Some surprisingly good soups and stews can be prepared in advance and easily transported in a cooler. A few of my Midwest hunting pals introduced me to the wonders of a slow cooker and I learned how to have a hot and tasty hors d'oeuvre waiting when we returned to camp at night, cold and tired. Even if a local motel is our base camp, we almost always include a fancy little spread of hors d'oeurves and a few good drinks as a pleasant relaxation before we explore the local eateries.

Over the years in camps and motels, some of the more elaborate hors d'oeurve spreads would have rivaled any gala cocktail party. Some of the more interesting included:

A collection of unique salsas and exotic chips gathered from across the American Southwest.

A collection of a half-dozen interesting cheeses the hunter had first tasted around the world, then purchased in the United States with complementary crackers.

A barbecue grill laden with spicy sausages, marinated shrimp, garlicky fingers of Korean steak and smoked pork strips.

A spread of tangy barbecue specialties brought from a local barbecue shop: ribs, sausages, chicken and turkey.

A huge spread of Tex-Mex food, refried beans, guacamole, ground beef, taco shells and chips.

A large platter of freshly cut vegetables: carrots, celery, broccoli, cauliflower and green peppers with several different kinds of dips.

A casserole of Val Mikula's delicious and hearty beef and broccoli dip.

VAL MIKULA'S BEEF AND BROCCOLI DIP

Valerie Mikula swears this recipe is foolproof and tastes great on a variety of different crackers or over toast. She calls this a dip, but team it up with a tasty salad and some hearty bread and it makes a truly memorable hot meal. The recipe is also great made with shredded pheasant rather than ground beef. It serves six as a meal or twelve for hors d'oeurves.

- 3 **pounds lean ground beef, browned**
- 1 **cup chopped onion**
- 3 **10-ounce packages of frozen broccoli, drained**
- 3 **cans cream of celery soup**
- 2 **cans of cheddar cheese soup**
- 1 **can nacho cheese soup**
- 1 **tablespoon chopped jalapeño or Tabasco to taste**

Combine all ingredients in a large slow cooker. Heat for a few hours and enjoy.

ELIXIRS

Almost all roughshooters seem to have the same pattern of refreshment after a hard day in the field. It is de rigueur to have a cold beer to slake the thirst from many hours of dusty, long-distance trekking while the dogs are fed and the birds cleaned and a "big red" wine always accompanies dinner. But between the beer and the wine, a glass of strong liquor eases the aches. By far the most common elixirs found in camp are sour mash whiskey, bourbon and scotch. On occasion a bottle of good vodka—Absolut, Stolychnaya or Finlandia—will show up. In all my years afield, I have never seen a bottle of gin or tequila on the sideboard. Of course, in Canada the standard bottle of rum is always present.

American bourbons and sour mash whiskeys like Wild Turkey and Jack Daniels have long been a part of southern quail hunting traditions and have by association been transferred to the prairies and woods. Their strong flavors fit well in the rugged atmosphere of camp. Fine scotch is an integral part of the British hunting scene, and it seems to be the drink of choice for American grouse shooters. The dark amber and strong-tasting blended scotches like Johnny Walker, Pinch, Famous Grouse and Chivas Regal seem to be preferred in a hunting lodge over the lighter blends

LIBATIONS

Some of the more interesting libations that partners have brought along on hunting trips have included:

Three bottles of unique single-malt scotches that are not sold in the United States, all brought back from a trip to Scotland.

A beer feast, two coolers stocked full of four great imported beers, each of a very different taste and style. This hunter had learned to enjoy these beers while traveling the world.

A block of ice with two holes: one for a bottle of Pepper Stolychnaya and one for a bottle of Citron Absolut.

Some of my closest friends and I have developed a deep affection for some of the unique single-malt scotches. Some, like Glenlivet and Glenfiddich, are available in the States but some of the very interesting ones can only be found in the British Isles. Anyone who brings along a bottle of unique or untried single-malt scotch whisky is sure to be a hit in hunting camp.

With my hunting crowd, packing a spread of good food and drink has become standard practice and now most of the guys keep an eye peeled all year for the kinds of foods that fit the bill: good, classy and easily prepared without undue effort.

WINE RECOMMENDATIONS

Nidal Zaher is a certified wine sommelier and the cellar master for the Merchant of Vino Company, an eight-store retailer of fine wines. Nidal is also the past director of the Detroit International Wine Auction and a guest lecturer at the Michigan State University School of Hotel and Restaurant Management. The following are his recommendations for wines that complement game recipes as well as some interesting suggestions for good wines to drink with hearty camp foods.

Nidal Zaher stands amid the huge and extensive wine inventory stocked by the Merchant of Vino. At a store of this size, the many types of wine that complement game dishes are usually part of the regular stock.

WINES WITH GAME BIRDS

Game	Cooking Method	Wine
Pheasant	Fresh or lightly aged	Cru-Beaujolais or Pinot Noir Côte de Beaune
	Well aged, gamy	Older "Bordeaux" Full bodied "Pomerol"
	With sweeter sauces or glazes	High acidity wines White Rioja (Spain) Pinot Blanc (Alsace)
Grouse	In white sauces	Tokay Pinot Gris (Alsace)
	In brown sauces	Crozes Hermitage (Rhone) Chateauneuf-du-Pape Grange Hermitage (Australia) expensive
Quail	In sweet sauces (rice/ raisins/orange/glazes)	Cru-Beaujolais Côtes-du-Rhone (inexpensive) Pinot Noir (California)

Game	Cooking Method	Wine
	In white sauce or cream sauce	Chardonnay Pouilly-Fuisse Vouvray (French, low cost)
	In brown sauces	Pinot Noir (full bodied) Côte-de-Beaune Burgundy Merlot (California)
Woodcock	Any style	Rioja (Red-Spain) Châteauneuf-du-Pape Cabernet Sauvignon (California) Pinot Gris (White-Alsace) Grange Hermitage (Australian)

HEARTY FOODS

Food	Cooking Method	Wine
Steaks	(grilled)	Cabernet Sauvignon or Merlot Australian or California
Burgers, casual meats		Inexpensive Italian Reds: Chianti Dolcetta D'Alba Barbera D'Alba Dolcetta D'Acqui Sangiovesi Di Ronagna Valpolicella
Chili		Dolcetto D'Alba Amarone or Cold Beer

TO WARM UP BY THE FIRE

Port

Tawny Port

Amarone

Shooting Sherry

HEARTY CAMP FOOD

IOWA CHILI

Serves 6–8.

2 tablespoons oil
1 large onion, chopped
2 cloves garlic, chopped
2 pounds ground beef
2 cans beans (Brooks Chili Beans), 16 ounces per can
2 cans tomatoes (chopped, stewed), 16 ounces per can
5 dry chilis
1 tablespoon red wine
1 tablespoon honey
$^1/_2$ teaspoon oregano
1 teaspoon paprika
1 heaping tablespoon ground cumin
2 tablespoons chili powder
1 teaspoon pepper
$^1/_2$ teaspoon salt
$^1/_4$ teaspoon cayenne
Tabasco sauce (optional)

Sauté onion and garlic in small amount of oil until translucent. Add beef to onion and garlic mixture and brown. Add remaining ingredients and cook 2 hours over low heat to blend flavors.

HENRY HENRIQUES'S GROUSE SUPREME

This basic recipe works equally well with quail, pheasant and Chukar. Serves 6.

3 grouse, cleaned, soaked in salt water $^1/_2$ hour,
   then rinsed. Remove shot carefully.
$^1/_2$ cup flour
2 tablespoons dried parsley
2 tablespoons ground ginger
2 tablespoons paprika
1 tablespoon dry mustard
4 tablespoons walnut oil

> **4** tablespoons margarine or butter
> $^{1}/_{2}$ cup honey
> $^{1}/_{2}$ teaspoon ground black pepper
> **2** tablespoons Worcestershire sauce
> $^{3}/_{4}$ cup Madeira wine

Split birds in half. Season flour with 1 tablespoon of the parsley, 1 tablespoon of the ginger, 1 tablespoon of the paprika and mustard. Dry birds well, roll in seasoned flour and shake off excess. Heat walnut oil and lightly brown each bird. Remove birds and set aside.

After browning in separate saucepan, strain and pour remaining walnut oil. Add butter (or margarine). Melt over low heat. Add honey and dissolve. Add all dry ingredients, except flour. Add Worcestershire sauce. Stir for 2 minutes and add Madeira. Continue to stir until near boiling point. Add seasoned flour to thicken as you like. Do not let sauce boil (just a few bubbles).

Turn birds breast down. Pour sauce over top. Bake in oven at 350° for 20 minutes. Reduce heat to 200° for another 20 minutes. Remove, turn birds breast up. Place back in oven for another 10 minutes at 300° or until brown.

MILLIE SYLVESTER'S EQUINUNK WOODCOCK

Two to three birds per serving.

> **12** woodcocks
> $^{1}/_{2}$ pound ground bacon (at room temperature)
> **2** tablespoons garlic powder
> **1** $^{1}/_{2}$ tablespoons marjoram
> **3** $^{1}/_{2}$ tablespoons parsley flakes
> **1** $^{1}/_{2}$ to **2** pounds bacon
> Salt and pepper
> Toothpicks

Clean woodcock of all feathers and innards. Wash in cold water. Spread ground fat back (it will be easier to work at room temperature) in a 1/3-inch layer on cutting board. Sprinkle with the garlic powder, marjoram and parsley flakes. Work ingredients into fat back with a French knife by cutting into mixture, turning and cutting again until seasonings are blended. Should be grayish-green in color.

Take one woodcock at a time and season to taste with salt and pepper, inside and out. Place a rounded teaspoon of fat back mixture in cavity of bird, also place a dab of mixture (a little less than a teaspoon) on breast, spread out a little. Wrap entire bird with bacon and fasten with toothpicks. May require 1 1/2 slices per bird.

Place birds on a rack in roasting pan; cover pan with foil. Bake at 325° for 1 1/2 hours, basting occasionally. Uncover and continue baking until bacon is browned; turn birds and let underside brown.

WEEZIE SCHIRMER'S ROAST PHEASANT WITH PURPLE PLUM SAUCE

Serves 4.

2 young pheasants
1 onion, halved
2 stalks celery, sliced
1 apple, sliced
4 slices bacon
　Plum Sauce (below)
　Salt and pepper

Place onion, celery and apple inside birds. Layer 2 strips of bacon over each breast. Season with salt and pepper. Roast at 350° in the oven for 2 hours, basting with Plum Sauce during the last half hour. Serve remaining sauce in sauce boat.

PLUM SAUCE

1 one-pound can purple plums
$^{1}/_{4}$ cup butter or margarine
$^{1}/_{4}$ cup chopped onion
3 tablespoons lemon juice
$^{1}/_{4}$ cup brown sugar
2 tablespoons chili sauce
1 teaspoon Worcestershire sauce
$^{1}/_{2}$ teaspoon ginger

Drain plums and reserve liquid. Remove pits from plums and puree in blender. Melt butter in small saucepan; add onion and sauté until golden. Stir in remaining ingredients including plums and liquid. Simmer 30 minutes.

WEEZIE SCHIRMER'S WILD RICE CASSEROLE

Serves 8.

- 1 ¹/₂ **cups wild rice**
- 4 **10.5-ounce cans beef bouillon**
- 1 **cup chopped onion**
- 1 **cup chopped green peppers**
- 1 **cup fresh sliced mushrooms**
- ¹/₄ **cup soft butter or margarine**
- 1 **cup heavy whipping cream**
  Salt and pepper to taste

Wash rice then cook in bouillon or beef broth until most of the liquid has been absorbed. Sauté onions, peppers and mushrooms in butter. Add cream, salt and pepper to taste. Add to cooked rice and put into a casserole dish. Bake at 350° for 20 minutes. May be prepared ahead, but increase baking time to heat through.

Even in a spartan motel, a well-stocked sideboard and a spread of hors d'oeuvres can add to the ambiance of the surroundings.

CHAPTER 32

ROUGHSHOOTING STYLE

There is a passion for hunting, something deeply implanted in the human breast.

—CHARLES DICKENS
OLIVER TWIST

There are many ways to hunt besides roughshooting and most are far less physically taxing. Roughshooting involves miles of walking through briars and brush, climbing hills and jumping streams in all kinds of weather. In many ways roughshooting is more akin to hiking, jogging and cross-country skiing than to some of the more sedentary types of shooting. Dr. Harry B. Bigelow of Concord, Massachusetts, once summed it all up in six words when he said, "Guns don't kill grouse. Legs kill 'em." And although there are many ways to describe the lure of roughshooting, I think it was best explained in 1950 when Roderick L. Haig-Brown wrote in his book *The Measure of the Year:*

> Wingshooting was another matter and I stayed with it, liking the close, intricate work of the dogs, the companionship of a good friend, the long days of walking the rocky hills. The roads were few and scattered in those days and hunters were few—it was easy to pick country where one could walk steadily through a whole day and see no one else. It was good and necessary to be out in the fall days, working over logged and discarded country, watching the start of new growth, crossing ridges, finding creeks and swamps unseen and untrodden by humans between hunting seasons. (See chapter 33 for complete publication information.)

Together Bigelow and Haig-Brown capture the primitive physical calling of the hunt that must somehow reach back into our Paleolithic origins.

THE EVOLUTION OF YOUR STYLE

When you're walking ten miles a day on a South Dakota pheasant drive, it is great to be surrounded by a fun-loving group of safety-minded, hard-driving hunting companions.

The lure of roughshooting is not just physical and athletic, but mental and spiritual as well. The commingling of these urges leads each of us in different directions, to pursue the quarry of our choice in our own style in widely divergent geographic dispersion. Some people would have you believe there is only one real way to roughshoot (usually their own), but in reality the style that gives you the most enjoyment is the right way. It is easy to fall in with groups that have "our way" of approaching the sport. Sometimes it is lonely to stand apart from the crowd, but as long as you come home at night refreshed and rejuvenated by the experience of the day, you are the winner. You may need to fend off some urgings to follow the local crowd. You'll hear phrases that put subtle but poorly camouflaged pressure on the hunter like, "Pointer owners are all rednecks," or, "Only the tweeds and pipe smokers own spaniels," or, "Pump guns are best used by a swat team."

Don't listen to all that baloney. I've watched with open interest as many hunting acquaintances experimented with dogs, guns, places and birds, modifying or switching persuasions until finally they evolved a style of their own. My own style feels uniquely my own, but obviously many others like the same dogs, places, pursuits, methods and guns that I do. It is also the unique mixture of skills, actions and motivations that completely defines your style. How you hunt is as important as what and where you hunt.

Good friends and camaraderie are often an important part of roughshooting, but there are other ways to partake of the joys of bird shooting and the outdoors, and I'm always surprised to learn that many avid hunters have never spent a single day afield alone, with just a dog as a companion.

> *If I'd known I was gonna live this long, I'd have taken better care of myself.*
>
> —EUBIE BLAKE, 1883–1983

USE IT OR LOSE IT

A cross-section survey of the U.S. population would yield some interesting insights into our physical fitness situation. At a time when we hear daily news reports about the waning physical condition of the population in general and the term *couch-potato* is part of our daily vocabulary, others within the population are in the best shape of their lives. Gyms and health clubs are on every corner and joggers, walkers and bicyclers pound out mile after mile, day after day, along our busy streets. Visit any state or national park and you will see the trail head

Since his accident (described in this chapter), Frank Sylvester can't pound out the miles like he once did, but he keeps moving and is still very effective using his strain of northeastern grouse setters.

parking lots full of hikers' cars, while their drivers roam the mountains and valleys in search of scenery and physical testing. When you are ten miles up a mountain trail and meet a gnarled seventy-five-year-old, you know you can keep moving, too.

Roughshooting, unlike duck hunting, deer hunting or turkey hunting, makes you sweat. America has coined phrases to describe it: *Use it or lose it*; *If you rest, you rust.* I can see it in my friends, some in their eighties, still going strong; some in their fifties, resting and rusting.

> *After the game, the king and pawn go into the same box.*
> —ITALIAN PROVERB

ENJOY EVERY DAY

People that are fun to be with and wear well are a great source of life's satisfactions. Frank Sylvester, an old friend from northeastern Pennsylvania, is such a fellow. As a consummate hunter and a no-nonsense brush buster, Frank sallied forth nearly every week of hunting season rain or shine. He hunted the whole northeast corner of the United States as if it were his backyard. Frank always invited along a core group of tried and true buddies to share the bounty of hunting excitement and camaraderie.

Unfortunately, this man that measured the passing of the years by the quality of the hunting fell victim to a freak accident that ended his ability to walk the endless miles each season. Contemplating the depth of this void in Frank's life made me recognize my own vulnerability. Something as simple as a severely damaged knee or a ruptured disc could prematurely end the many years of outdoor enjoyment that I have planned to save for my future. In Frank's case it came after a grisly accident. While he and a friend were working on the roof of his hunting cabin, both of them fell off a two-story scaffold and the bones in Frank's ankle were shattered. For a long while, it looked like the accident would forever end his ability to walk without a cane. It's pretty hard to hobble through the woods on a cane and respond in a split second when a grouse flushes. But with lots of surgery and rehabilitation Frank is now back in the woods. Not like the old Frank, but at least he can still hunt.

In my own case I had never even considered the possibility that I might in some way be slowed down. A sudden unexpected knee injury hobbled me for an entire season and a slow recovery from surgery created doubts in my mind as to whether I would ever be able to plow through, over and around the brush, briars and hills as I always had. This recognition of the vulnerability to age, injury or accident has strongly infected my psyche with the need to use and enjoy my physical capabilities while they last. Far too many of my friends and associates have pushed the enjoyment of their favorite things into the future, which, presumably less pressure in their lives, will allow them to enjoy many days in the field. Unfortunately, some of them never reached that point in life. Today is the time to enjoy your life, not tomorrow.

> *And stay right here 'cause these are the good old days.*
> —CARLY SIMON, *ANTICIPATION*, 1970

I have been planning this trip in my mind for years, but I've never found the time or the right travel partner to make it happen. I'm going to spend a couple of weeks winding my way across the great plains of western Canada and the United States in the big places like Montana and Saskatchewan, searching for pheasants and on the way finding surprising pockets of sharp-tail grouse and Hungarian partridge. Once there, in the quiet waning light of a Tuesday afternoon, I'll quietly slip into a little pot hole cove and jumpshoot a few pintail ducks. While I'm at it I'll find a hidden spot where the dog and I can watch as a small flock of Canada geese set their wings and glide over us, barely treetop high.

We'll eat eggs and gravy at the Main Street Diner in Moose Jaw, and cheeseburgers with the green-capped farmers at Bob's Cafe in Havre. And they'll take time to visit and ask where I'm from and how I'm doing and give me political advice. And as the drive wanders across the border into the Dakotas I'll chart the sun's course across the sky and savor its

It was a cold December day with a hint of snow squall in the air when we embarked on a few hours of a solo hunt; just my favorite dog Ruffy and me. It was just the right tonic to relieve the stress of a lifestyle that often seems too hectic.

nightly finale as it blazes a hole into the horizon. As I lean back in a worn but comfortable chair in a Holiday Inn or Red Roof or Motel 6—the best accommodations in these parts—I crack open the Johnny Walker Red and splash a bit over ice then sip it slowly to soothe the sweet ache of miles of prairie hiking that echo in my knotty old calves. In the morning, with a deep and restful eight hours of sleep in my body and after a hot shower loosens the tightness in my old bones, the dogs will shake and whine to be out of their crates as a spray of frost diamonds leaps from the scraper on the windshield.

You bet. Two weeks exploring the solitude of the endless prairie, of walking for hours and hearing only the sounds of nature, save the distant whine of a combine, is on my agenda—soon as I can find the time. One of these days!

A friend is one before whom I think aloud.

—RALPH WALDO EMERSON

CHOOSE YOUR TRAVEL PARTNERS CAREFULLY

Good friends, honest, easy to be with, funny, interesting and compatible can be the best thing about hunting. But bores, louts, braggarts, know-it-alls, unsafe, cheap, dishonest or unethical shooters ruin the trip. A long trip with an interesting and interested friend is mile after mile of stories and ideas, taxing the mind and lifting the spirit. There is an old saying that a good companion makes the journey shorter. But a long trip, with a bad companion, is a grueling, two thousand miles of discomfort that fosters an intense longing for home and solitude. I've learned to separate my hunting partners from business associates that like to hunt. Too many business associates bring the office along in their head, and I don't want to work when I'm at the top of a grouse ridge in Ontario.

It isn't easy to find good hunting partners whose schedules match your own and whose interests are compatible. So sometimes we take on unknowns and test the concept of friendship severely with several days of intense travel. Over the years I've made some good choices and some bad, a few bad enough to seriously diminish an otherwise fine trip. As I've gotten older I've become more interested in the ambiance of the experience, the scenery, the social situations of the isolated little places where we hunt and the farmer friends I've made along the way. I now count Dale and Norma, Larry and Ginger,

Good friends add a lot to the hunt, and I have made many fast friends hunting coast to coast and far into Canada. Jerry Babin and Pat McAvoy have a laugh before a day in the "bush." Those are coffee cups from the local donut shop—just in case you wondered. In some places in Canada the donut shops outnumber the people.

Bill and Lloyd and Leon and Billy—all farmers and land owners—as some of my closest friends, and I think of them and talk to them throughout the year, not just at hunting season. We call and write and send Christmas cards and ask about the kids. They are my friends.

I am not young enough to know everything.

—OSCAR WILDE

WHY DO WE HUNT?

Lately almost every outdoor magazine I pick up has an article or letter to the editor explaining or justifying our right to hunt. Many of these treatises are well written and work toward condensing the prohunting viewpoint into an easily understood and soundly rationalized argument for sport hunting. Frankly, I get lost in the rhetoric. Usually I can wrestle through the logic of a complex social argument, but in this case I just know what I believe and what I enjoy. I am also realistic enough to realize that I am just another predator in a very complex and sophisticated food chain—a chain so intermeshed that any slight change can throw it out of balance. Do I hunt because I am hungry? Of course not. I hunt because I love the physical and mental tests of the sport; I love watching the dogs work; I love the effort and the sweet dull ache of the muscles after a hunt. I love the friendships and the camaraderie; I love being outdoors under the big sky, regardless of the weather; I love the isolation and I love the challenge of the shooting.

I view roughshooting as a physical outlet that is intensely personal and requires a very complex set of skills. Other forms of hunting that do not involve intense physical exertion and complex dog work hold little appeal. But those are my tastes and I have no intention of urging my own preferences upon others.

Wild bird hunting in its most natural and realistic form is a taxing and testing sport. Yes, the hunted birds do die as the result of the sport, but man is a carnivore and to condemn sport hunting and ignore the 250 million hamburgers eaten in this nation every day is the kind of logic that only the antihunting proponents almost seem to believe is rational.

Robert Wehle, renowned Pointer breeder and owner of Elhew Kennels, is reported to have said, "The essence of the sport is not the killing of game, but the pursuit of it." That is what hunting is all about.

Solitary trees, if they grow at all, grow strong.
—WINSTON CHURCHILL

THE JOYS OF HUNTING ALONE

I'm always surprised when an avid hunter tells me that he has never spent a single day in the field alone. Good friends and camaraderie are an important part of roughshooting, but hunting alone has rewards, too. When I reflect on my years of hunting, some of my most enjoyable and memorable moments occurred when I was hunting by myself.

Some things in life are planned, but many are simply the result of circumstance. I first experienced the joys of hunting alone after my company transferred me to Des Moines, Iowa, as manager of one of its smaller offices. After years of living in major cities, I found Des Moines to be a neat, clean, safe oasis. The people were sincere and honest almost to a fault! Fine homes cost a fraction of the price in New York or Chicago, and membership in a world-class country club was available for a song. Surprisingly, a decent schedule of concerts and Broadway road shows hit town at reasonable prices and easy availability and prime hunting was nearby. I moved to Iowa as a golf addict and left with the bird-hunting fires of my youth fully rekindled.

Hunting alone in Iowa was at first a matter of convenience. With prime hunting only a thirty-minute drive away, I didn't always want to go through the hassle of calling a friend, loading the vehicle and making arrangements. It was much easier to just jump in the car with my dog and a gun and hit the road.

As a single, I could hunt tiny, hidden patches that might be passed up by a party. Most farmers would say yes to a lone hunter. They could quickly size up one person and assess my character and willingness to act in a sportsmanlike manner. The same farmer might say no to two or three hunters. I could also hunt at my own pace, crashing through a slough or dawdling to watch a sunset with only myself to please.

Of course, hunting alone is not new. When I was younger and more people lived near their hunting fields, I remember seeing old Doc Baker's car parked off the turn around by the Buffalo Ford bridge, while he was down in the alder whips with his dog looking for the woodcock flights. Or if Sam White's truck was pulled off on the side of the road over by Liberty Corner Church, I knew that he and Mike were checking out the quail population back in the northeast forty of the Totten farm. Both men hunted alone in a time when lifestyles made it easier and more common. Today it is a rare occurrence but a simple pleasure, too easily missed.

I still frequently hunt all alone with my dogs. Often these are just day trips, two or three hours from home and more relaxed than an extended hunt in another state. I find that on these occasions I tend to shoot far less and work the dog more carefully. With no one to impress, no shooting courtesies to address and fewer safety needs to consider, I tend to relax and more thoroughly enjoy all the sensory signals of the day's environment. These are the days when I can purposely take the time to let a young spaniel eagerly run back and forth over a hen pheasant's track and give the dog the necessary time to learn from doing. I can spend more time letting my young dog learn how to use the wind and take pleasure in watching the youngster's instincts kick in. I can take the time to sit cross-legged with my back against a fence post, the warm sun on my face and an old friend of a dog curled up beside me with its head in my lap. These are the times when a brace of woodcock and a brisk walk adds just the right amount of exercise to a life that is all to often spent in offices, meeting rooms and airplanes.

At such times you really begin to learn if you like yourself enough to spend the day alone. Today you set the rules, the standards and the pace. My guess is that in such a situation you, too, will slow down, pay more attention to the world around you, enjoy the little victories in your dog's performance, view your gun as a comfortable old tool cradled in your arm, smoothed and worn by years of handling. Alone, shooting a limit will become less important than the quality of the experience.

It is often easier to fight for principles than to live up to them.
—ADLAI STEVENSON

HUNTING WITH CLASS

For some reason the aesthetics of bird hunting (although reasonably lofty) have never approached the almost reverent pinnacle of fly fishing. Of course, fishing has so many levels and variations, from cane pole and worms fishing to midging in spring brooks. In Howell Raines's 1993 book *Fly Fishing Through A Mid-life Crisis* (William Morrow & Co: New York), the author frequently refers to the "Red Neck Way" and goes on to explain it as the southern fishing urge to catch every fish in the stream and hang them on a stringer to die, regardless of one's needs or desires for eating the catch. I remember when fishing was a contest to catch as many as possible by any method, and even dynamite was ethical as long as you could show off a big stringer of fish.

Bird hunters today run the same gamut, from crude to esoteric. In the far north it is still common for the local woodsman to "ground swat" or "tree pop" any partridge (ruffed grouse) dumb enough to show its face near a gravel road. In Iowa the locals "road hunt" pheasants as they cruise into town for a cup of coffee. The boors and the louts and the "no muffler" crowd march off into the fields to follow the birds they've seen scurry off the roads, ignoring "no hunting" signs, tramping fences and bursting forth with five-shot volleys. There is little chance that that group will even be offended by what I write. Words on paper are as despised by that crowd as an ATF (Alcohol, Tobacco and Firearm) agent to a moonshiner!

The essence of bird shooting is not the shooting. It is finding an appropriate bit of cover, and there to lovingly work with a well-trained manageable dog. It is the smell of the air, the feel of a step, the sound of the brush on your clothes. It is a beloved gun, like an old friend cradled in the crook of one's elbow and a pocket full of confident shells. It is the crackle of a shooting vest that summons forth so many memories and the snug support of a pair of fine boots. It's lunch on the hood and a glass of good scotch at the end of a wonderful day.

Bird hunting is not ground swatting or tree popping or road hunting. Those are corruptions and profanities to be endured within the society of the sport. But if the sport is to survive, we roughshooters, like the fly-fisherman, must come to its rescue and stand up for the highest levels of sportsmanship.

A difference of opinion is what makes horse racing and missionaries.
—WILL ROGERS

SAM WHITE

Sam White must be a common name. I've known six or seven Sam Whites over the course my fifty years, but most were fairly nondescript. Only two stand out. One Sam White was the big-time Oldsmobile dealer from the southwest side of Houston, a spectacularly successful businessman who built a car-selling empire and a national reputation. The other notable Sam White was a carpenter and bricklayer turned small town businessman who in the early years of his midlife had a consuming love for high school basketball and quail hunting. His taste in bird dogs ran to setters and he had some good dogs, especially one named Mike. Sam's dogs were well known around the little town he called home and all summer the big, feathered setter would sleep sprawled out on the cool concrete floor of Sam's Feed and Lumber Store.

Sam had about everything going his way when it came to bird hunting. With a bird dog in the truck, a shotgun behind the seat and a talking acquaintance with every farmer in the county, Sam's only limitation was a business that needed constant attention, six days a week. Even so, he always found a way to slip off for an hour or two of hunting several days a week.

I lost contact with Sam for about twenty years. I went off to college and then I worked on both coasts, while he continued to run a string of small businesses in my old home town. Somewhere along the line Sam stopped hunting and I always thought it was due to Sam's deteriorating health. Then, twenty-five years later, one Thanksgiving weekend while visiting my farm, we were working some bird dogs and invited Sam out to watch. Sam walked along and surveyed the proceedings as our Springers worked up pen-raised pheasants. I offered him a chance to do some shooting but he declined, saying his doctor had ruled out anymore hunting.

HUNTING AND ANIMAL RIGHTS

After the training session was over and we were discussing the dog work over a round of Diet Cokes, I brought the subject back to Sam's hunting days. He talked for a while about his dogs, now long dead; his favorite old shiny Winchester Model 12 pump that still leans in the corner of his bedroom closet and the small patches of bird cover that dotted the farms of that bygone era. Then he surprised me, as he told the real story of why he stopped hunting. He stopped hunting because it deeply upset his teenage daughter. In an effort to improve their relationship and show his deep respect for his daughter's viewpoints, he gave up his favorite pastime. I didn't ask Sam about his daughter's views about hunting today. His hunting days are far behind him, so what would have been the point?

My own daughter deeply resents my hunting, and in line with the way we raised her, to freely and openly express her opinions, she frequently lets me know about her disdain for my hobby. It hasn't caused a rift in our relationship, but we sure know where we stand. Whether her views will change as she matures, I don't know. I do know that if I stop hunting while she grows to adulthood, my hunting days will be long gone by the time she may decide otherwise. So we have a truce. I'm not sure my daughter and I will ever come to terms on the animal rights issue. Her viewpoints might change as she grows older but mine are fairly firm.

I doubt that the animal rights issues will fade away in the near future. As hunters we have an obligation to pursue our sport in an ethical manner and treat the resource we seek with the utmost respect and sportsmanship. At some point you, too, will come face to face with a daughter, son, sister, friend, secretary or co-worker who honestly disagrees with hunting as acceptable recreation. You will be expected to handle the debate in a calm and logical way and you have as much right to your view as they do theirs.

You can't put off being young until you retire.

—PHILLIP LARKIN

SHOOT YOUR BEST GUNS

Any thinking person should at some point come face to face with his or her own mortality. With that often comes the recognition that the prospect of enjoying life is an immediate thing. For me, that recognition dawned while I was sitting quietly at the funeral services for a favorite aunt. I suddenly realized that a finite number of years remained in my life. Further, it is most obvious that many of the pursuits I enjoy the most—mountain hiking, fly fishing, following a fine bird dog over a mountain ridge, snap shooting at a fleeting grouse, all physical activities—will be enjoyed at a diminishing rate as I grow older. By the time I retire, I expect my physical capacity to enjoy many of these activities will be lessened.

Later, as I watched the survivors divvy up my aunt's possessions accumulated lovingly over the seventy-five years of her life, I realized that many of her most prized possessions had not been enjoyed to the fullest. In her frugal, careful, Germanic way she had always saved the best for "special occasions." The best china was almost never out of the hutch. The best silver was seldom used, the best linens were only for guests. All these things, which she had worked so hard to acquire, were not a part of her daily life.

When I returned from her funeral, I took a long, hard look in the mirror and asked myself three questions:

1. When are the good times supposed to begin?

2. What am I saving it for?

3. What does it cost to go first cabin?

Starting that day I reached into my gun safe and took the best guns I own, a 5E L. C. Smith, a mint Parker and a couple of nice old English guns, and moved them to the front of the cabinet. My new motto became, "Good guns should be used, as often as possible."

I went to the closet in the basement and pulled out the eight or ten bottles of unique single-malt scotch that I'd been saving for some occasion (I don't know what) and put them on a shelf in the kitchen to be enjoyed by the fire with my best friends and not just on special occasions.

Finally, I called the travel agent and booked that trip to the Pacific Northwest for my wife and our family to hike the Olympic Peninsula, Mt. St. Helens and Mt. Rainier, like we'd been discussing for years.

I love using those guns on a weekly basis and I have no regrets at all about the few wear marks and scratches they have acquired. Most of the scotch has been imbibed with good friends or quietly by a warm fire, and more has been restocked on the shelf. The trip to Washington State was wonderful and we still talk about it often, but it was just the start of an intense family interest in mountain hiking and our annual trip to some unique place to hike is one of the best things we share in life. Since then we've hiked many other places around the world. I'm no longer saving life until I have time to enjoy it; I'm spending at least some part of it every day as I go. Life is for the living: Use it every day. It is not like my aunt's fine china, only to be enjoyed three times a year.

Old and young we are all on the last cruise.

—ROBERT LOUIS STEVENSON

THE LIFESTYLE SIDE OF ROUGHSHOOTING

An article by Jan Hoffman in *The New York Times* travel section included the following quote: "You know you have slumped to a new low when life becomes a serious impediment to *lifestyle!*" He further explained, "Certainly there's nothing like a mortgage and a steady job with a mingy vacation plan to interfere with what I used to live for: travel."

If you insert roughshooting or fly fishing or field trials for travel, those two sentences say a lot. Except for the fortunate few who live alongside wild bird habitat, roughshooting is time consuming and so its enjoyment is severely limited. The only solution is to get your priorities in order and make time.

No one ever rasped out with his dying breath, "I wish I'd spent more time in the office."

C H A P T E R   3 3

BOOKS TO READ

Some books have a way of getting into your soul, reaching into your mind, and altering your understanding. Sometimes it will be the author's approach, at others it will be his words and sometimes his unique thoughts will strike a chord. I have a special respect for the words of Robert Haig-Brown who lived what he wrote. In 1950 he authored *Measure of the Year,* an insightful book that captured my attention and has helped cement my most basic beliefs as an outdoorsman. It is still in print but it won't be easy to find. The publisher is Lyons and Burford, of New York.

I would also highly recommend the classic environmental and nature book *A Sand County Almanac,* by Aldo Leopold. The book is deceptive in its simplicity, but carefully pulls one's mind into the understanding of the complex interaction of humans and nature. The book was completed in 1948, less than a month before Leopold's death. The publisher is the Oxford Press, New York.

Another of my favorite books has nothing to do with roughshooting, but everything to do with enjoying life's little pleasures in food, drink, friends or culture regardless of where you find it. Peter Mayle chronicled a wonderful and colorful zest for life in his book *A Year in Provence.* The scenery and the cuisine of Iowa may not match Provence, but your zest for life can. I try to travel with a bit more style and flair and to savor the local color a bit more since I read Mr. Mayle's words. This significant book was published by Random House, New York, in 1990.

My favorite gun book is a battered old copy of *The Good Shot* by R. Frasier Willett. It is the only copy I have ever seen anywhere and I found it on a sale table at a New Jersey book store for $1.98. Willett is a British author, but his ideas are fully relevant to American roughshooting situations. The book delves deeply into some rather complex shooting and gun fit issues in a way that is simple and straightforward. It was published in 1979 by A. S. Barnes and Co., South Brunswick, New Jersey.

Some other books that I have found to be very informative include:

Boothroyd, Geoffrey. *Boothroyd on British Shotguns.* Amity, Ore.: Sand Lake Press, 1993.

Brister, Bob. *Shotgunning: The Art and Science.* Tulsa, Okla.: Winchester Press, 1976.

Burroughs, Franklin. *Billy Watson's Croker Sack.* New York: Houghton Mifflin Co., 1991.

Duffey, David Michael. *Expert Advice on Gun Dog Training.* Tulsa, Okla.: Winchester Press, 1977.

Goodall, Charles and Gasow, Julia. *The New Complete English Springer Spaniel.* New York: Howell Book House, 1984.

Lewis, Jerry A. *Wings for the Heart.* Corvallis, Mont.: West River Press, 1991.

Tarrant, Bill. *Training the Hunting Retriever.* Howell Book House: New York, 1991.

Walrod, Dennis. *Grouse Hunters Guide.* Harrisburg, Penn.: Stackpole Books, 1985.

Wolters, Richard. *Game Dog.* New York: Penguin Books/USA, 1983.

Zutz, Don. *The Double Shotgun.* Tulsa, Okla.: Winchester Press, 1978.

PERIODICALS

America is the land of special-interest publications, although a trip through any foreign airport could convince you that the whole world is caught up in the craze as well. Some of the British outdoor magazines like *Shooting Times* are very well done and relevant to our sport. Some of the French outdoor magazines have beautiful photos but I can't negotiate the language.

The knowledgeable roughshooter in America tends to bypass the big-volume national outdoor magazines in favor of the more specialized and in-depth periodicals that focus only on bird hunting. The best example is *Gundog,* published bimonthly by Stover Publishing (800/435-0715). This is a well-done and well-respected special-interest magazine. By and large it is a "how-to" magazine with straightforward advice on gundogs.

Another periodical you may want to investigate is *Gunlist* (800/258-0929); just what you would expect, an extensive listing of thousands of guns for sale. *Gunlist* features categories for all types of shotguns. If you can't find the firearm you're looking for in *Gunlist,* it must really be rare!

Double Gun Journal (800/447-1658) *is* unabashedly fancy and specialized to a fault, but carries many hunting and shooting articles about double guns: side-by-sides and over-unders, American and imported.

Association periodicals from the conservation organizations you should support include *Ruffed Grouse Society Magazine, Ducks Unlimited Magazine* and others.

The esoteric magazines include *Grey's Sporting Journal* (800/458-4010) and *Shooting Sportsman* (800/666-4955). They are fancy, slick and photographically perfect, but short on detail. These are designed to let your mind fill in the blanks.